MURDER
AT THE SUPREME COURT

MARTIN CLANCY AND TIM O'BRIEN

MURDER
AT THE SUPREME COURT

LETHAL CRIMES
AND
LANDMARK CASES

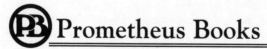 Prometheus Books

59 John Glenn Drive
Amherst, New York 14228–2119

Published 2013 by Prometheus Books

Cover images © 2013 Media Bakery
Cover design by Grace M. Conti-Zilsberger

Inquiries should be addressed to
Prometheus Books
59 John Glenn Drive
Amherst, New York 14228–2119
VOICE: 716–691–0133 • FAX: 716–691–0137
WWW.PROMETHEUSBOOKS.COM

17 16 15 14 13   5 4 3 2 1

Library of Congress Cataloging-in-Publication Data

Clancy, Martin.
    Murder at the Supreme Court : lethal crimes and landmark cases / by Martin Clancy and Tim O'Brien.
        p. cm.
    Includes bibliographical references and index.
    ISBN 978-1-61614-648-1 (cloth : alk. paper)
    ISBN 978-1-61614-649-8 (ebook)
    1. Capital punishment—United States. 2. United States. Supreme Court—Cases. 3. Discrimination in capital punishment—United States. I. O'Brien, Tim. II. Title.

KF9227.C2C54 2013
345.73'0773–dc23

                                                                    2012040642

Printed in the United States of America on acid-free paper

CONTENTS

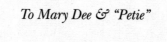

To Mary Dee & "Petie"

INTRODUCTION
A HOUSE OF SECRETS

*T*ransparency is a political catchword for open government in Washington, the spawn of both policy and public relations. It most closely resembles the latter. The White House holds daily on-camera briefings and regularly publishes a list, once closely held, of official visitors; meanwhile, the real work goes on behind guarded doors. C-SPAN beams sessions of the Senate and House around the globe; so while the mysterious ingredients of legislation are mixed privately, floor action is at least on public display. The United States Supreme Court, on the other hand, makes no pretenses toward transparency concerning its deliberations.

The third branch of government, arguably the most potent and definitely the most permanent, operates mostly out of public view. The Court, which followed the Congress from New York to Philadelphia and then to Washington, was housed first in the basement of the Capitol, then on the ground floor of the Senate. In 1935 it was moved to its present marble palace, on First Street NE, across from the Capitol. All of its homes have been houses of secrets.

Supporters of the system argue that secrecy at the Supreme Court is minimal and essential to allow the institution to function; the degree of openness is obviously in the eye of the beholder. The work of the justices can indeed be seen performed publicly from October through April in the splendor of the mahogany and marble Court Chamber, where they hear arguments and announce decisions in about one hundred cases each year. But the Court's real work is performed in the justices' private offices—and, most profoundly, in the Conference Room on the building's second floor, where cases are discussed and decided in absolute secrecy.

The room has a huge fireplace and a wall of bookshelves bearing hundreds of volumes of *U.S. Reports*, containing all the precedents—thousands of decisions—crafted by generations of justices. For more than seventy-five years, those decisions have been crafted in this very room. It was here that the nine incumbents of the Court assembled for a momentous life-or-death discussion on March 9, 1969. But while the justices were sequestered out of public sight, the eyes of the world were elsewhere.

One hundred thirty miles above the earth, astronaut Rusty Schweickart was suiting up aboard *Apollo 9* for a spacewalk that would last forty minutes and would electrify the nation. In Pompano Beach, Florida, Ted Williams was preparing for his debut later in the day as the newly minted manager of the Washington Senators; his team would lose the exhibition game but have its first winning season in seventeen years. On college campuses, new sexual boundaries were being drawn: parents at Vassar went to court that morning to prevent male visitations to their daughters' dorms, and the Air Force announced that women would be admitted into its ROTC programs.

The justices were isolated from these outside events. There was a bleak view of Second Street through the windows of their Conference Room, but the justices were in a cocoon of their own making. No clerks or other staff members were present; no telephone calls were allowed. At the long, rectangular table, under three gleaming chandeliers, the justices focused on the fate of a condemned Alabama convict named William Maxwell. The case turned on the constitutionality of Alabama's procedures, but a Supreme Court decision concerning Maxwell could potentially affect all death-penalty jurisdictions.

The justices would vote on that March morning to vacate Maxwell's sentence on constitutional grounds—a vote that might have been the precursor of a death knell for capital punishment throughout the United States. How that vote came about, and how the case evolved, is a revealing case study of the inner workings of the highest court in the land.

The Court would begin in this case to grapple with the issue of whether juries should be required to determine sentences in capital cases separately from deciding guilt; essentially, whether juries' decisions on the death penalty should take into account particular circumstances about the crime and the criminal in determining the sentence.

Chief Justice Earl Warren, a generally liberal Republican and former California governor just two weeks shy of his seventy-eighth birthday, began the discussion. He told his colleagues he felt that the Alabama procedures followed in the Maxwell case violated the Constitution on two grounds: the jury issued a single verdict (guilty and death) rather than determining guilt and punishment in separate deliberations, and the jury acted without any guidelines or restraints on sentencing.

"The only issue attacked here is the death penalty," said Warren. "I would not reverse the conviction, but simply convert it to a life sentence."

We know what Warren told his fellow justices in the sacrosanct privacy of their Conference Room through the work of a meticulous scholar named Del Dickson. Dickson, now teaching at the University of San Diego, has compiled a revealing and well-annotated collection of notes taken by the justices over more than forty years of closed Conference sessions.[1]

As was the practice, the most senior associate justice, Hugo Black, spoke next. He didn't speak long. Black, who had turned eighty-three the previous week, was in his thirty-second year on the court. Though a darling of liberals, Black saw few constitutional barriers to the death penalty. A native of Alabama, he was familiar with its practices and jurisprudence—and he was firm in his resolve about the Constitution and capital punishment. "The Constitution gave states the power," he said, "and we can't overrule them."[2] As Black's colleague William Brennan would say years later, "He just couldn't believe that anyone would seriously argue that the death penalty was unconstitutional."[3]

Justice William O. Douglas, a feisty seventy-year-old and proud liberal, was the next voice at the table. He echoed Warren's arguments that unbridled jury discretion—the jurors were given no standards by which to make decisions—and the lack of a bifurcated verdict were constitutional defects requiring the court to vacate Maxwell's conviction.

John Marshall Harlan told his colleagues he believed the sentence should be overturned based on the single-verdict issue. Harlan, a year younger than Douglas and about to mark his fourteenth year on the court, was a conservative who famously believed the Supreme Court should not be considered "a general haven for reform movements."[4] He was surrounded by precedents bearing his family name: his grandfather had served on the Court, and many of the senior Harlan's opinions were contained in the volumes of *U.S. Reports* lining the Conference Room's west wall. "I reverse on the issue of punishment," he said.[5]

Justice William Brennan, an outspoken liberal with a gentle demeanor, was about to turn sixty-three. He agreed with Warren and Douglas on concerns over jury standards and a single verdict. He would later urge Douglas, as draft opinions on the case circulated among the justices, to sharpen his argument against the single-verdict system. "A unitary trial," he wrote in a personal note, "unconditionally prejudices the defendant by compelling him to forego his privilege against self-incrimination by taking the stand to make his case on punishment."[6]

Justices Potter Stewart (fifty-three years old) and Byron White (fifty-two), next in seniority, had known one another since their days as fraternity brothers at Yale Law School; neither subscribed to either a liberal or a conservative agenda. They both took a unique and narrower view of the Maxwell case than their colleagues: they felt Alabama's jury selection violated the Court's recent (1968) decision in *Witherspoon v. Illinois*. In that case, the Court threw out an

Illinois law that allowed prosecutors to dismiss any prospective juror who had scruples against capital punishment. The Court found that that would "stack the deck" against the defendant. Maxwell's lawyers claimed the Alabama jury was stacked just that way.[7]

Justice Stewart was also bothered by the lack of evidentiary standards and direction given to the jury. This case reminded him, he said during oral argument, of one that his father, James Garfield Stewart, a distinguished Ohio attorney and jurist, brought to the Supreme Court in the 1920s, "when I was a little boy." Then, as now, he said, the issue was what guidance the jurors should be given. The issue in the earlier case, a first-degree murder conviction from Ohio, was whether the jury should have been allowed to hear an argument for mercy.

Justice White had also expressed concern about the jury's unbridled discretion. During arguments, he asked if a judge in Alabama, unlike a jury, would have been bound by constraints in deciding upon a sentence of death. He was told no, but that the judge was at least a "professional sentencer."

Justices Abe Fortas and Thurgood Marshall were the last to contribute during this first turn around the table. Fortas, age fifty-eight, an appointee of his friend Lyndon Johnson, was an unabashed liberal. So was Marshall, sixty-one, a veteran of the civil rights movement who had successfully argued for the NAACP before the Court in the landmark school-desegregation case *Brown v. Board of Education*. Fortas and Marshall agreed that Maxwell's conviction should be overturned because of the lack of a bifurcated trial. Neither of them joined in the arguments against jury guidelines or selection.

Having made the rounds of the table, Warren opened the floor for wider discussion. As he described the procedure, "If, after the first canvassing of the Court, there was a difference of opinion, the case was open for debate. We did not observe Robert's Rules of Order."[8]

There are no notes on the discussion that followed, and therefore no further guidance about what took place. But we do know that when the topic was exhausted and the chief justice polled the table—in reverse order of the discussion, proceeding from the most junior justice to the chief justice—there were eight votes to spare Maxwell's life and declare that capital-punishment procedures in Alabama were unconstitutional. Hugo Black was alone in his dissent.

The vote could have produced a seismic shift of the Court's direction on capital punishment. Given the questions the case presented, and the determination of some of the Justices to reexamine capital punishment itself, the potential was there for a landmark ruling ending the practice once and for all.

While this little-known case was specific to Alabama, by extension a definitive finding would affect much of the South, where similar practices were in place. And the justices had come to their conclusions by differing routes that converged on constitutional vulnerabilities that could have proved fatal to the death penalty if the momentum were sustained. It was not to be.

The coalition of interests wouldn't hold together for even twenty-four hours. On Friday morning Justice Harlan sent the chief justice a note that he was "not at rest with my yesterday's vote."

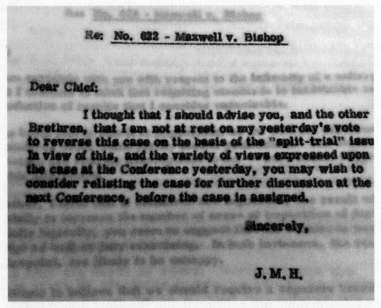

Re: No. 622 - Maxwell v. Bishop

Dear Chief:

I thought that I should advise you, and the other Brethren, that I am not at rest on my yesterday's vote to reverse this case on the basis of the "split-trial" issu In view of this, and the variety of views expressed upon the case at the Conference yesterday, you may wish to consider relisting the case for further discussion at the next Conference, before the case is assigned.

Sincerely,

J.M.H.

Figure I.1. Justice Harlan's note to Chief Justice Earl Warren.

Harlan's defection was the first step in a series of events that would totally unravel the justices' initial vote, keeping it from both the Court's decision docket and the history books. As Stuart Banner, the historian and close student of the Court has observed, "Had Harlan been more decisive, a five- or six-justice majority would have invalidated most capital punishment sentencing schemes in the country on the bifurcated trial issue."[9]

But the justices' consideration of *Maxwell* amounted to one of the most serious challenges to capital punishment of the era, and the Conference vote was a harbinger of the uncertainties about the death penalty that would haunt the Court, or at least several of its members, for the next half century. Harlan's vacillation was just one indicator of those uncertainties.

After the initial round of draft opinions and memos circulated among the justices' chambers, further consideration of Maxwell's case came to a halt, stalled by outside events. The makeup of the Court changed: Abe Fortas resigned as the result of an ethics scandal, and Earl Warren retired. The case was put off for reargument the following term.

The new Court, under Chief Justice Warren Burger, spared Maxwell's life, focusing narrowly on the method of jury selection under *Witherspoon*. The decision was silent on the other constitutional issues raised in the initial conference discussion. The case had other unique facets that the Court did not address at all: Maxwell, a black man, had been convicted of raping a white woman. It would be years before the Court took up the issues of race and non-lethal crimes in the imposition of capital punishment.

The discussion and vote on that Thursday morning in 1969, a near-miss in the annals of constitutional law, is but one of several little-known occasions on which capital punishment came under withering scrutiny in the secrecy of the justices' Conference Room. The crimes that bring landmark capital-punishment cases to the Court are similarly little known, the range of violence and harm often obscured by legal terms and constitutional rhetoric. In the chapters that follow, we hope to lift the curtain on both arenas.

Over the course of the half century since the Conference first took up *Maxwell*, the Court has considered hundreds of capital-punishment cases, some of them truly horrible crimes. Behind the curtain of Court secrecy, the justices themselves have wrestled with both the law and their own consciences. In at least one case you will read about, a justice made an end-run around his colleagues to stop an execution he had voted to carry out. In other cases, justices have changed their opinions about the death penalty after years of voting to uphold it.

The justices, despite their exalted positions and gilded workplace, suffer doubts and fight prejudices like the rest of us. Jeffrey Toobin, the writer for the *New Yorker* and astute student of the contemporary Court, notes that Americans labor under "a magnificent illusion—that the Supreme Court operates on a higher plane than the mortals who toil on the ground."[10] An illusion indeed, as the following pages will illustrate.

Capital punishment continues to have widespread popular support from a public that is repulsed by violent crime. Yet many still struggle with the idea of state-sponsored killing, including the justices who sit on the Supreme Court. Ten of the fifteen cases we profile in this book split the Court 5–4. The U.S. Department of Justice reports that there are currently around twelve thousand homicides in the United States ever year. However difficult the decision whether to have the death penalty, deciding who among twelve thousand murderers may qualify for a death sentence has turned out to be considerably more daunting. If nothing else, this book will illustrate the difficult road the Court has set for itself in allowing states to go forward with capital punishment.

In the courts and legislatures of the country, where the legal levers of execution are located, flaws in the system are being closely, sometimes agonizingly, examined. This book is about people rather than policy; it is about the human intersections of crime and punishment.

A word of caution. Some of the photographs in this work are disturbing, and some readers are apt to find them offensive. We thought long and hard about what to use and what to discard. We were influenced in our decision-making process by, among other things, our discussions with a number of prosecutors who routinely introduce into evidence material far more graphic than anything we would ever consider for publication. They have made a credible case that jurors who are charged with determining the punishment must fully understand the magnitude of the offense.

That principle may also be applied to the general debate about capital punishment. As we explain more fully in the chapters that follow, retribution has become a leading—if not *the* leading—justification for the death penalty. Retribution, however, for *what*? We believe that some of the photos we have chosen for this book will help the reader understand why many Americans feel the punishment for murder must be severe. All the crime-scene photos, and many more, were admitted into evidence for the jury to see. We do understand that many readers may still find them disturbing, as do we. Forewarned is forearmed.

Throughout the book, we'll call your attention to videos about specific stories, issues, or cases available by following a hyperlink or by scanning a "QR" code with your mobile device. All of the videos, other documents, and a blog that continues the dialogue begun here are available at our website. For example, follow this link or scan this code:

 http://murderatthesupremecourt.com

1
THE ROAD TO THE DEATHHOUSE

He that upon pretended malice, shall murther or take
away the life of any man, shall bee punished with death.
No man shal commit the horrible, and detestable sins
of Sodomie upon pain of death; and he or she that can
be lawfully convict of Adultery shall be punished with
death. No man shall ravish or force any woman, maid or
Indian, or other, upon pain of death.
—*Articles, Lawes, and Orders, Divine, Politique,*
and Martiall for the Colony in Virginea, first established by Sir Thomas Gates Knight, Lieutenant
General, on May 24, 1610

O
dd as it may seem, the prison system in the United States, now
straining at the seams and ripe for reforms, came into being
as a reform itself of corporal and capital punishment. The merits
and faults of capital punishment have been debated from Plymouth
Rock to Capitol Hill, with great passion and without resolution. The
Supreme Court, the ultimate arbiter of constitutionality, has grap-
pled with the legitimacy of the death penalty since 1879.[1] The Court
has banned "cruel and unusual punishment," forbidden by the
Eighth Amendment, but struggles with the definition of that term
and its application to capital punishment. It is a struggle that has its
roots deep in the country's history.

The first known execution on what is now American soil occurred in 1608. Captain George Kendall was put to death on charges of spying for Spain; the execution was by firing squad. Fourteen years later, Daniel Frank was hanged in Jamestown for stealing a calf; this execution was the first sanctioned by colonial law and was carried out by a hangman.

The first murderer to be put to death was John Billington, a pilgrim on the Mayflower known as a troublemaker even before he set foot in the Massachusetts Bay Colony. In 1630 Billington killed a neighbor and was, in the words of Governor William Bradford, "both by grand and petty jury found guilty of willful murder, by plain and notorious evidence."[2] Billington died by the noose, which became the preferred method of execution as other colonies moved to implement capital punishment. By the time the colonies joined together to rise up against King George, most of them had established death as the penalty for a host of crimes ranging from murder to counterfeiting, arson, rape, and horse theft.

After the colonies gained their independence, fresh voices were heard on the issue of capital punishment. In Virginia, Thomas Jefferson proposed limiting capital punishment to the crimes of murder and treason. The legislature initially defeated the measure but narrowed capital offenses several years later. The limitations didn't prevent the commonwealth from keeping its executioners busy for the next two centuries: Virginia leads the nation with 1,386 executions since 1608.[3]

Early in our history, there were a dozen executions carried out by "breaking on the wheel," six by gibbeting (hanging the criminal's body in public for weeks or months after execution), and sixty-six by burning. Firing squads accounted for 144 executions, including three in modern-day Utah.[4] Hanging, however, was the predominant instrument of execution throughout the United States until the

1920s. It was also the method used by vigilantes, racists, and unruly mobs—but those lawless instances are more properly categorized as "lynchings" and are outside the scope of this book.

Execution by hanging was a public spectacle for many years, often a raucous and rowdy event. Contemporary accounts used such terms as *drunken frenzy* and *carnival of brutality* to describe them.

Figure 1.1. The public hanging of John Morgan on December 16, 1897.

The last public hanging in West Virginia occurred in 1897 in the Jackson County seat of Ripley, population five hundred. Arriving on horseback or wagons, an estimated five thousand people came from sixty miles around, from five surrounding West Virginia counties and one in Ohio, to see a murderer named John Morgan hanged by the sheriff. According to an eyewitness account in the *Jackson Herald*, the party atmosphere started two days early:

> Ripley is a temperance town. It is against the law to sell any liquor there, but there isn't any law against drinking it. . . . Let the reader imagine a town built around a public square covering perhaps five acres. . . . Fill the square with men, women and children . . . some

of the women with babies in their arms . . . and punctuate that part of the turmoil with the loud shrieks of a hundred or more youthful fakirs on foot, each with a bundle of printed matter in his arms and each shouting, "Last and only true confession of John F. Morgan." "Here you are, only 5, 10, 15 cents," as the case might be.[5]

The crowds aside, the general public attitude toward hanging was not enthusiastic. Death on the gallows could be an untidy process: incorrect placement of the rope or a miscalculation of the prisoner's "drop" resulted in some agonizingly slow deaths. There were cases where the rope broke, resulting in a second hanging; there were also several decapitations.

A new method of execution, one that held out the promise of less cruelty and more certainty than hanging, had its roots in an accidental electrocution in Buffalo, New York.

There, in 1881, a dentist named Alfred P. Southwick heard an interesting story from the local coroner, an acquaintance of his and fellow amateur scientist. The coroner had just conducted an autopsy on a man who had, while intoxicated, stumbled against a generator terminal in a power plant. The coroner was struck by the immediacy and apparent painlessness of the man's death, and Southwick, who clearly had a macabre side to his personality, saw a possible application of electricity to the business of execution. He thought that electrocution could be a more humane form of execution than the gallows.

To explore his theory, Southwick built a miniature electrocution chamber and volunteered his services to the Buffalo Society for the Prevention of Cruelty to Animals. Up until this point, the society had been disposing of hundreds of stray dogs and cats each year by placing them in bags and submerging them in Lake Erie. It took some grisly trial and error on the part of the experimenters, but soon Southwick's machine was declared a success.

Southwick had an engineering background and strong political connections, and he employed them both in order to push for a government study to investigate the application of the new method to state executions. A three-man commission (on which Southwick served) unanimously reported that electrocution was "the most humane and practical method of carrying into effect the sentence of death."[6] The state legislature agreed.

What followed was a study in brawling egos and cutthroat commercial competition. Thomas Edison, the father of electricity, had a huge stake in direct current (DC), with which much of Manhattan was wired. George Westinghouse had discovered a way to produce alternating current (AC), a form of electricity that could be more easily and widely distributed. Neither man wanted his product to be used for executions, and both mounted political and public-relations wars to protect their "brands."

Edison won. His canny campaign resulted in the selection of alternating current for the new electric chair being installed at Auburn State Prison. But Westinghouse didn't go down without a final, novel legal battle—which he conducted by proxy.[7]

The first person condemned to death under the new New York State law was William Kemmler, who had confessed to the murder of his girlfriend. He went to court not to prevent his execution, but rather his electrocution. His lawyers, apparently surreptitiously paid by Westinghouse, argued that the electric chair constituted cruel and unusual punishment. The litigation went all the way to the United States Supreme Court, which ruled unanimously that death by the electric chair was not inhumane. The Supreme Court upheld the trial court's view of electrocution as "in keeping with the scientific progress of the age."[8]

Figure 1.2. Kemmler execution as reported in the *New York Herald* on August 7, 1890.

The *New York Times* described what followed as "a disgrace to civilization":

FAR WORSE THAN HANGING

KEMMLER'S DEATH PROVES AN AWFUL SPECTACLE.

THE ELECTRIC CURRENT HAD TO BE TURNED ON TWICE BEFORE THE DEED WAS FULLY ACCOMPLISHED.

Figure 1.3. *New York Times* article from August 7, 1890.

After the initial jolt of electricity, Kemmler was pronounced dead by the attending physician. But as Warden Durston began to remove the electrode from Kemmler's head, the condemned man began to breathe. Durston reattached the electrode and signaled for another burst of electricity. The *Times* reporter described what happened next:

> Again came that click as before, and again the body of the uncon-
> scious wretch in the chair became as rigid as one of bronze. It was
> awful, and the witnesses were so horrified by the ghastly sight that
> they could not take their eyes off it. . . . An awful odor began to
> permeate the death chamber, and then, as to cap the climax of this
> fearful sight, it was seen that the hair under and around the elec-
> trode on the head and the flesh under and around the electrode
> at the base of the spine was singeing. The stench was unbearable.[9]

After the second jolt of electricity, Kemmler was again pronounced dead. This time, the doctor was right.

George Westinghouse felt vindicated. He told the *New York Times*, "It has been a brutal affair. They could have done better with an axe."[10]

The experience did not cause New York State authorities to shut down the electric chair; instead, technical procedures were reworked. On the morning of July 7, 1891, they confidently threw open the doors of a new execution chamber at Sing Sing prison in Ossining, thirty-five miles north of New York City, and invited the press to witness a marvel of efficiency: four executions in a row, conducted within just two hours.

New York's innovation attracted the attention of legislators across the country. Over the course of the next two decades, fourteen more states wired up their own electric chairs; by 1950 electrocution had spread to twenty-five jurisdictions. The new method was initially less popular in the American West, where hanging remained the political and cultural choice, but electricity became the dominant preference for execution chambers in the rest of the nation.

The "humaneness" of electrocution was under continuing attack by death-penalty opponents over the years, but the method had strong defenders with firsthand experience. The authors met one of them, Warden Frank Blackburn of Louisiana's Angola Penitentiary, in 1985. Blackburn, who oversaw the execution of four prisoners during his tenure, said the chair was humane and efficient: "I think the electrical chair, the electricity, the voltage, and so forth that we have here, it's instantaneous," he said in an interview that took place in the tiny building known as the Death House, which housed the state's electric chair, known as "Gruesome Gertie."[11]

Blackburn told us the key was planning and preparation. During the interview, he was totally relaxed, chomping on a long cigar, as he took the role of a condemned prisoner and eased himself into the Gruesome Gertie's seat to demonstrate the process.

Figure 1.4. Warden Frank Blackburn of Angola State Penitentiary sits in the electric chair demonstrating the role of the condemned prisoner.

"We have what we call our strap-down people. And we'll select an employee of about the same height and the same weight of the inmate that's to be executed, and the whole purpose is to test the straps, to make sure the chair is still, you know, firm and things of this sort." When asked if he'd ever had a botched execution, Blackburn said, "We've had no problems."[12]

 To see the interview with Warden Blackburn and a video report on the electric chair, go to: http://murderatthesupremecourt .com/blackburn

That electric chair is no longer in the Death House; it was last used in 1991 and is now on display in the prison's museum. Gruesome Gertie and many of her counterparts in other states have been retired in favor of the gurneys and crucifix-shaped tables used for executions by lethal injection. However, lethal injection did not immediately displace the electric chair as the most widely used method of execution.

In the search for "more humane" methods, eleven states adopted the use of lethal gas for varying periods of time. In this procedure, cyanide gas would be generated when the executioner threw a remote lever to drop pellets of cyanide into a bucket of acid in a sealed chamber. The chemical reaction produced a toxic gas that is fatal when inhaled. San Quentin State Prison's Clinton Duffy, the warden who presided over gas-chamber executions ninety times, from 1940 to 1952, said the executioner liked gas better than the electric chair "because he didn't feel so directly responsible for the death of the condemned."[13]

The unspoken element in the search for "more humane" methods of execution was the effect on executioners, prison staff, and witnesses, not simply the pain of the condemned. For many, lethal injection fit the bill.

The process of deliberate death through chemistry goes back through recorded time at least to Socrates. The men who would concoct a modern framework for its use in executions were two Oklahoma doctors named A. Jay Chapman and Stanley Deutsch. Chapman was the state's chief medical examiner and Deutsch, an anesthesiology professor. The recipe called for poison that would stop the heart after an injection of quick-acting barbiturates that would put the condemned prisoner to sleep. "Having administered these drugs for approximately 20 years, I can assure you that this is a rapid, pleasant way of producing unconsciousness," wrote Deutsch.[14]

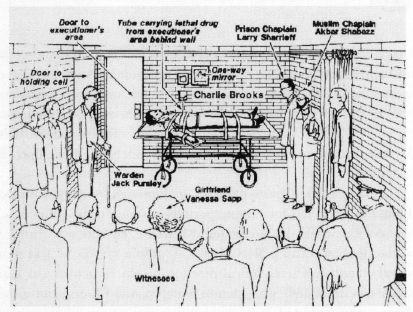

Figure 1.5. Execution by lethal injection of Charles Brooks
on December 7, 1982. © Bettman/CORBIS

Oklahoma was the first state to officially adopt lethal injection, but Texas carried out the first execution. On the night of December 6, 1982, forty-year-old Charles Brooks Jr. ate a final meal of steak, french fries, ketchup, Worcestershire sauce, biscuits, peach cobbler, and iced tea at the "Walls Unit" of the Texas State Penitentiary in Huntsville. Just after midnight, he was rolled into the new execution chamber on a gurney, connected to an intravenous tube, and put to death. The drugs were injected at 12:09 a.m., and Brooks was pronounced dead at 12:16 a.m.

One of the witnesses, Dick Reavis of *Texas Monthly* magazine, said that after the anesthetic began to enter Brooks's body, "he moved his head as if to say 'no.' Then he yawned and his eyes closed, and then he wheezed. His head fell over toward us, then he wheezed again."[15]

Lethal injection came to Louisiana's Angola Penitentiary in 1993, under the administration of Warden Burl Cain. Cain is a supporter of the method and an advocate of capital punishment. He has put seven prisoners to death at Angola. A gurney sits where Gruesome Gertie was once installed, and Cain took Barbara Walters for a tour of the Death House in 2001. He said that a condemned prisoner is startled by the sight of that gurney. "When he sees it for the first time, the reaction is, it shocks him," Cain said, "literally shocks him. And you immediately think of the victim. That's how the victim probably felt when he had the gun to their head, or whatever he used to kill them, at their last minute. Then he sees it and he feels what they felt."

Death comes quickly. "He's going to breathe two breaths," Cain told Walters. "Pshh. Pshh. It's not painful at all, I wouldn't think." Cain says most prisoners ask to hold his hand. "What can I say?" he asked, adding that he's been tempted to respond. "But who held the victim's hand?"

"I think of that, you know," Cain said. "But I have to think, I'm here with him. I couldn't be with the victim." He says he'll signal to the executioner to begin the flow of chemicals, then turn to the prisoner and speak the last words he will ever hear: "Get ready to see Jesus' face. Here we go."[16]

Figure 1.6. Warden Burl Cain in Angola's execution chamber.

 For the interview with Warden Cain and a visit to the Angola Death House go to: http://murderatthesupremecourt .com/cain

At this writing, capital punishment is on the books of thirty-three states. There are more than 3,100 condemned prisoners on the death rows of those states. Many of them have been behind bars for years; some will die of natural causes before their legal remedies are exhausted. The others await a last meal and a warden's final words.

2

THE DEATH PENALTY LIVES AGAIN

Excessive bail shall not be required, nor excessive fines
imposed, nor cruel and unusual punishments inflicted.
—Eighth Amendment of the United States
Constitution, ratified 1791

On April 11, 1967, thirty-seven-year-old Aaron Mitchell tried to cheat California's executioner out of his life. Mitchell slashed his own left arm with a razor blade smuggled into his cell on death row, digging deep into the flesh just below his elbow, in an attempt to avoid execution in San Quentin's gas chamber the following day. He failed.

Prison medical personnel bound up his wound, and the next day guards strapped Mitchell, bandage and all, into the metal chair where he would die breathing fumes from hydrogen cyanide. He was the first prisoner to be executed in California in four years, a prospect on which he wryly remarked toward the end of his days on death row. "I kind of hate having that distinction," he said.[1] Aaron Mitchell had another distinction coming (and he would have *really* hated this one): he became the last prisoner to be executed in California for twenty-five years. He was also the next-to-last inmate in the entire country to be executed for a ten-year period following his death.

Colorado's Luis Monge had the dubious honor of being the last prisoner put to death before a decade-long national moratorium began. Condemned for murdering his pregnant wife and three of their children, Monge died in the Colorado State Penitentiary's gas chamber on June 2, 1967. Ironically, Wayne Patterson, the warden who pulled the lever releasing the lethal gas, was an opponent of capital punishment. "It was a terrible experience," Paterson said, "but if you want to be the warden, you do the warden's duty."[2]

The moratorium on capital punishment was shaped by many forces, but none as powerful as a legal campaign that had its roots in a Georgia murder. That murder took place in Savannah, just seventy days after Monge was executed.

As 1967's calendar flipped to August 11, the day before his thirtieth birthday, William Micke came home just after midnight from the Tiffany Lounge, where he moonlighted as a waiter. Micke's fulltime career was in the U.S. Coast Guard; he was a Machinist's Mate 2nd Class, stationed at the nearby Coast Guard Air Station. He worked the two jobs to support ten children: six by his wife's first marriage, three by his own former marriage, and one child they had together. The baby was fourteen months old.

The Mickes, who were white, lived in a blue-collar area just blocks from an invisible neighborhood boundary; on the other side the residents were black and poorer. There was little racial tension, but there was a pattern of larceny—those who had less preyed upon those who had more.

Around 2:00 a.m., William Micke was in bed but still awake when he heard noises coming from the kitchen. His wife's eleven-year-old, Jimmy, had a habit of sleepwalking, and Micke assumed the boy was at it again. He got up and headed to the kitchen. When he got there, he found an intruder who immediately fled. But in the process, a pistol the man was carrying discharged, and a .22 caliber bullet hit Micke in the chest.

How the gun was fired would later become a bone of contention, but that was of little consequence to William Micke—he died on his kitchen floor before help arrived.[3]

Sergeant G. W. Spivey of the Savannah Police Department was the first officer on the scene. He organized a neighborhood manhunt, which uncovered muddy footprints leading across the invisible border to nearby Sherman Street. There, hiding in a crawl space under his uncle's house, officers found twenty-four-year-old William Furman. He had a .22 caliber handgun in his pocket.

Furman was black, a sixth-grade dropout, and had absolutely no talent for burglary. He'd been caught and convicted of that crime four times. Released on parole several months before, he was living with his mother and was a regular at Ruby's Two Spot, a neighborhood bar. Three weeks earlier, he had bought the pistol on the street for twenty-five dollars. "It was a good buy," he told police.

Furman's statement to police that night, which he refused to sign, would come into question later. In it, according to detectives, he admitted to firing one shot back toward his pursuer as he fled the house, assuming the homeowner was armed. "He came after me. I knew he was going to shoot," Furman was quoted as saying.[4] At the Micke home, Sergeant Spivey and crime-scene investigators found a hole near the latch of a screen door on the porch and signs that the intruder had gone through a kitchen window from the porch, climbing over a washing machine to gain entry. They also gathered fingerprints that, together with ballistics evidence matching Furman's gun to the bullet in William Micke's chest, would help prosecutors build a solid case against Furman. They moved quickly.

Furman was charged with felony murder. It was a capital offense for which, under Georgia law, intent to kill was not a factor: killing was murder, whether by accident or design, when it occurred in the commission of a felony. William Henry Furman would go on trial for his life.

Furman's family could not afford to hire an attorney, but he was fortunate in the court appointment of B. Clarence Mayfield to defend him. "Bobby" Mayfield was one of the few black attorneys in town, active in the struggle for civil rights, and a fierce opponent of the death penalty. Mayfield empathized with the victim's family—he was himself the father of nine children—but he would use every legal tool to save William Furman's life.[5] He knew the evidence was stacked against his client, and he knew the racial realities in Savannah.

"It was black on white. A black man killed a white man. That did it," Mayfield would say later. "It wouldn't have been so with black on black, or white on black, or white on white. I could almost guarantee you that in any of these combinations the charge would be less than murder. No capital crime. No electrocution."[6]

Whatever the quality of justice in Savannah, it was swift. The entire trial took place in one day, on September 20, 1968. Starting at 10:00 a.m., a panel of sixty in the jury pool was whittled down to a twelve-man jury, followed by the presentation of evidence. Closing statements by both sides were delivered after lunch, Judge Dunbar Harrison instructed the jury by midafternoon, and a verdict was returned at 5:00 p.m.

The prosecution presented nine witnesses in quick succession; the defense, only one—William Furman. Rather than have him be subject to cross-examination, Mayfield succeeded in having the defendant present an "unsworn statement" to the jury. In it, Furman testified that the shooting had been a fluke, that he had tripped over the washing machine's power cord while fleeing, and that the gun had discharged by accident:

> They got me charged with murder and I admit going to these folks' home and they did caught me in there and I was coming back out, backing up, and there was a wire down there on the floor. I was coming out backwards and fell back and didn't intend to kill nobody. I didn't know they was behind the door. The gun went off and I didn't know nothing about no murder until they arrested me, and when the gun went off I was down on the floor and I got up and ran. That's all to it.[7]

The jury, eleven whites and one black, would have to weigh this account against the testimony of police officers about Furman's statement to them on the night of the crime, when he allegedly admitted to firing back at Micke. But the judge's instructions held out little hope for Furman; they made it clear that Micke's death during the burglary, not Furman's intent, was the issue. "If you find that such killing was the natural, reasonable and probable

THE DEATH PENALTY LIVES AGAIN

consequence of such breaking and entering," Judge Harrison told the jurors, "then I instruct you that under such circumstances you would be authorized to convict the defendant of murder . . . whether the defendant intended to kill the deceased or not."

Harrison told the jurors that if they were to find Furman guilty, they had two options. If they recommended mercy, the defendant would be imprisoned for life. If they made no recommendation, he would be sentenced to death. The jury began its deliberations at 3:35 p.m., but the foreman sent back a telling question just forty-five minutes later. He said the members wanted to know if the judge, rather than the jury, could decide on punishment in the event of a guilty verdict. The jurors clearly wanted this cup to pass, but Harrison would have none of it. "No, sir," he told the foreman. "I have given you the forms of the verdicts. It's up to the jury to determine."

An hour later, the jury returned a guilty verdict with no recommendation for mercy. Judge Harrison delivered the sentence, first to a crowded courtroom and then in a signed judgment: "It is therefore considered, ordered and adjudged that the said William Henry Furman be delivered to the Director of Corrections for electrocution at such penal institution as may be designated by the Director." The jurors went home in time for dinner.

The verdict was exactly what Bobby Mayfield had feared. He immediately filed a motion for a new trial, citing alleged Miranda violations the night of Furman's arrest and protesting the dismissal of a potential juror who opposed the death penalty. That motion was denied, and Mayfield then organized a full-scale appeal to Georgia's Supreme Court. For months, Mayfield had been working for nothing; the $150 fee allowed by his court appointment had long ago been spent.

The Georgia Supreme Court saw no merit in any of Mayfield's arguments. It found no Miranda violations; it ruled that the juror's exclusion was permissible under U.S. Supreme Court guidelines (*Witherspoon v. Illinois*), that fingerprint and ballistic evidence was properly obtained, and that Georgia's death-penalty statute was not cruel and unusual punishment. The state court's concluding sentence left no room for hope: "Having considered every enumeration of error argued by counsel in his brief and finding no reversible error, the judgment is affirmed."[8]

Bobby Mayfield had done his best; now it was time to call in the cavalry. A legal team mounted by the NAACP Legal Defense Fund (LDF) had both the resources and the talent to take Furman's case to the court of last resort. The LDF team included Jack Greenberg, who had helped argue the landmark civil rights case *Brown v. Board of Education* before the Supreme Court, and Anthony G. ("Tony") Amsterdam, who at just thirty-six years of age was considered one of the country's premiere courtroom advocates. The LDF team began focusing its appeal on the issue of cruel and unusual punishment.

Unknown to the lawyers on either side of the Furman case, the issue of cruel and unusual punishment had been simmering within the marble confines of the Supreme Court for several years. The flame had been lit by two men no longer in the building, Justice Arthur Goldberg and his then twenty-four-year-old clerk, Alan Dershowitz.

In the summer of 1963, in Goldberg's first year on the Court, he was faced with six petitions for hearings in death-penalty cases. None of the cases specifically raised the Eighth Amendment issue of cruel and unusual punishment, but Goldberg felt that a test of that issue was due. He assigned Dershowitz, a Brooklyn-born legal prodigy who had been first in his class at Yale Law School, to research the issue. The result was a memorandum, polished by Goldberg and presented to his colleagues on the Court, that urged the abolition of the death penalty on Eighth Amendment grounds.

The memorandum did not accomplish its immediate purpose—Goldberg was not able to garner the four votes necessary to grant a hearing in any of the cases that had been petitioned—but it did stir discussion. Goldberg noted that public opinion might still favor capital punishment, but that "standards of decency" were evolving, and the justices should lead the way. "This Court has traditionally guided rather than followed public opinion," he wrote, "in the process of articulating and establishing progressively civilized standards of decency."[9]

Also behind the scenes, the justices were actually shopping for cases to decide "once and for all," as Justice Douglas put it, whether state laws and practices concerning capital punishment violated the Eighth Amendment. The justices felt a need for clarity after a muddled 1971 decision in a California due-process case (*McGautha v. California*), and they appointed William Brennan and Potter Stewart as a two-man committee to cherry-pick promising appeals. They selected four cases, of which *Furman* would become the keystone.[10] Goldberg and Dershowitz were both gone from the Court for several years by the time the LDF argued cruel and unusual punishment in its briefs for the *Furman* case. Goldberg had acceded to Lyndon Johnson's persuasion and accepted the post of ambassador to the United Nations in 1965; Dershowitz had gone to Boston to begin a career on the Harvard Law School faculty that has flourished for almost half a century. But they had planted a seed that *Furman's* defense team would nourish.

The LDF lawyers built their constitutional case against the death penalty not only around the Eighth Amendment claim of "cruel and unusual" but also on the Fourteenth Amendment's guarantee of equal protection, tracing that guarantee all the way back to its legislative roots.

In introducing the proposed constitutional amendment on the floor of the Senate on May 23, 1866, Senator Jacob Howard of Michigan told his colleagues: "It does away with the injustice of subjecting one caste of persons to a code not applicable to another. It prohibits the hanging of a black man for a crime for which the white man is not to be hanged."[11]

The LDF briefs claimed that, beyond issues of race, defendants were deprived of equal protection by the way jurors were selected, how those jurors made decisions, and the instructions judges gave to jurors.

- The exclusion of "scrupled" jurors, those with reservations about the death penalty, skewed a jury, said the LDF.
- The practice of determining guilt and sentence in one trial was arbitrary and unconstitutional. Sentencing should be considered separately, the LDF argued, with guilt or innocence the single focus of a jury's first deliberations.
- A lack of instruction about sentencing allowed jurors unbridled discretion. Judges often provided careful instructions regarding evidence that would be considered regarding guilt or innocence, the briefs asserted, but judges generally did not provide jurors with sufficient guidance concerning life or death.

On the morning of January 17, 1972, Tony Amsterdam stepped to the lectern before the nine justices of the Supreme Court. He would argue two of the cases accepted by the Court to address challenges to the death penalty: that of a horrific killer in California named Ernest James Aikens Jr. and that of William Furman. Furman's case was more palatable in that an accident was a possible explanation for William Micke's death, and because Furman had been diagnosed with a "mental deficiency" after his trial. The Aikens case—that of a man who was convicted of raping two women and then stabbing them to death—had no redeeming qualities.

Amsterdam made the case that the punishment was at issue, not the crimes. Concerning the Eighth Amendment, he argued that the death penalty was cruel under evolving social standards; it was unusual, he said, because it was now being applied with less frequency. (There was an obvious irony in that argument, given that LDF legal efforts were largely responsible for the drop in executions.)

The death penalty, he told the justices, was also being applied unevenly—that is, unequally—and all defendants, regardless of their crime, race, or social status, should be protected from it by the Fourteenth Amendment. Amsterdam presented well-organized, compelling arguments. Justice Byron White, notoriously a tough audience, would later tell his clerks it was possibly the best oral presentation he had ever heard.[12]

The Aikens case would disappear from the justices' radar; the California Supreme Court overturned Aikens's death sentence, making his case before the U.S. Supreme Court moot. But the issues in *Furman* would present a major stress test to the Court's proud tradition of collegiality.

At the Conference held four days after the arguments, a consensus on a decision began to coalesce, but it came from widely diverse points on the legal compass. Chief Justice Warren Burger, along with Justices Lewis Powell, Harry Blackmun, and William Rehnquist, voted to affirm Furman's sentence, though they were not in lockstep on their reasons. On the other side, Justice Douglas told his colleagues that the death penalty "is used primarily against minority groups. . . . If it is discriminatory in practice, it is 'unusual' under the Eighth Amendment."[13]

Justice Brennan used a broader brush, citing Eighth Amendment arguments made in the Goldberg/Dershowitz memorandum. "The death penalty is a highly suspect penalty," he told the Conference. "Even if the death penalty were restricted to a select form of murder, it would fail."[14]

Justices Byron White and Potter Stewart also voted to reverse Furman's sentence.

Thurgood Marshall, who had helped birth the LDF's campaign against the death penalty before he joined the Supreme Court, did no gloating in the Conference. "The Eighth Amendment," he said simply, "was intended to be considered in light of contemporary history. I reverse."[15]

If the justices had set a course at that January Conference, their nine oars were not being wielded in synch. Despite several more meetings, telephone consultations, and the distribution of numerous drafts, no two justices could agree on the rationale of an opinion. The result was a brief, one-page unsigned opinion setting aside Furman's death sentence, followed by nine separate opinions explaining why the decision was right in the view of five of the justices and why it was viewed as wrong by the four others. Overall, the decision totaled more than 230 pages, almost eighty thousand words—one of the longest decisions in Supreme Court history.

Given the disarray of the opinions, it was left to Chief Justice Burger, who had voted to affirm Furman's death sentence (and death sentences in two other consolidated cases) to announce the decision that would set it aside: "The Court holds that the imposition and carrying out of the death penalty in these cases constitutes cruel and unusual punishment in violation of the Eighth and Fourteenth Amendments."[16]

The majority of justices agreed that the death penalty was "cruel and unusual punishment," but each made his own argument. Justice Stewart, citing the arbitrary nature of capital punishment, made a striking comparison: "These death sentences are cruel and unusual in the same way that being struck by lightning is cruel and unusual."[17] Justice Blackmun, in dissent, was not to be outdone in eloquence, admitting to "an excruciating agony of the spirit." He wrote, "I yield to no one in the depth of my distaste, antipathy, and, indeed, abhorrence for the death penalty . . . and of moral judgment exercised by finite minds."[18] But Blackmun felt that the Court had overstepped constitutional boundaries. "It has sought and achieved an end," he said.[19]

The Stanford University scholar Robert Weisberg called *Furman* "a badly orchestrated opera, with nine characters taking turns to offer their own arias."[20] Edward Lazarus, whose academic knowledge was enriched by firsthand experience as a clerk at the court, was more scathing: "For five justices to issue one of the most far-reaching constitutional rulings in the Court's history without even agreeing among themselves on a legal rationale," he wrote, "betrayed the very rule of law they claimed to be upholding."[21]

The *Furman* decision was hugely controversial. Although the justices failed to come together on any single rationale, opponents took heart that the country's highest Court was finally casting doubt on capital punishment and generating some hope that a decision to do away with the practice forever might be within reach. After all, the Court historically moves slowly on many issues, and this was, in their view, at least a step in the right direction.

Proponents of capital punishment, particularly legislators in those states that permitted the death penalty, saw the decision quite differently. For one, the decision was razor thin, 5–4. Only two Justices—William Brennan and Thurgood Marshall—rejected the death penalty outright. A third, William O. Douglas, was close, finding the practice inherently discriminatory. But the two other justices voting to set aside Furman's death sentence, Potter Stewart and Byron White, made it clear they could embrace state death-penalty laws if procedures could be put in place to make death sentences less arbitrary, if greater attention were paid to the circumstances of the specific crime and the character of the individual defendant.

On November 12, 1975, there was another development that further encouraged death-penalty proponents. One of the justices sharply critical of capital punishment, seventy-seven-year-old William O. Douglas, retired from the Court. Douglas, who had become one of the most liberal justices ever to sit on the Supreme Court, had suffered a debilitating stroke a year earlier. President Ford named John Paul Stevens to succeed him. Stevens was highly regarded for his lucid, scholarly opinions as a judge on the U.S. Seventh Circuit of Appeals, and he was easily confirmed on a 98–0 vote in the Senate. Stevens, it was believed, would surely be less doctrinaire than Douglas and more receptive to the will of the popularly elected branches of government. As it turned out, he was.

The *Furman* decision would, however, stay the executioner's hand for years. Lawyers and state legislators spent the time parsing the individual opinions to divine a workable path for reintroducing capital punishment. By 1976, thirty-five states had drafted new death-penalty laws designed to satisfy the high Court's concerns. Congress had also enacted a federal law allowing the death penalty for a specific crime: airline hijackings resulting in death.[22] The time was ripe for reconsideration, and a number of appropriate cases would soon be on the Court's doorstep. Among them was *Gregg v. Georgia.*

Troy Leon Gregg had been born into a family ravaged by alcoholism and violence. His great-grandfather had slit his wife's throat; his grandmother and three cousins were shot to death by his uncle. Gregg, by the time of the crime that would write his name into legal history, was twenty years old and rootless. He had been working a variety of construction and landscaping jobs, staying on the move. "I was a wanderer," he said.[23]

On November 21, 1973, Gregg and a sixteen-year-old companion, Sam Allen, hitched a ride on the Florida Turnpike from "Tex" Moore and Fred Simmons. Gregg and Allen were broke; they had only eight dollars between them, but hoped to get to North Carolina. Simmons and Moore appeared to be good ole boys with money to spend and beer to drink. They did a bit of both on their journey north. Their car broke down about 240 miles north of Miami, but with the help of a Florida Highway patrolman, they got to a used-car dealer and purchased a 1960 red-and-white Pontiac, paying cash. The trip resumed with Gregg doing much of the driving while Simmons and Moore did much of the drinking.

At the intersection of I-10 and I-75 in north Florida, this motley quartet picked up yet another hitchhiker, identified as Dennis Weaver, on his way to Atlanta. The five of them continued the trip until about 11:00 p.m., when Weaver was dropped off in the Druid Hills section of Atlanta. In a statement to police, Gregg's young companion, Sam Allen, recounted what happened next.[24]

Simmons and Moore wanted to stop at a rest stop to relieve themselves and did so at the intersection of I-85 and Highway 20 in Gwinnett County, Georgia. Gregg told Allen to get out of the car, saying "We're going to rob them." As Simmons and Moore returned from the gas station rest room, said Allen, "Gregg lay up on the car with a gun in his hand to get good aim and fired three shots. . . . One of the men fell, the other staggered." Gregg then circled around the back of the car and approached the two men, both lying in a drainage ditch. Gregg placed the gun to the head of one of the men and pulled the trigger. He then went quickly to the other man, placed the gun at his head, and again pulled the trigger. A subsequent crime-lab report showed that Simmons had been killed by a shot to the right corner of the right eye, in the temple region, and that Moore had been shot once on the right side of his face and again in the back of his head. Gregg then took their money and whatever else they had in their pockets, according to Allen, then told him to get in the car. They drove away.

Two days later, the other hitchhiker, Dennis Weaver, went to a Druid Hills restaurant to have breakfast and read about the double homicide on the front page of the *Atlanta Constitution*. Weaver called the police and told them about his contact with Gregg and Allen, and that he believed they were headed toward Asheville, North Carolina. Law enforcement officials in Gwinnett County notified their counterparts in Asheville, who arrested Gregg and Allen the next day, still driving the 1960 red-and-white Pontiac. They found $107 in Gregg's pocket and a .25 caliber automatic pistol. Ballistics tests established that it was the same gun used in the shooting deaths of Simmons and Moore.

Gregg initially confirmed Allen's recollection of events to police, telling a Gwinnett County detective, "By God, I wanted them dead."[25] Later, however, he changed his story and claimed that the shootings were in self-defense. Gregg had hoped that Allen, only sixteen years old, would back up his self-defense account. He even wrote a prompting letter to Allen, asserting they both had "feared for their lives"; he asked Allen to memorize the letter and then destroy it. Allen did neither, instead handing the letter to authorities. It would be used as evidence in Gregg's murder trial.

The trial in Gwinnett Superior Court lasted less than a week. The prosecutors had Gregg's admission, the murder weapon, and the testimony of Gregg's fellow hitchhiker, Sam Allen. The jury deliberated less than an hour before returning a verdict: guilty of first-degree murder. Right after the verdict, the judge convened a hearing on sentencing as required by Georgia's new death-penalty statute.

The prosecutor painted Gregg as malicious and without remorse. Defense Attorney G. Hughel Harrison urged mercy and warned against an irrevocable mistake. Jurors, he said, would not want to look back after an execution and say, "Well, maybe I was a little bit mistaken."[26] The judge carefully charged the jury about how they must consider both aggravating and mitigating circumstances, as required by the new statutes, and the twelve members returned to the jury room. This time, their deliberations took nearly four hours. They returned to the courtroom with a verdict of death.

Under the new Georgia law, death sentences were automatically reviewed by the state supreme court, which, on October 17, 1974, affirmed Gregg's conviction and death sentence. In denying his appeal, the Georgia court specifically rejected Gregg's claim that his various confessions should not have been allowed into evidence because fourteen hours had expired between the time he was warned of his Miranda rights and the time he made his final incriminating statement.

Internal memoranda of the U.S. Supreme Court reveal that the Court was actively searching for death-penalty cases that could be used to address the myriad questions left unanswered by the Court's decision in *Furman v. Georgia*, and to resolve the constitutionality of the newly enacted death statutes.

"There are now thirty-four states and the federal government which have enacted post-Furman capital punishment statutes," wrote James B. Ginty, the Court's senior counsel, in a memorandum to the justices designed to help them select the cases to be heard. "It is possible to identify four basic approaches taken by state legislatures in enacting these statutes—'aggravating only'; 'aggravating-mitigating';

'quasi-mandatory aggravating-mitigating'; and 'mandatory.'"[27] The Court would have to parse with care.

Gregg's case was on that list, with a recommendation that it not be accepted because the Miranda issue might somehow muddy the waters or even prevent resolution of the death-penalty questions. In the end, however, *Gregg v. Georgia* was among five cases the Court accepted for review, the others involving death-penalty laws in North Carolina, Florida, Louisiana, and Texas.[28] *Gregg*, however, would become the lead case.

Courts do not write legislation; legislatures do. But the Supreme Court seized these five cases to at least provide a blueprint for the states on how to write a death-penalty statute that would comply with the Court's view of the U.S. Constitution. The stakes in this new round of cases could not have been higher—literally life or death. Not just one life or death, but hundreds. Attorneys for the condemned inmates would be asking the Supreme Court to go beyond the Furman case and declare the death penalty cruel and unusual, and thus unconstitutional, once and for all.

The death penalty is, of course, a political issue as much as it is a constitutional one, and the Ford administration supported capital punishment. The Justice Department also had a horse in this race: the validity of the Federal Air Piracy statute was on the line along with the five state death-penalty statutes. This allowed the Ford administration to dispatch its top courtroom lawyer, Solicitor General Robert Bork, to argue the government's case as a "friend of the Court."

Bork was a scholar with conservative views and a compelling courtroom manner. His own nomination to the Supreme Court by Ronald Reagan would be shot down in the Senate ten years later, but on the morning of March 31, 1976, Bork had the full attention of the Court. He argued that capital punishment served society's legitimate interest in deterrence, retribution, and its expression of moral outrage. He pressed the point that the death penalty could not be unconstitutional because "the men who framed the Eighth Amendment [prohibiting cruel and unusual punishment] framed the procedures which must be followed in inflicting it."[29]

There are, however, some forms of punishment that were permissible at the time the Bill of Rights was adopted that would be unacceptable today, leading Justice Potter Stewart to ask, "What if a state said for the most heinous kind of first-degree murders we are going to inflict breaking a man on the wheel and then disemboweling him while he is still alive and then burning him up. What would you say to that?" Bork responded:

> I would say that that practice is so out of step with modern morality and modern jurisprudence that the state cannot return to it. That kind of torture was precisely what the framers thought they were outlawing when they wrote the cruel and unusual punishment clause.[30]

Bork also addressed the claims by Justice Stewart and Byron White in *Furman* that the death penalty was being applied in a "wanton and freakish" manner:

> Counsel's real complaint is not that anybody is freakishly convicted and executed but, rather, that some murderers are freakishly spared and given life imprisonment. In other words, the fault in the system which makes it unconstitutional to inflict the death penalty is that it errs, if it errs at all, on the side of mercy and the side of safety, and that is what we are told makes it unconstitutional.[31]

Bork's passion for his argument was apparent. Scholar and historian Stuart Banner suggests that passion was deeply rooted, writing that Bork "viewed opposition to capital punishment as a symptom of moral decay, and . . . was motivated even more by a visceral disgust for the constitutional philosophy of Justices Brennan and Marshall."[32]

Given the new composition of the Court—with Justice Douglas gone and replaced by the decidedly more moderate Justice Stevens—and the closeness of the vote in *Furman* (5–4), it was highly unlikely that the Court would throw out the death penalty altogether. But it did use the five cases before it to refine its mandate in *Furman*, that a death sentence be based on objective criteria and on the individualized consideration of both the crime and the criminal who committed it.

The death penalty statutes in North Carolina and Louisiana were rejected largely because they permitted mandatory death sentences in some cases, leaving the jury (or judge) no discretion to reduce the sentence. The Texas, Florida, and Georgia statutes were upheld, however, with the Court pointedly noting in the *Gregg* decision how the Georgia statute had satisfied the concerns the justices had raised in *Furman*.

As with the *Furman* decision, again there was no majority opinion. But Justice Stewart announced the judgment of the Court and the rationale of the Court in upholding Gregg's death sentence:

> The new Georgia sentencing procedures . . . focus the jury's attention on the particularized nature of the crime and the particularized characteristics of the individual defendant. While the jury is permitted to consider any aggravating or mitigating circumstances, it must find and identify at least one statutory aggravating factor before it may impose a penalty of death. In this way, the jury's discretion is channeled. No longer can a jury wantonly and freakishly impose the death sentence; it is always circumscribed by the legislative guidelines. In addition, the review function of the Supreme Court of Georgia affords additional assurance that the concerns that prompted our decision in *Furman* are not present to any significant degree in the Georgia procedure applied here.[33]

Stewart also observed that any death penalty in Georgia was subject to automatic review in the state supreme court, which must consider whether the sentence was influenced by passion, prejudice, or any other arbitrary factor. It also must consider whether the sentence is disproportionate to sentences imposed in similar cases, considering both the crime and the defendant. Should the state supreme court affirm the death sentence, it must include in its decision reference to the similar cases it has considered. The vote was a lopsided 7–2, with only Justices Brennan and Marshall dissenting.

The Georgia death-penalty statutes would become a model for the nation. For a fuller understanding, see the actual text in Appendix A.

Many of the thirty-four other states to reenact their death penalty laws had done so in a fashion much like Georgia. And those that didn't were generally quick to follow Georgia's lead. The death penalty was back. From 1976 through September 2012, the Court's decision in the *Gregg* case and in the related cases has allowed for the execution of more than 1,300 convicted murderers.[34] Paradoxically, Troy Gregg was not one of them.

Gregg stretched out his date with death at the Georgia State Penitentiary at Reidsville, Georgia, as best he could. There were still some additional appeals available, and he filed a number of complaints with corrections officials about the prison conditions, which he claimed were inhumane.

As might be expected on death row in any state, Georgia's was populated by the worst of the worst—and Gregg, over the years, got to know his neighbors quite well. Among them was Carl Isaacs, sentenced to death for the massacre of six members of a farm family in Seminole County, Georgia, including a young woman who had been savagely raped before being shot in the back and head. Isaacs had previously escaped from a minimum-security prison on Maryland's Eastern Shore. He took great pride in the escapade and was hoping to repeat the achievement at Reidsville with a carefully selected coterie of fellow murderers.

Troy Gregg was one; Tim McCorquodale, another. McCorquodale, a member of a violent North Carolina biker group calling themselves the "Outlaws," had been convicted of the torture, rape, and murder of a twenty-year-old woman—a crime often described as one of the most gruesome in Georgia's history.

There were five inmates on the team. Isaacs had been orchestrating the escape for more than a year. Among other things, Isaacs was an accomplished tailor; he hoped to duplicate the uniforms of prison guards using pajamas, belts, black shoes, and even the insignias from actual uniforms, most of which had to be smuggled into the prison. Isaacs managed to have hacksaw blades smuggled in as well, concealed in gift items such as portable radios. The men worked in shifts and in stealth to cut through the bars on their cells, masking the cuts with gum and spit and shoe polish.

Isaacs loved attention and shared some of his exploits, including his plan to break out of prison, with Charlie Postell, an editor at the *Albany Herald* newspaper. He even tried to get Postell to assist—it is unclear to what extent, if any, he did. But Postell did publish his interviews with Isaacs and was well known to the other inmates.

Time, however, was running out for Gregg. He was scheduled to be put to death in the electric chair at Reidsville on July 29, 1980. His escape was planned for the previous day, the early-morning hours of July 28.

Time did run out, ironically, for the mastermind of the plot, Carl Isaacs. Two hours before the escape was to begin, Isaacs heard footsteps along the catwalk. Seconds later, a guard stopped in front of his cell, "Pack up your stuff," he said. "You're being transferred this morning."[35] Isaacs figured it would be better to let the others go without him rather than risk blowing the operation. He did not object or try to move up the escape.

At approximately 5:30 in the morning on July 28, Gregg, McCorquodale, and two other convicted murderers staged probably the most daring escape in Georgia history. It was a scenario worthy of Hollywood, with script and costumes by the absent Carl Isaacs. A car was waiting for them in the prison parking lot, keys in the sun visor as planned, the gas tank full. The prisoners made their way out of the prison in their guard disguises unchallenged, and they drove away. They were free.

Gregg was so proud of himself, he could hardly wait to break the news to Charlie Postell, the *Albany Herald* editor. Postell called the prison to alert them to the escape and was told he was mistaken, that all four inmates were accounted for. Prison officials learned to their horror a short while later that Postell had it right.[36] An all-points bulletin circulated throughout the southeastern United States. (Postell and his wife Judi wound up being charged by authorities as accessories to the escape. The charges were later dropped.)

The dragnet for the escaped inmates, four of the most ruthless killers in Georgia's prison system, was growing rapidly. McCorquodale maintained ties with his Outlaws biker group, which had members in the Charlotte, North Carolina, area. It's not exactly clear how law enforcement found them, possibly on a tip. But find them they did, in a small, four-room brick home on the shores of Lake Wylie, just southwest of Charlotte. After a four-hour siege, police fired tear gas into the home and then watched as McCorquodale and two other fugitives came stumbling out. Troy Gregg, however, was not among them.

The mystery of Gregg's whereabouts was solved a few days later; his body was found floating in Mountain Island Lake, about twelve miles away from where his cohorts were captured. During the manhunt, Gregg, McCorquodale, and some of McCorquodale's former Outlaw biker buddies were having drinks at the Old Yellow Tavern, a biker bar on the banks of the Catawba River. Arrogant and something of a braggart, Gregg made an unflattering remark about the girlfriend of one of the bikers and a fracas ensued.[37]

Court testimony established that McCorquodale, who was six feet three and weighed about three hundred pounds, knocked Gregg down and began stomping on him, that he brought his right foot down with all his weight on Gregg's upper chest, throat, and head. Authorities said Gregg died from suffocation due to swelling from a blow or blows to the throat, all less than twenty-four hours after his scheduled execution at Reidsville. The man whose case had laid the groundwork for the execution of more than 1,300 inmates over the next thirty-five years, would be spared execution by the state—but not by a fellow inmate.

Tim McCorquodale and Carl Isaacs were eventually put to death in Georgia's electric chair. The other two escapees later had their death sentences overturned; they are serving life terms in the Georgia prison system.

The initial plaintiff in this life-and-death chronicle, William Furman, is behind bars—but not for murder. His initial sentence was changed to life in prison after the Supreme Court decision; in

Georgia, that meant he could eventually be eligible for parole. He made it on his fourth try, and was released on parole in 1984. He stayed out of trouble for two decades but was arrested in 2004, at the age of sixty-two, for burglarizing a home in Macon, Georgia. He is serving a twenty-year prison sentence.

Figure 2.1. Troy Gregg.

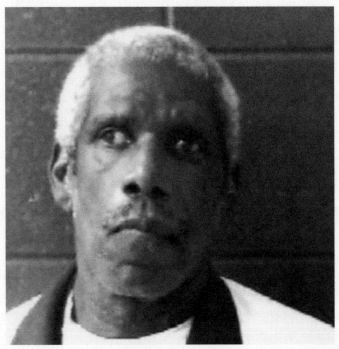

Figure 2.2. William Furman.

3

GOOD GUY/BAD GUY? SAME GUY?

PROPORTIONALITY AND THE DEATH PENALTY

*The need for treating each defendant in a capital case
with the degree of respect due the uniqueness of the individual is far more important than in non-capital cases.*
—Chief Justice Warren Burger, ruling in
Lockett v. Ohio, 438 U.S. 586 (July 3, 1978)

In *Furman v. Georgia,*[1] the U.S. Supreme Court rejected capital punishment not because the justices found it to be per se unconstitutional, but rather because of the way it was being implemented.
The broad, unlimited discretion that juries seemed to enjoy resulted
in their returning death sentences in vastly different circumstances.
There was no way of predicting just what would bring about a death
sentence, leading the Court to conclude that its application was "arbitrary and capricious." The Court made it clear in *Furman,* and again
in *Gregg v. Georgia,*[2] that the ultimate sanction should be reserved
for the worst offenders having committed the worst crimes and that
it must be imposed in a more consistent and rational manner. The
"character and record of the individual offender and the circumstances of the particular offense"[3] should be an indispensable part of
the sentencing process.

Some three dozen states responded by rewriting their death-
penalty laws with the "guided discretion" the Court appeared to have
demanded. These new laws identified the specific aggravating circumstances that might bring a death sentence, such as the murder of

a law-enforcement officer in the performance of duty, murder while in prison, or murder in the course of another violent felony such as kidnapping. Some states made the death penalty mandatory for certain offenses. And many states also identified mitigating circumstances, factors about the offense or the offender that might help a capital defendant escape a death sentence.

In the same breath, the Court appeared to be demanding not only greater consistency but also individualized, case-by-case analysis. There developed among the justices a quiet but troubling concern that the Court might have boxed itself in with its decision in *Furman* and therefore might have made it even more impossible for states to enact death-penalty laws that would be both rational and constitutional.

In this chapter, we will examine two extraordinary cases: first, *Lockett v. Ohio* (1978), a landmark ruling that challenged the various formulas the states had adopted for capital sentencing, and second, *Pulley v. Harris* (1984), a remarkable case from a variety of standpoints that challenged the Court to apply and clarify its decision in *Lockett*.

Sandra Lockett was a twenty-two year-old African American woman with a troubled past. A high school dropout with an addiction to heroin, she had a five-year-old son, Albert Young. His father wasn't around much, and Sandra had no real means to take care of him. Since dropping out of school, she also had had a number of minor scrapes with the police in her hometown of Akron, Ohio. The offense that would ultimately make her name familiar to the country's death-penalty lawyers occurred in May 1975. It began with an offer to help some friends, Al Parker and Nathan Dew, whom Lockett had met a few weeks earlier in New Jersey. The three spent some time together in New Jersey and eventually drove back to Akron together.

Parker was soon getting itchy to return to New Jersey but needed money. Dew suggested that all Parker had to do was pawn the fancy gold ring he was wearing. But Lockett thought the ring was beautiful. Lockett had another idea that would allow Parker to keep the ring and get the money he needed: they would rob either a grocery store or a furniture store in the area, maybe both. She warned that the operator of the grocery store was a "big guy who carried a .45. We'd have to work fast."[4]

It's unclear which shop they decided to hit first, but as night began to fall, both stores closed and the trio robbed neither. Later that evening, Lockett's brother, James, joined the conspiracy and offered what he thought might be a better target. Pawn shops have a lot of money; why not hit a pawn shop? He and Dew would enter the shop and pretend to pawn Parker's ring. Parker, who had only bullets but no gun, would then enter the pawn shop and ask to see a gun for possible purchase. Parker would then load the weapon and announce the holdup, and the three would take whatever cash they could get. Sandra Lockett knew the pawnbroker, Sidney Cohen, and he knew her. So she would stay out of sight in the getaway car.

It all went like clockwork until Parker announced the stickup and Cohen tried to wrestle the gun away. In the ensuing struggle, the gun went off. Parker's finger was on the trigger. He had just shot Cohen dead.

The timing of all this could not have been worse. Just two weeks earlier, on New Year's Day, a new death penalty law had gone into effect in Ohio,[5] one that was designed to respond to the concerns the U.S. Supreme Court had articulated in its *Furman* decision. Lockett played no direct role in the murder; she wasn't even there. Further, she never intended for anyone to be killed, nor had she reason to believe that that would happen. Yet she fit squarely within the requirements of the new Ohio law and would be Ohio's first candidate for the death penalty under it.

As stated in the previous chapter, the Court found in *Furman v. Georgia* that the death penalty was being applied in an entirely irrational and unpredictable manner. In the memorable words of Justice Stewart, "these death sentences are cruel and unusual in the same way that being struck by lightning is cruel and unusual," a phenomenon Stewart attributed to the unlimited discretion accorded to judges and juries to decide who shall live and who shall die. What was needed, the Court said, was better guided discretion, and that's what Ohio sought to provide with its revamped death-penalty law.

Ohio's new death-penalty law identified seven specific aggravating factors, any one of which, if found to exist, would require a death sentence (with only a handful of narrow exceptions). If none of the aggravating factors could be found, death would be impermissible. One of the seven factors included the murder of the president, the vice-president, the state's governor or lieutenant governor, or the candidate for any of those offices. A death sentence would be required if any murder was committed for hire, if the offender was already confined in prison, or if the victim was a police officer acting in the performance of official duties.

None of these aggravating circumstances could be applied to Lockett, but two others could. The law also required a death sentence in cases where either the murder was committed in the course of some other violent felony (such as aggravated robbery), or the murder was committed to avoid getting caught for some other felony (in this case, the robbery).

To better guide the judge or jury, the Ohio statute also specified three mitigating circumstances. The defendant could not be sentenced to death if (1) the victim had induced or facilitated the offense, (2) it was likely that the defendant would not have committed the offense but for the fact that he or she "was under duress, coercion, or strong provocation," or (3) the offense was "primarily the product of the defendant's psychosis or mental deficiency."[6]

Lockett would be tried separately. Two weeks before jury selection, the prosecutor offered to permit her to plead guilty to voluntary manslaughter and aggravated robbery, offenses that each carried a maximum penalty of twenty-five years' imprisonment. But she would have to cooperate and testify against Parker, Dew, and her brother, James. She rejected the offer. Prosecutors knew that it was Parker who fired the fatal shot, and he was the defendant they wanted to get the most, but they were uncertain they had enough evidence to convict any of them without a confession. So prosecutors offered deals to all the defendants, and Parker—the most vulnerable to a death sentence—did not share Lockett's apprehensions. He agreed to tell all in exchange for a life sentence.[7]

There was the question of what, if anything, to make of the fact that Lockett never pulled the trigger and wasn't even present when the shooting occurred. The judge instructed the jury that before it could find Lockett guilty, it had to find that she had purposely killed the pawnbroker while committing or attempting to commit aggravated robbery. Purposely? The judge explained that one who

> purposely aids, helps, associates himself or herself with another for the purpose of committing a crime is regarded as if he or she were the principal offender and is just as guilty as if the person performed every act constituting the offense.[8]

The judge's definition of the word *purposely* embodies the common law doctrine that an accessory before the fact is as guilty as the principal who later commits the crime. The doctrine has since been rejected in most states, and whether it could be applied in death cases was unclear at the time of Lockett's trial.

Regarding the intent requirement, the court instructed:

> A person engaged in a common design with others to rob by force and violence an individual or individuals of their property is presumed to acquiesce in whatever may reasonably be necessary to accomplish the object of their enterprise. . . .
>
> If the conspired robbery and the manner of its accomplishment would be reasonably likely to produce death, each plotter is equally guilty with the principal offender as an aider and abettor in the homicide. . . . An intent to kill by an aider and abettor may be found to exist beyond a reasonable doubt under such circumstances.[9]

The jury found Lockett guilty as charged, and it found the two aggravating circumstances: the murder occurred in the course of another violent felony and for the purpose of escape. That's called *aggravated murder* in Ohio, and it required the trial judge to impose a death sentence unless he or she could find one of the mitigating factors specified in the death-penalty statute. But there was no evidence here that Cohen had "induced or facilitated" his own murder. Nor could it be said that Lockett was acting "under duress, coercion, or strong provocation" or that the offense was "primarily the product of [Lockett's] psychosis or mental deficiency."

A careful look at the crime might lead one to believe that if anyone deserved the death penalty, it would have been Parker. But it turned out that Lockett, who arguably was the least culpable, was the only one of the four to end up on Ohio's death row. By pleading guilty, Parker received a life sentence. Dew escaped a death sentence because of what the court found to be his diminished mental capacity. And Sandra Lockett's brother, James, had his death sentence commuted to life in prison because of the failure of the government to turn over relevant evidence to the defense.[10] In Sandra Lockett's case, it was a reluctant sentence. The judge told Lockett that he had "no other alternative . . . whether he liked it or not."[11] There was an automatic appeal to the Ohio Supreme Court, which affirmed the conviction and sentence.

Although the murder that January night in 1975 did not receive a great deal of attention at the time, there seemed to be little question that once Lockett's case reached the U.S. Supreme Court, the outcome could have a significant impact on the death penalty throughout the United States. Proponents of capital punishment saw the case as an opportunity to expand on the Supreme Court's decision in *Gregg* and to send a green light to Ohio and all states to resume implementing the death penalty in a large way. Civil rights lawyers saw opportunities as well. The Court could use Lockett's case to ban death sentences for those who participate in a felony but play no direct role in taking another's life. (This question has since been resolved; see Chapter 9.) Did race play a part in the sentencing (all the defendants in the Lockett case were African American and the victim was Caucasian)? Was the "guided discretion" that was deliberately built into the Ohio law so narrow as to preclude the jury from considering other factors that might be relevant in determining whether a death sentence was justified? The answers to these questions had the potential to affect laws in all states, all drafted with the common goal of meeting the Court's latest pronouncements on capital punishment in *Furman v. Georgia.*

The NAACP Legal Defense Fund (LDF), then and now the nation's premier civil rights law firm, offered to spearhead Lockett's Supreme Court appeal. The organization was founded in 1940 by Thurgood Marshall, who, a quarter century later, would become the country's first African American Supreme Court justice and one of its fiercest opponents of capital punishment. Jack Greenberg, who had succeeded Marshall as executive director of the LDF, would head up the defense team, although the Lockett case would actually be argued by legendary death-penalty lawyer Anthony "Tony" Amsterdam, the same lawyer who had successfully argued the *Furman* case and, four years later, had also argued *Gregg v. Georgia* (with less success). Amsterdam, a former law professor at Stanford University, knew the law and he knew the Court. Sandra Lockett would be in good hands.[12]

Amsterdam got off to a shaky start. His plan was to challenge not only Lockett's death sentence but also the conviction itself, arguing that the death of the pawnbroker was never part of the plan. Chief Justice Burger stopped him short, "They had bullets in the gun, did they not?" Amsterdam pointed to Parker's confession in which he had stated, "It was only supposed to be a robbery. The killing—that was not part of the plan." Burger responded: "I suppose on that theory, the perpetrators would not need any bullets in the gun if they had no intention. . . . Would an empty pistol not have done just as well?"[13]

Figure 3.1. Professor Anthony Amsterdam.

Getting nowhere, Amsterdam moved on to what he saw as another flaw in Lockett's trial. Lockett never testified. She had planned to testify but, at the last minute, her mother talked her out of it. It turned out there was no one else who either could or would testify on her behalf. The defense had no defense at all. After the prosecution rested, so did the defense. The Fifth Amendment guarantee against self-incrimination gives a criminal defendant an absolute right not to testify, and prosecutors are forbidden from suggesting to the jury that doing so in any way indicates guilt. In his closing argument in the Lockett case, however, the prosecutor repeatedly referred to the "un-refuted" and "un-contradicted" evidence that the state had presented. Amsterdam found those remarks sufficiently close to commenting on Lockett's decision not to testify as to violate her Fifth Amendment right against self-incrimination, tainting the conviction and requiring a new trial. Again he got nowhere, this time running into opposition from someone he considered an unlikely source: it was an incredulous Thurgood Marshall—one of only two justices on the Court (the other being William Brennan) who opposed capital punishment in all cases. "What do you mean?" thundered Marshall. "Let us just state one point: Of course you can always say it is un-contradicted. . . . I just do not see how you can do that." Amsterdam answered: "Well . . . Your Honor . . ." Justice Marshall again: "I do not see how you can muzzle the prosecutor by your trial tactics."

Amsterdam was not only losing his case, he was also wasting precious argument time when Justice Potter Stewart leaned in with a helpful hint: "I trust, Mr. Amsterdam, you are not going to consume all of your time on this question. There are other questions."

To Amsterdam, and to those most closely following the case, the fact that Lockett played no role in the actual murder appeared paramount. While states can clearly say that those who participate in a crime are as culpable as the principle for all foreseeable consequences—the felony-murder rule—the Court had never squarely addressed whether someone who did not personally commit the murder but was still involved in the crime was sufficiently culpable to face a death sentence. The robbery scheme may have been Lockett's idea, but the only actual role she played in the offense was to drive the getaway car. Did this make her culpable enough that she should pay with her life? Amsterdam thought not, especially in this case where the Ohio statute appeared to preclude the jury from *even considering* Lockett's relatively minor part as a mitigating circumstance. The fact that she wasn't even in the store when the murder occurred and had had no reason to expect anyone would be killed was not encompassed by any of the mitigating factors specified in the Ohio law.

Justice Harry Blackmun watched with interest. He had previously written about his personal distaste for capital punishment and vowed that as a state legislator he could never vote to authorize it. But as a judge, he saw nothing about the death penalty that might be inconsistent with the Eighth Amendment guarantee against cruel and unusual punishment or any other provision of the Constitution. As a judge rather than a policy maker, Blackmun found himself duty bound to uphold the death penalty. But Amsterdam's argument was taking hold on Blackmun, who was never much of a fan of Tony Amsterdam. Blackmun's recently released papers show a more than passing disdain dating back to when Blackmun was on the U.S. Court of Appeals for the Eighth Circuit. After reading one of Amsterdam's briefs, Blackmun scrawled in the margins, "I suspect I am too far removed from academic days to understand the professorial mind."[14] Later, in his Supreme Court bench notes, Blackmun observed that Amsterdam's "voice squeaks." He summed up Amsterdam's performance in one argument with a single word: "Ugh!"[15]

But on this occasion, Blackmun found in Amsterdam's argument an easy way out of the case. Blackmun contemplated a narrow decision stating simply that before sentencing someone to death, the jury (or judge) must be allowed to at least *consider* that the defendant did not actually pull the trigger, that he or she did not immediately kill the victim or intend physical harm. (The Court did not take up whether the Eighth Amendment would actually prohibit executing a non-triggerman for another four years.)

As a former lower court judge, Blackmun had considerably more experience than any of his colleagues, and he thought that Chief Justice Warren Burger, a childhood friend and best man at Blackmun's wedding, would assign the writing of the opinion to him. When the case came up for conference, however, Blackmun found that some of his colleagues wanted to go further and rule not only that the sentencing authority—judge or jury—be allowed to consider the degree of involvement of the defendant but also be allowed to consider anything about the defendant or the crime that might make a death sentence inappropriate. Burger was acutely aware that the Court had become deeply divided over capital punishment and was unable to speak with a single voice. In the *Furman* decision, the Court issued a brief, unsigned opinion finding the death penalty unconstitutional *as applied*, and then all nine justices weighed in with separate opinions totaling 232 pages, one of the lengthiest Supreme Court decisions in history (and one of the most confusing). The chief justice thought for once he could get four of his colleagues to agree, resulting in an actual majority opinion—a "decision of the Court"—and, with that in mind, assigned the writing of the opinion to himself.

Burger initially felt he could draft a decision along the lines suggested by Blackmun, but it became apparent at the Conference on the case that he could not. Justice Lewis Powell felt that, given the severity of the punishment, all possible mitigating factors should be considered, not just the degree of involvement of the defendant. This was not what Burger had in mind. Justices Potter Stewart and John Paul Stevens were lining up behind Powell. A week after the Lockett case had been argued, Burger wrote his colleagues about the divisions within the Court on capital punishment and about his own effort to find common ground:

> Although I did not agree with the views of the plurality in our preceding cases, I am now prepared to yield with the hope that there can be a majority opinion here. With deference, I feel that our plurality opinions on the death penalty have created uncertainty and instability in an area which deserves the greatest certainty and stability that can be provided, and this calls for a [majority] Court opinion.

The chief's goal of bringing the Court together on a controversial issue turned out to be elusive. Blackmun himself responded to Burger:

I suspect that . . . I shall not be able to join the opinion that evolves. The [initial] position at conference was that a sentencing authority must be permitted to consider the degree of a non-triggerman's involvement. It would follow that the Ohio statute was unconstitutional as applied to Sandra Lockett on that fairly narrow ground.[16]

Blackmun goes on to express dismay that five justices could not agree to join in a single opinion (his) stating just this point.

No justice's opinion could garner five votes. The Lockett case would result in yet another plurality opinion, although that turned out to be enough to set aside Lockett's death sentence. The chief justice, writing for himself and Justices Stewart, Powell, and Stevens, concluded that

the sentencer, in all but the rarest kind of capital case, must not be precluded from considering, as a mitigating factor, any aspect of a defendant's character or record and any of the circumstances of the offense that the defendant proffered as a basis for a sentence less than death.[17]

Justice White couldn't join the opinion of either Blackmun or the chief and, in dissent, saw both opinions as an invitation to further muddy the waters:

By requiring as a matter of constitutional law that sentencing authorities be permitted to consider and in their discretion to act upon any and all mitigating circumstances, the Court permits them to refuse to impose the death penalty no matter what the circumstances of the crime. This invites a return to the pre-Furman days when the death penalty was generally reserved for those very few for whom society has least consideration."[18]

White saw Burger's *Lockett* decision as undoing whatever the Court had thought it had accomplished in *Furman* and *Gregg*. Justice Antonin Scalia, who would not join the Court for another eleven years, later scoffed at the *Lockett* decision as predicating the death penalty on "two quite incompatible commands: the sentencer's discretion to impose death must be closely confined. . . . But the sentencer's discretion *not* to impose death (to extend mercy) must be unlimited."[19]

Justice William Rehnquist dissented, writing, "The Court has gone from pillar to post, with the result that the sort of reasonable predictability upon which legislatures, trial courts and appellate courts must of necessity rely has been all but completely sacrificed."[20] Justices Rehnquist and White would have allowed Ohio to go forward with Sandra Lockett's execution.

The immediate effect of the *Lockett* decision was to set aside ninety-nine death sentences in Ohio and many more around the country. In the years that followed, however, the decision appeared to be of little help in deciding which capital defendants should live and which should die, nor did it advance the Court's demand for consistency in the death-penalty process. On this point, the views of Rehnquist and White turned out to be prophetic.

But for Sandra Lockett, the Court's decision on July 3, 1978, was a huge victory. Her death sentence was reduced to life in prison. She would be eligible for parole in fewer than ten years.

Two Days Later
July 5, 1978
Mira Mesa, California

It was a lazy summer afternoon in Mira Mesa, California, a middle-class suburb of San Diego. Teenagers John Mayeski and Michael Baker lived on the same quiet street and were best friends. And they knew just how to spend this fine day: by fishing on a nearby lake. But first, a bite to eat. They stopped by a Jack in the Box fast-food place down the street and picked up a bag of hamburgers.

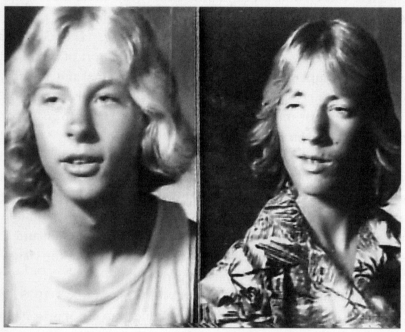

Figure 3.2. Murder victims John Mayeski, fifteen *(left)*, and Michael Baker, sixteen *(right)*.

Across the parking lot sat another pair of young men, Robert Harris, who was twenty-five, and Daniel ("Danny"), his eighteen-year-old brother. Robert and Danny were trying to hotwire a car. On this particular afternoon, the Harris brothers would rob a bank together. Robert would be the teacher; Danny, the pupil. "I told him I'd whip his ass if he didn't do it," the elder Harris later recounted. Lesson number one: You don't use your own car for the getaway. When Robert couldn't get the car started, he looked across the parking lot to see Mayeski and Baker sitting in their green Ford LTD and told his brother, "We'll take that one."

Figure 3.3. Robert *(left)* and Daniel *(right)* Harris.

John and Michael were just beginning to dig into their burgers when Robert went up to their open window, pointed a 9mm Luger pistol at John's handsome blond head, and told the boys they were going for a ride. There would be no fishing today. Robert then crawled into the back seat and told John to drive east. Danny followed in his older brother's 1963 Ford. When they got to a remote canyon a few miles away, John and Michael were ordered out. Robert told them he was going to use their car in a bank robbery and assured them that they would not be hurt. He might even leave a few bucks for them for the use of the car. The boys tried to be accommodating, given the circumstances, and they agreed to wait on top of a little hill for a while and then walk into town and report the car stolen. Michael then turned to leave, hoping he could simply walk away. John, also turning as if to leave, wished his abductors "Good luck." Just then, Robert slowly raised the Luger and shot John in the back.

Danny described the scene to police:

Just as I heard a shot and I looked back and the blond-haired guy—I don't know what his name was—he spun around and looked at me.

Blood was coming out of his mouth. His eyes were real big, he fell to the ground and, I started to get sick. All of a sudden, I hear the other guy run up to the bushes up ahead of me. And he was screamin' at my brother, "Don't shoot me."[21]

Robert then chased Michael down a ravine and caught up with him, and then—after ordering him to "stop crying like a baby"—shot him four times in the head and chest.[22] Michael was still breathing when Robert climbed back up the hill. Robert walked over to the boy, knelt down, put the Luger to his head, and fired.

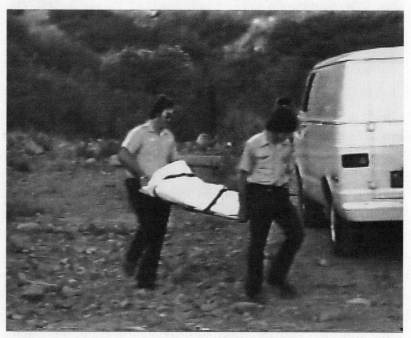

Figure 3.4. One of the boys' bodies being removed from the scene, July 5, 1978.

In an interview years later,[23] Daniel said, "God, everything started to spin. It was like slow motion. I saw the gun, and then his head exploded like a balloon. . . . I just started running and running. But I heard Robert and turned around. He was swinging the pistol in the air and laughing." Robert Harris drove the car to a girlfriend's house where he and Daniel were staying and there, fifteen minutes after the double murder, began eating what was left of his victims' hamburgers. Laughing, Robert offered his younger brother an apple turnover. Daniel says he became nauseous and ran to the bathroom. But Robert continued to appear unfazed. Smiling, he told Daniel it would be amusing if the two of them were to pose as police officers and inform the parents that their sons were killed. What fun!

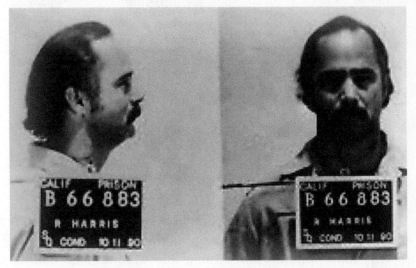

Figure 3.5. Mug shot of Robert Alton Harris.

Later that afternoon, the Harris brothers did return to the Mira Mesa branch of the San Diego Savings and Trust Bank, donning maroon ski masks, and they did rob it as planned, netting $3,009 in cash. It turns out that the sister of one of the victims, Tammy Baker, was in the bank at the time. The Harris brothers' portraits were captured by the bank's roving cameras, although the police would not need the video for evidence. Robert Harris's cleverness in using someone else's car was offset by the not-so-clever escape, driving straight from the bank to his girlfriend's home in Mira Mesa. He was followed by a bystander who then called police. Within half an hour, a squad of armed police officers was on the doorstep.

Figure 3.6. Robert Harris arrested.

Robert and Danny surrendered without resistance and were even captured on police video coming out of the house with their hands up. They were promptly advised that they were suspects in a bank robbery. One of the arresting officers was Detective Steven Baker, who would later learn that there was a lot more to this crime than a robbery, that it was a double murder and that his own son, Michael, was one of the victims.

Both Harris brothers had been advised of their Miranda rights, the right to remain silent, to have a court appointed lawyer, and so on. They had been arrested at 1:00 p.m. for the bank robbery. Three hours later, Daniel finally told the police all about the murders; at 6:30 p.m., he confessed in a tape-recorded statement, portions of which were promptly played back for Robert. Robert then himself confessed. Later that evening, Dr. William Griswold, a psychiatrist for the State of California, was with police during further questioning.

Griswold wanted to know why the elder Harris believed it was necessary to kill the two teenagers.

> *Harris:* I don't know why I did it.
> *Griswold:* Would you fear that they could identify you or what?
> *Harris:* No. They said "Take the car" and they wouldn't say anything. They'd say a nigger did it. I don't know why I killed them.
> *Griswold:* Did you derive any pleasure from shooting them?
> *Harris:* I started laughing.
> *Griswold:* Started laughing? It seemed to give you some pleasure at the time?
> *Harris:* Well, it seemed funny at the time.[24]

The elder Harris subsequently told a fellow inmate at the San Quentin State Prison why he had killed the boys: "I couldn't have no punks running around that do that [identify him], so I wasted them."[25]

Danny Harris agreed to cooperate with prosecutors, pleaded guilty to a single count of kidnapping, and was sentenced to six years in state prison. He was discharged in 1983. That Robert Harris would be charged with capital murder was all but a foregone conclusion. The only question seemed to be whether there might have been some mitigating circumstances about Robert Harris that could have outweighed the aggravating circumstances identified in the California law—that is, murder in the course of another murder, and murder in the course of a robbery or kidnapping. Could the state demonstrate that it was implementing capital punishment with the kind of consistency the Supreme Court required in its *Furman* decision?

Early on, Robert Harris was not the kind of kid you'd want living next door. When asked about his childhood, he boasted, "I used to take cats up on this big water tower and throw them off." His first brushes with the law began when he was only seven years old, and after that, it wasn't long before he was spending every weekend in some jail or detention center on some new charge.

At the penalty phase of his trial, the jury learned that Harris had been convicted of voluntary manslaughter for the beating death of a neighbor who had slighted him; that he was on parole for the homicide at the time of the double murders; that he had sodomized his cellmate while in jail and threatened the cellmate's life were he not to return the favor; and that twice he was caught in prison in possession of deadly weapons, first a knife, then a garrote.

Harris presented evidence of his dismal childhood, including severe beatings and denials of paternity by his alcoholic father (who had been sent to prison for sexual offenses against Harris's sister). When he was only fourteen, Harris had been abandoned by his mother, herself an alcoholic and a convicted bank robber. It wasn't enough. The jury returned a verdict of death; the trial judge declined to modify it; and, on March 6, 1979, Harris was formally sentenced to die.

The basis of Harris's initial appeal was that California had failed to undertake any kind of proportionality review to guarantee that the death sentence met the consistency the Supreme Court had demanded in *Furman,* that there were other murderers in California who had committed objectively worse crimes and had received only life sentences. Such discrepancies, argued Harris's lawyers, meant the death penalty was still being applied in an unconstitutionally cruel and unusual fashion.

The U.S. Court of Appeals for the Ninth Circuit agreed with the defense, ruling that California would have to undertake some kind of "proportionality review" before imposing a death sentence in Harris's case or in any other. The crime and the criminal in each case would have to be compared with other earlier capital cases before a death sentence could be returned. Harris's execution was, at minimum, put on hold until the U.S. Supreme Court could review the Ninth Circuit's decision.

It was a tough ruling for California law-enforcement officials, particularly Detective Steven Baker, who candidly shared his sentiments with the authors: "As far as the rights go, they're all for the criminal.

My son had no stay of execution. My son did not have a Supreme Court to stop his execution. Nor was my son executed by a simple injection. He was blown away. I believe some day Robert Harris will get his due. I have requested to be one of the twelve witnesses when he is executed."[26]

Figure 3.7. Detective Steven Baker: "My son had no stay of execution."

Once again, it would be the highly regarded Tony Amsterdam who would argue on behalf of the condemned inmate.[27] Could there really be crimes worse or even comparable to those committed by Robert Harris? Indeed maybe there were. In his Supreme Court brief on behalf of Harris, Amsterdam offered a laundry list of brutal murders, arguably as bad as or worse than those committed by Harris, which brought only life sentences.[28] Among them was the case of *People v. Zimmerman*. Zimmerman was convicted of the axe murders of an eighteen-year-old boy and his twelve-year-old sister during a burglary in Los Angeles. The girl was also raped and sodomized. Despite a prior burglary conviction, Zimmerman got only life.[29] Then there was the case of *People v. Thomas*.[30] Willie Thomas was convicted of the execution-style murders of four people, including a two-year-old girl, apparently in retaliation for a slight received in a family feud. He had previously served time for armed robbery. Thomas received only a life sentence.

Paul Roberts also was sentenced to life for the murders of a San Bernadino homeowner and his daughter, killings committed in the course of a burglary.[31] Roberts had stalked the victims and, after he killed the daughter, had "spontaneously" committed necrophilia on the body. He, too, received a sentence of life in prison.

The list went on and on, crimes that shocked the conscience and broke the heart yet brought only life in prison. Is this the kind of consistency the Supreme Court demanded in *Furman v. Georgia*, asked Amsterdam. Michael Wellington, California's deputy attorney general, told the Court that the kind of proportionality review that Amsterdam was seeking was "simply not possible. . . . It is simply not possible for any one court to compare the hundreds of cases that would be before them . . . [or] for this Court to do it . . . some 1,200 nationwide . . . in all of their particulars."[32]

Dividing 7–2, the Supreme Court agreed with Wellington and upheld Harris's conviction and death sentence. In the cases that followed *Furman* (most particularly *Gregg v. Georgia* and *Lockett v. Ohio*), the Court had made it clear that death-penalty laws must give juries some guidance to prevent arbitrary sentences and to ensure at least some consistency and individualized consideration of each case. In Harris's case, the Court found that by requiring the jury to find at least one "special" (aggravating) circumstance and by allowing consideration of any and all circumstances that work in the defendant's favor along with appellate review of the jury's decision, California had largely satisfied that requirement. But just as each case is different, so, too, is each jury; therefore, absolute consistency in sentencing is not required.

Figure 3.8. California deputy attorney general Michael Wellington.

The Court did acknowledge, however, that proportionality must be considered in the sense that the punishment must fit the crime. As the Court had held in *Coker v. Georgia*[33] (discussed in greater detail in Chapter 8), the death penalty may be disproportionate to the crime in cases where the victim does not die. The Court, however, had settled in *Gregg v. Georgia* that a death sentence is not disproportionate for murder and that, while many states may choose to compare different murders and the sentences they bring, the Constitution does not require such review. Justice Byron White, writing for a seven-judge majority, concluded, "Any sentencing scheme may occasionally produce aberrational outcomes. Such inconsistencies are a far cry from the major systemic defects identified in *Furman*. As we have acknowledged in the past, there can be 'no perfect procedure for deciding in which cases governmental authority should be used to impose death.'"[34]

Only Justices Brennan and Marshall, who opposed the death

penalty in all cases, dissented. They concluded that proportionality review "would serve to eliminate some, if only a small part, of the irrationality that currently infects imposition of the death penalty," and that alone would justify requiring such review whenever a capital defendant, having been sentenced to die, requested it.

Figure 3.9. Michael Wellington surveying the crime scene with coauthor Tim O'Brien.

The Court's decision was announced on January 23, 1984, almost six years after the deadly shootings in Mira Mesa, and one might have reasonably thought, after review in the nation's highest legal tribunal, that that would have been the end of it. Robert Harris was able to put off execution for another eight years with a succession of new appeals, some more serious than others. He and his lawyers challenged the quality of his psychiatric evaluation; he argued that the jury should have been allowed to consider that he was the victim of fetal alcohol syndrome as a result of his mother's alcoholism (she eventually drank herself to death). He also argued that the death penalty in California discriminated against younger killers, males, and those who killed whites. In each of these cases, the lower courts ruled against Harris. Several of these issues were appealed to the U.S. Supreme Court, which denied review, allowing the lower court decisions to stand, but each claim further stalled Harris's execution.

Eventually, all appeals were exhausted, or so it again seemed. Harris was scheduled to die at 12:01 a.m. on April 21, 1992. It would be the first execution in California in more than twenty-five years. There were numerous death sentences after California reenacted its death penalty statute, but with no one being executed, the ranks of death row had swelled to 323 inmates, second only to Texas with 370 death-row inmates.[35] Death-penalty opponents feared that Harris's execution would open the floodgates. Mother Teresa was among those urging clemency. Famed 1960s folk singer Joan Baez was among dozens of activists who staged protest rallies outside San Quentin State Prison, where Harris was to be put to death that night. And Harris's lawyers did not give up, seeking one stay after another. The final hours ended up as a bizarre, cross-country duel by telephone and fax machine between the U.S. Supreme Court and the lower court judges in California.

Six hours before Harris was to be executed, an appeals court judge in San Francisco issued a stay of execution based on a claim that Harris's brother Danny may have fired the first shot. Even before the Supreme Court could rule on that, the appeals court issued another stay based on Harris's contention that the gas chamber, the only method of execution in California at the time, was cruel and unusual. When the Supreme Court overturned the first stay and began considering the second, the appeals court issued a third. Three hours after the execution was to have taken place, the high Court acted on the remaining issues. The eyewitnesses were put on buses and taken to the gas chamber. It was now 3:51 a.m. Finally, Harris was strapped in and was apparently prepared to die. Then the phone rang. Yet another delay. Ninth Circuit Court of Appeals judge Harry

Pregerson determined that Harris was entitled to a hearing on his claim that death in California's gas chamber was cruel and unusual.

In the confusion of the night, Pregerson was apparently unaware that the Supreme Court had already rejected Harris's argument about the gas chamber. The Supreme Court again stepped in to vacate Pregerson's stay with two justices, Blackmun and Stevens, dissenting. But as the matter was reverberating between Washington and San Francisco, Harris was unstrapped and taken back to his cell, the first time in San Quentin history that a condemned prisoner was removed from the gas chamber alive.

Figure 3.10. Last-minute reprieve.

In its order setting the stage for Harris's execution, the justices added another order that was unprecedented: "No further stays of Robert Alton Harris' execution shall be entered by the federal courts except upon order of this court."[36] The justices were clearly irritated by Harris's last-minute appeals. The unsigned order referred to them as "abusive" and "a last minute attempt to manipulate the legal process."[37] Using its supervisory powers over lower federal courts,[38] the Supreme Court essentially told the federal judges in California it was time to butt out.[39]

For his last meal, Harris requested and was given two large pizzas, a twenty-one-piece bucket of Kentucky Fried Chicken, a six-pack of Pepsi, a bag of jelly beans, a double serving of ice cream, and a pack of Camel cigarettes. At 6:01 a.m., he was again led back to the chamber. He was described as looking resigned to his fate and was fully cooperative with the guards who led him the fifteen paces from his cell. He was strapped into the metal chair, and a stethoscope was taped to his chest. The door to the gas chamber was closed and sealed, and at 6:05 a.m., he began breathing deeply, staring ahead, and he appeared to be mouthing the words "It's all right" and "I'm sorry."

At 6:07 a.m., a prison official operated the lever, slowly lowering the pellets of cheesecloth-wrapped sodium cyanide into the small vat of sulfuric acid beneath Harris's chair to create the lethal hydrocyanic gas. Harris took a number of deep breaths and for several minutes appeared to gasp and twitch convulsively. His head snapped back and then dropped as he strained against the straps. After a minute his hands seemed to relax. His mouth was open and his face flushed . . . and then turned blue. Three minutes later there was a cough and a convulsion. At 6:21 a.m., Warden Daniel Vasquez declared Harris dead and announced the last words—a poem—Harris had chosen to be remembered by. Misquoting the Keanu Reeves film *Bill and Ted's Bogus Journey*, Harris recited, "You can be a king or a street sweeper. But everybody dances with the grim reaper."[40]

Among some fifty witnesses was Michael Baker's sister, Tammy, and his father, Detective Steven Baker. In an interview later in the day, Baker told CNN, "He appeared to look for me in the gallery . . . and the minute he made eye contact with me, he quit looking for anybody else. And he looked me right square in the eye and he mouthed the words, 'I'm sorry.' And I nodded my head at him, so as to acknowledge it, and then he looked straight forward again. I'm satisfied that Harris has been punished for the crime he committed."[41] Baker died six years later of cancer but not before cofounding the Crime Victims Bureau in San Diego to assist the victims of violent crime and their loved ones.

Harris's lawyers had raised a multitude of legal issues, some of which lingered on long after the execution. Among those lasting issues was whether death in California's gas chamber was cruel and unusual punishment. Federal judge Marilyn Patel had quietly allowed Harris's execution to be videotaped so that it could be used later as evidence in a lawsuit filed on behalf of death-row inmates by the American Civil Liberties Union. Believed to be the only video-tape ever made of an execution in the United States, the tape had been kept in a court vault and had apparently never been shown. It has since been destroyed on Judge Patel's order after state lawyers agreed not to present testimony from additional witnesses should, for some reason, the case have to be retried.[42]

Before ordering the tape destroyed, Judge Patel ruled that the gas chamber "is inhumane and has no place in civilized society" and must be shut down.[43] In her ruling, Patel said that doctors' reports and eyewitness accounts indicated that inmates remained conscious from fifteen seconds to more than a minute after being exposed to the cyanide gas, and that during that period, an inmate likely experienced intense physical pain. Patel's decision was affirmed by the U.S. Ninth Circuit Court of Appeals[44] but was summarily reversed by the U.S. Supreme Court without even hearing formal argument in court.[45] California now uses lethal injections for its executions, but, like a handful of other states, officials keep its gas chamber up and ready should lethal injection be successfully challenged in court.

While the jury did hear about Harris's troubled childhood, there are some things about him it did not hear. How could anyone have done the things that Harris did and laugh about them? In an interview,[46] Barbara Harris, one of Robert Harris's sisters, put her palms over her eyes and said softly, "I saw every grain of sweetness, pity and goodness in him destroyed. It was a long and ugly journey."[47]

Harris was born January 15, 1953, several hours after his mother was kicked in the stomach by her insanely jealous husband. She was six and a half months pregnant at the time, and the elder Harris had come home drunk and accused her of infidelity. Harris's father and mother were both alcoholics. His father had twice been convicted of sexually molesting his two daughters, Robert's sisters. His mother had been arrested several times, once for bank robbery. The father frequently beat his children and often caused serious injury. All of the children had monstrous childhoods. But even in the Harris family, the abuse Robert was subjected to was unusual.

Harris's sister Barbara recounted, "I remember one time we were in the car and Mother was in the back seat with Robbie in her arms. He was crying and my father threw a glass bottle at him, but it hit my mother in the face. The glass shattered and Robbie started screaming. I'll never forget it," she said. "Her face was all pink from the mixture of blood and milk. She ended up blaming Robbie for all the hurt, all the things like that. She felt helpless and he was someone to vent her anger on."

Harris had a learning disability and a speech problem, but there was no money for therapy. When he was at school, he felt stupid and classmates teased him, his sister said. "He was the most beautiful of all my mother's children; he was an angel," she said. "He would just break your heart. He wanted love so bad, he would beg for any kind of physical contact." The child who had cried at the movies when Bambi's mother dies had evolved into a man who was arrested several times for abusing animals. He killed cats and dogs, according to his younger brother Daniel, and laughed while torturing them with mop handles, darts, and pellet guns.[48]

In all, there were nine children, and Barbara says that all nine are psychologically crippled because of their father. But Robert, she says, was too young and the abuse lasted too long. In his sister's mind, he never had much of a chance to recover.[49]

While even among abused children Robert's case may stand out, he shared many of the same characteristics of his fellow residents on death row in California and around the country. All death-penalty cases now have separate trials, the first to determine guilt and, if a guilty verdict is returned, a second trial to assess punishment by weighing the statutorily specified aggravating circumstances against any and all mitigating circumstances. The penalty phases of these trials have now given the world new insight into the environment that often gives birth to future killers. In literally hundreds of cases we reviewed, three characteristics stand out prominently: abject poverty, little or no education, and abuse in early childhood.[50]

Justice Department statistics show that more than half of the inmates on death row in the United States never finished high school.[51] The prevalence of abuse in early childhood is more subjective and less quantifiable, but it does show up with striking consistency in the penalty phase of death-penalty trials. There are many studies showing a correlation between childhood abuse and adult violence,[52] particularly among those sentenced to death.[53] Quite often, as in the Robert Harris case, all three factors—abject poverty, little or no education, and early childhood abuse—are present.

These characteristics figure prominently in the ongoing philosophical debate over the extent, if any, a defendant's background might diminish responsibility for his offense and, if it does, how that might relate to the wisdom and fairness of the death penalty itself.[54] There is the colloquialism "abuse excuse," but no one is really suggesting that the environment in which these defendants were raised should be considered an excuse; all would agree that these offenders should be punished. Given the remarkable prevalence of poverty, substandard education, and early childhood abuse, however—all conditions beyond the defendants' control—the question becomes to what extent, if any, are we putting people to death because of who their parents were and what their parents did? No argument is made that these largely uncontrollable factors *cause* children to turn into monsters, only that they contribute to the phenomenon more than mere poverty.

The flip side of all this is that society does have a right, indeed an obligation, to protect itself from its worst offenders, and that retribution is generally accepted as a legitimate function of our law.[55] If our laws fail to take retribution into account, bereaved loved ones—who might care little about the childhood difficulties of the murderer—may be more inclined to seek retribution on their own, thus promoting more lawlessness. To some, Harris's disastrous upbringing may be more interesting than relevant in determining how he should be punished. California governor Pete Wilson, in rejecting Harris's bid for clemency, may have summed it up in a single line: "As great as my compassion for Robert Harris the child, I cannot excuse nor forgive the choice made by Robert Harris the man."[56] The governor was speaking from Sacramento to a statewide television and radio audience. In San Diego, Michael Baker's mother, Sharon, cried as she listened to the governor's speech on her car radio while riding home from a shopping trip. She later told the *Los Angeles Times*, "Today is a joyous day. I'm very pleased with the governor's decision. With all his compassion, he did make the right decision."[57]

Robert's younger brother Daniel grew up in the same household but did not appear to suffer either the same level of abuse or the psychopathic inclinations of Robert. The evidence produced at trial at least seemed to support his defense that he never intended to hurt anyone and that he was quite shaken by the way events unfolded. In some respects, he was in the same position as Sandra Lockett, who never pulled the trigger but still faced a possible death sentence for her involvement. After dancing around the issue of the death penalty for non-triggerman defendants, the Supreme Court finally addressed the issue in a series of cases beginning with *Enmund v. Florida* in 1982[58] and ending with *Tison v. Arizona*[59] (see Chapter 9). The rule that emerges is that the non-triggerman can be sentenced to death only if prosecutors can prove beyond a reasonable doubt that the defendant played a principle role in the underlying felony and acted with reckless indifference to human life.

There is no question that Daniel Harris played a principal role in the kidnapping that ended in the deaths of Michael Baker and John Mayeski. It could not have occurred without his assistance. But did he act with reckless indifference to human life? Only Daniel can answer that question. A *San Diego Times Union* story published in 1992 says that, since his release from prison, Daniel Harris had not gotten so much as a speeding ticket.[60] But you never know what goes on behind closed doors. A canvas of the inmates currently housed by the California Department of Rehabilitation and Corrections shows the name of Daniel Marcus Harris, convicted of sexually molesting his stepdaughter over an eleven-year period, beginning when she was only seven years old. It's the same man. Fifty years old as of this writing, Daniel Harris is currently completing a thirty-five-year prison term at the California State Prison at Corcoran.[61]

Figure 3.11. Daniel Harris mug shot, September 21, 2011.

Akron, Ohio, 2011

Sandra Lockett was released on parole in 1993 after serving eighteen years in prison. Two years later, she was back in jail. This time she was serving in the Summit County Jail in Akron for thirty-two days after she stole cosmetics from a local drugstore, a misdemeanor.[62]

In 1997, she was ordered back to prison for parole violations, including a refusal to submit to urinalysis as part of a substance-abuse program. She is now free and focusing her attention on her son, Albert Young, whom she left for prison when he was only five.

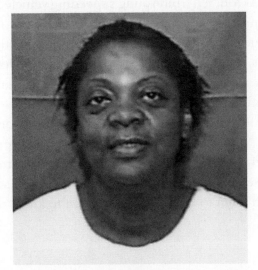

Figure 3.12. Sandra Lockett, August 14, 2002.

Figure 3.13. Albert O. Young.

In 1986, while Lockett was still incarcerated, seventeen-year-old Albert, along with a cousin and a friend, tried to rob and abduct a college student from the parking lot of an Akron bowling alley. Twenty-two-year-old Susan Soldierson, an accounting major at the University of Akron, fell from Young's speeding vehicle and sustained fatal head injuries. She died at Akron City Hospital two days later after emergency brain surgery. The three boys were tried as adults, and each was sentenced to thirty years in prison for involuntary manslaughter, aggravated robbery, and kidnapping. As of this writing, all three are still in prison.[63]

Getting Albert out of prison now is a driving force in Sandra Lockett's life. "I don't want them to come out [of] here 40 or 50 years old," said Lockett, now fifty-seven. She believes the three young men risk being "useless to society" if they aren't released soon.[64] Sandra Lockett would seem to be in a good position to know.

4
BLACK ON WHITE
RACE AND THE DEATH PENALTY

*Apparent disparities in sentencing are an inevitable part
of our criminal justice system.*
— Justice Lewis Powell, ruling in
McCleskey v. Kemp, 481 U.S. 279 (1987)

On a Saturday morning in 1978, Warren McCleskey and three of his friends drove around Marietta, Georgia, in a beat-up blue Pontiac, predators looking for likely prey. They found it in Atlanta, instead, after lunch.

The quartet, all African American and with spotty criminal records, had gone to Marietta, a suburb of Atlanta, to case a jewelry store. They decided not to rob it, later picking what appeared to be a better target downtown: the Dixie Furniture store, which sat on a commercial strip of Marietta Street. McCleskey parked the Pontiac nearby and, while his three partners waited, went to check out the store.[1]

He talked with Dixie cashier Marie Thomas about a fictional gift purchase while looking over the store and the whereabouts of its employees. Afterward, McCleskey returned to the car and worked out a plan with the others; the four men then piled out of the car and headed for the store. McCleskey entered the front door, carrying a .38 caliber Rossi nickel-plated revolver; one man, holding a sawed-off shotgun, went in the back door accompanied by the other two, both of whom were carrying pistols.[2]

The nine Dixie employees were herded to a back room, tied

up with tape, and forced to lie down on the floor. Owner William Dukes handed over $4,100 from the store safe, along with his watch and the six dollars in his pocket.[3] Somewhere in this process, one of the employees managed to activate a silent alarm. It would summon Officer Frank Schlatt, a white policeman, to his death.

This kind of alarm call was common for police officers. "You can answer three or four a night and there'll be nothing to them," said Philip Autrey, who regularly patrolled the downtown area in a squad car. Officers would respond alone. "With the current shortage of police officers, we're patrolling one man in a car, and we do not send backups," said Atlanta police lieutenant B. G. Hodnett shortly after the incident. "It's a bad situation for us."[4]

Frank Schlatt, thirty-one years old, had been on the force for five years. His colleagues regarded him as cautious and careful; he was no cowboy, they said, but he tried to be prepared for trouble. He had his gun in his hand when he entered the furniture store.[5]

Figure 4.1. Officer Frank Schlatt.

Warren McCleskey fired first—two quick shots. One of the .38 caliber bullets ricocheted harmlessly from a cigarette lighter in

Schlatt's pocket. The other hit him full in the face and killed him. McCleskey and his accomplices fled, leaving Frank Schlatt mortally wounded, bleeding out on the store's floor. He was so badly injured that Hodnett, his supervisor, did not recognize him when he arrived at the scene. Schlatt left behind a wife and a young daughter.

Figure 4.2. Officer Schlatt's family at graveside.

The manhunt was massive. Police got their first break after McCleskey was arrested in connection with another armed robbery in nearby Cobb County. During questioning, he admitted to participating in the Dixie robbery, but he denied shooting Schlatt. McCleskey would be done in, however, by his later admissions while in custody, to a codefendant and to an inmate in the next jail cell. Furthermore, two of his accomplices in the Dixie robbery would turn on him.

The evidence looked formidable to John Turner, hired by McCleskey's sister to defend him in the Dixie robbery case. An experienced former federal prosecutor, Turner urged McCleskey to plead guilty in exchange for a life sentence. "In a death-penalty case, if you can get a life sentence, you take it and run," Turner recalled years later. "But he didn't want to hear it. He was stubborn."[6]

Figure 4.3. Warren McCleskey.

The chief witness against McCleskey was Ben Wright, the accomplice who had entered the rear of the Dixie store with a sawed-off shotgun. An experienced felon—he had served fifteen years in prison for another armed robbery—Wright began building his defense strategy as soon as he heard the shots from the front of the store.

Wright was in the back, tying up one of the employees, according to the recollections of the prosecutor in the case, Russell Parker. "When the shots were fired," said Parker in an interview, "he told this person 'I'm taking your watch—you remember where I was at the time the shots were fired.'"[7]

"Ben Wright was a scary guy," said Thomas Thrash, then a young attorney assisting Parker. He remembers the two of them interviewing Wright about the details of the robbery over a dinner of fried chicken at police headquarters. "For a twenty-six-year-old kid two years out of Harvard Law School, this was a different experience than I was used to," Thrash told us.[8] Thrash is now a federal district judge in Georgia.

Wright was the star witness when the Dixie robbery case went to trial in the cavernous Fulton County courtroom of Judge Sam Phillips McKenzie. He testified that he was in the back room at the time of the shooting, but that McCleskey later told him what happened. "He said the police slipped up on him before he knew it," Wright testified, "and he said he shot him twice."[9]

McCleskey took the stand in his own defense, coming across as "cold and emotionally detached," according to Thrash.[10] The defendant said his admissions to police had been coerced, and he claimed he'd actually been playing cards elsewhere at the time of the robbery. There were no witnesses to back up his story, and McCleskey played a very weak hand from the witness stand:

Turner: Were you at the Dixie Furniture Store that day?
McCleskey: No.
Turner: Did you shoot anyone?
McCleskey: No, I didn't.
Turner: Is everything you have said the truth?
McCleskey: Positive.[11]

Marie Thomas, the Dixie cashier, was one of the picture cards in Russell Parker's deck. She identified McCleskey as the man who had talked with her about a purchase just before the robbery occurred, and she also said she was "one hundred percent sure" that he was the robber who later entered the store with a gun and shot Officer Schlatt.[12]

Then Parker played his ace. A jailhouse snitch named Offie Evans told the jury that he was in the cell next to McCleskey, that he gained McCleskey's confidence, and that McCleskey told him it was a simple case of shooting Schlatt or getting caught. He quoted McCleskey as saying, "It would have been the same thing if it had been a dozen of them."[13]

The game was over. The racially mixed jury took only two hours to return a verdict of guilty. "I don't think anyone in the courtroom was surprised," said Judge Thrash. "The evidence against McCleskey was overwhelming."[14]

In accordance with the 1976 Supreme Court mandate in *Gregg v. Georgia*, the jury then heard evidence in a sentencing hearing. Prosecutor Parker established two aggravating circumstances in connection with the murder: that it was committed during the course of another felony (the robbery) and that the victim was a police officer. Parker requested a verdict of death. "Have you observed any repentance by Mr. McCleskey?" he asked the jury. "Has he exhibited any sorrow? Have you seen any tears in his eyes for this act he has done?"[15] The defense, unaccountably, offered no evidence of mitigating circumstances on McCleskey's behalf.

There had been only one previous death sentence meted out in Georgia since the *Gregg* decision restored capital punishment, and Fulton County had a reputation for "liberal" juries. But Parker had some vigorous local support for his argument. "The law enforcement community felt very strongly that the death penalty was an appropriate punishment for the murder of a police officer struck down in the line of duty," recalled Judge Thrash.[16]

Again the jury deliberated for two hours, and the courtroom was hushed as the twelve members filed slowly back into the jury box.

The verdict slip was passed to Judge McKenzie, who read it silently and passed it to the clerk who would announce the jury's decision to the courtroom. "It was a moment filled with emotional tension, I would say," remembered Thrash. The clerk read the verdict: death. Sue Schlatt, widow of the slain policeman, wept.[17]

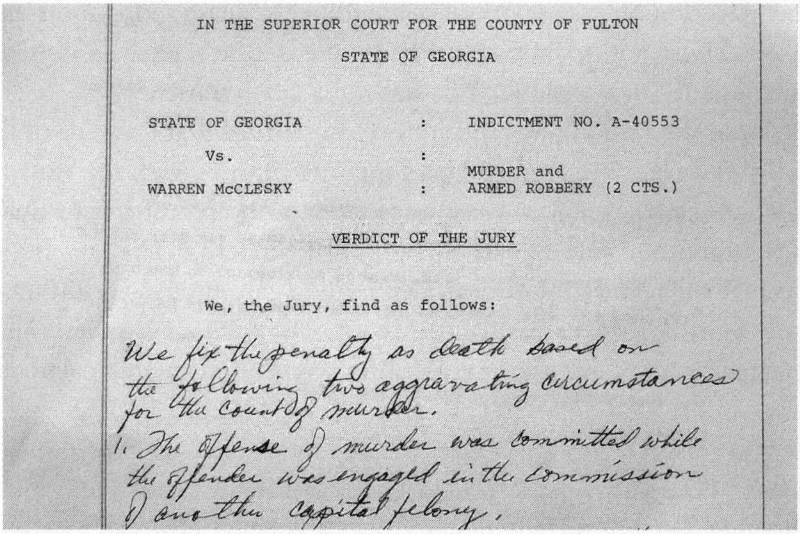

IN THE SUPERIOR COURT FOR THE COUNTY OF FULTON

STATE OF GEORGIA

STATE OF GEORGIA   :   INDICTMENT NO. A-40553

Vs.   :

WARREN McCLESKY   :   MURDER and
                                   ARMED ROBBERY (2 CTS.)

VERDICT OF THE JURY

We, the Jury, find as follows:

We fix the penalty as death based on the following two aggravating circumstances for the Count of murder.

1. The offense of murder was committed while the offender was engaged in the commission of another capital felony.

Figure 4.4. Jury verdict in *State of Georgia v. Warren McCleskey.*

Moments later, Judge McKenzie pronounced the formal sentence: death by electrocution.

The sentence was front-page news in Georgia, but, as is often the case, it attracted little press attention elsewhere in the country. But at 99 Hudson Street in Manhattan, the McCleskey sentence soon came under very close scrutiny. It was there, at the offices of the NAACP Legal Defense Fund (LDF), that lawyers were sifting through death-penalty cases in search of vehicles for testing the latest strategic weapon in the LDF arsenal: statistical research suggested a relationship between a defendant's race and being sentenced to death row.

The LDF had arranged foundation funding for a major statistical study of death sentencing, which was to be directed by the highly respected University of Iowa professor David Baldus. The study was designed to be independent, despite the LDF's role in its financing. But the results were clearly welcome on Hudson Street.

Baldus's researchers delved into 2,484 murder cases in Georgia between 1973 and 1979. They examined police, prison, and parole files, building a meticulous database that attempted to account for major statistical variables. Their findings on racial factors defied conventional liberal wisdom: blacks were not condemned to death more often than whites. There was no link, according to the statistical analysis, between a defendant's race and the probability of a death sentence.

What was striking was the study's conclusion that the race of the *victim* was a significant factor: defendants charged with the murder of whites were over *four times* more likely to be sentenced to death in Georgia than those charged with killing blacks.[18] The lawyers for the LDF viewed this statistical finding as a potential silver bullet in their fight against capital punishment. They decided—after much internal debate over the merits of its application in this particular case—to fire that bullet in defense of Warren McCleskey's life.

They used it first in a brief to Judge Owen Forrester of the U.S. District Court for northern Georgia. Forrester, a Reagan appointee who had already turned down a McCleskey request for a federal hearing, was an unlikely target. But the silver bullet had its desired effect: Forrester found Baldus's research intriguing enough to make it the subject of a full hearing.

In the end, despite extensive evidence and testimony offered by Baldus in Forrester's courtroom, the judge was not convinced. He determined that the evidence did not support the LDF argument that Georgia's legal system was so tainted by racial discrimination that its implementation of the death penalty should be declared unconstitutional. His ruling set the stage for further federal appeals on the bias issue that would eventually reach the U.S. Supreme Court.

As a curious sidenote, Judge Forrester developed doubts about testimony at McCleskey's trial made by the jailhouse snitch, Offie Evans. Forrester concluded that the jury should have been informed that detectives had offered to "speak a word" for Evans concerning his own charges in return for the testimony against McCleskey. This, despite the fact that everyone involved except for Offie had denied that he had been made an offer of any kind. A federal appeals court rejected Forrester's doubts.

But it was the Baldus research and the issue of racial disparity that earned McCleskey a slot on the Supreme Court's docket—but only by a whisker. Edward Lazarus, a former clerk to Justice Harry Blackmun and modern historian of the Court, discovered that *McCleskey* got the bare minimum of four votes necessary for a hearing: Justices Thurgood Marshall, William Brennan, Harry Blackmun, and John Paul Stevens. Not one of the Court's five conservative justices voted to accept the case.[19]

Inside the Court, Justice Byron White was already engaged in an examination of the Baldus study. Staying ahead of the game was typical of White's competitive approach to life; a former All-American turned professional football player, he had brought his sports ethic into the Court's marble palace. During breaks from work, White's chambers served as a putting green for him and some of his clerks. A putt would be hit in one office and have to travel across another to the justice's office, under the side of his couch, and out through its front legs. White won these contests with what some clerks viewed as a discouraging frequency.[20] They were a momentary escape from the weighty cases that consumed most of his working days.

Even before the McCleskey petition reached the clerk's office, White had begun a preemptive attack on the LDF's argument. Having become interested in the Baldus study when its results began to surface in 1985, he assigned one of his clerks to research it. Under White's microscope, the Baldus findings "cut no ice," as one of his clerks confided to Lazarus.[21] White didn't trust the statistics. He took the unusual step, before the case was heard, of sending a memo to his conservative colleagues urging a vote against *McCleskey*. He pressed Justices William Rehnquist, Lewis Powell, Sandra Day O'Connor, and Antonin Scalia to reject the LDF claims.[22]

White had lit a backfire before the LDF could light a match; the conservative justices conferred among themselves about his memo. By the time oral arguments were heard on October 15, 1986, the die was cast. "For all practical purposes," as Lazarus put it, "the fix was already in."[23]

Jack Borger, the LDF attorney who rose to make the *McCleskey* case that morning, had no idea of the odds against him.[24] He soldiered on. "There was a time," he told the justices, "before our nation's Civil War, when free blacks and slaves alike could be given a death sentence merely for the crime of assault on a Georgia white citizen. . . . Today, we are before the Court with a substantial body of evidence indicating that during the last decade Georgia prosecutors and juries . . . have continued to act as if some of those old statutes were still on the books."

Borger came under skeptical questioning from White, who leaned forward, scowling, as he challenged the LDF's position and the Baldus study. David Baldus watched helplessly from the gallery of the courtroom as he saw White's vote slip away. White, who had voted to overturn William Furman's death sentence, offered no hope in the *McCleskey* case.

White was not Borger's only challenger. Borger also got sharp questions from William Rehnquist, just installed as chief justice, Justice Lewis Powell, and newly appointed Justice Antonin Scalia. Scalia was at his most sardonic: "Now, what if you do a statistical study that shows beyond question that people who are naturally shifty-eyed are, to a disproportionate extent, convicted in criminal cases? Does that make the criminal process unlawful?"

And when Borger made the point that murderers of whites were more at risk of death than murderers of blacks, Justice O'Connor turned his logic on its head: "What's the remedy?" she asked. "Is it to execute more people?"

If the die was cast before oral arguments, it was hardened into steel by the time the justices convened in their second-floor Conference Room two days later. Justice White, taking nothing for granted, had circulated another memo urging that McCleskey's death verdict be affirmed. And it was, in Conference, by a vote of 5–4. The composi-

tion of the Court had changed since the case had been accepted—
Rehnquist moved into Burger's seat as chief justice, and Antonin
Scalia joined the Court to fill Rehnquist's place—but the balance on
the Court had not changed. Rehnquist, O'Connor, Powell, Scalia,
and White voted to affirm McCleskey's death sentence; Blackmun,
Brennan, Marshall, and Stevens voted futilely to overturn it.

White very much wanted to write the Court's opinion, Lazarus
tells us, but Rehnquist assigned it to Powell, who had rejected the
principal LDF-Baldus argument out of hand: "At most, the Baldus
study indicates a discrepancy that appears to correlate with race,"
Powell wrote. "Apparent disparities in sentencing are an inevitable
part of our criminal justice system. . . . We hold that the Baldus study
does not demonstrate a constitutionally significant risk of racial bias
affecting the Georgia capital sentencing process."[25] Justice Brennan
wrote the dissent, joined by Blackmun, Marshall, and Stevens, saying
the Baldus evidence "relentlessly documents the risk that McCleskey's
sentence was influenced by racial considerations."[26] Stevens concluded, in an additional separate opinion, that McCleskey would not
be on death row "if he had killed a member of his own race." He
continued, "This sort of disparity is constitutionally intolerable. It fla-
grantly violates the court's prior insistence that capital punishment
be imposed fairly . . . or not at all."

But no shadow of doubt appeared in Powell's opinion for the
majority: the verdict and the sentence were constitutional, and the
State of Georgia had every legal right to put Warren McCleskey to
death. The certainty is ironic, given the fact that Powell later regretted
both his opinion and his vote in the case. That vote would not only
have turned the case the other way, but it could have cast a pall of
doubt on all death sentences involving black defendants and white
victims. After his retirement, in fact, Powell said his views on capital
punishment had changed radically.

In a retrospective interview with his biographer, John Jeffries,
Powell was asked if he would change his vote in any of the cases that
came before him:

Powell: Yes, *McCleskey v. Kemp.*

Jeffries: Do you mean you would now accept the argument from statistics?

Powell: No, I would vote the other way in any capital case.

Jeffries: In any capital case?

Powell: Yes.

Jeffries: Even in *Furman v. Georgia?*

Powell: Yes. I have come to think that capital punishment should be abolished.[27]

Powell's turnabout came much too late for Warren McCleskey. He was pronounced dead in Georgia's electric chair at 3:13 a.m. on September 25, 1991—but his final hours were chaotic and confusing.

McCleskey had been scheduled to die the previous day. His head was shaved that afternoon to provide better conductivity for the lethal electricity. Shortly afterward, he was served the final meal he had requested: pizza pockets, pinto beans, corn bread, and Kool-Aid. But by that time, he was no longer hungry; there was a lot to distract him.

As the execution hour of 7:00 p.m. approaches, McCleskey's lawyers file a last-minute appeal in federal court with Judge Owen Forrester. The clock ticks on relentlessly.

6:45 p.m. Forrester grants a stay, but only until 7:30 p.m.

7:20 p.m. Forrester grants a second stay, this one until 10:00 p.m., so that he can hear evidence in the case.

9:30 p.m. Judge Forrester orders yet another stay, this one until midnight, while he continues to hear evidence.

11:20 p.m. Forrester denies McCleskey's appeal but allows yet a fourth stay, this one until 2:00 a.m., so that his lawyers can appeal to a federal court of appeals.

1:50 a.m. the court of appeals lifts the stay. Prison officials reschedule the execution for 2:15 a.m.

2:19 a.m. McCleskey is strapped into the electric chair, but as he begins to make a last statement, Warden Walter Zant interrupts him to announce that the U.S. Supreme Court has issued a stay. McCleskey is removed from the chair and taken to his cell.

2:42 a.m. the Supreme Court issues another stay—this one for only ten minutes.

2:52 a.m. the Supreme Court denies McCleskey's appeal.[28]

One minute later, McCleskey is once again strapped into the electric chair. He makes a final statement to the group of witnesses seated on three polished oak benches on the other side of the chamber's glass. "I want to say to the family of Frank Schlatt, I hope you find in your hearts to forgive me for my participation in the crime," he says. "I am ready to enter the kingdom of heaven."[29]

At 3:06 a.m., three unidentified state employees hit identical red buttons—but only one of them is operational. It sends two thousand volts through McCleskey's body. The electricity is turned off at 3:08 a.m., and doctors wait for a five-minute "cooling off" period before approaching the body and pronouncing McCleskey dead.[30]

 To hear an audio recording of the communications in the prison command post, go to: http://murderatthesupremecourt .com/mccleskey

The legal kabuki dance during McCleskey's last hours concluded with a gaggle of the nation's most senior judges in their pajamas, huddling by telephones to decide if a forty-four-year-old inmate would live to see the light of a new day. They decided he would not.

The incident disgusted Justice Thurgood Marshall, who had already announced his retirement and was serving until his replacement could be confirmed by the U.S. Senate. Ever an opponent of capital punishment, Marshall was particularly exercised about the Court's action—or lack of it—in McCleskey's final hours.

"In refusing to grant a stay to review fully McCleskey's claims," Marshall said, "the Court values expediency over human life. Repeatedly denying Warren McCleskey his constitutional rights is unacceptable. Executing him is inexcusable."[31] Jodie Swanner saw it differently. She was eleven years old when Warren McCleskey shot and killed her father, Officer Frank Schlatt, on Marietta Street. She said of McCleskey, "I never got to say goodbye to my father. This has nothing to do with vengeance. It has to do with justice."[32]

Recalling her father, Schlatt's only daughter said, "I remember my father as a good man. . . . He believed in the justice system, and it's about time the justice system takes up for my father."

5

MENTAL INCAPACITY AND "EVOLVING STANDARDS OF DECENCY"

It is indefensible to conclude that individuals who are mentally retarded are not to some degree less culpable for their criminal acts. By definition, such individuals have substantial limitations not shared by the general population. A moral and civilized society diminishes itself if its system of justice does not afford recognition and consideration of those limitations in a meaningful way.
 —Justice Lawrence Koontz, dissenting in
 Commonwealth of Virginia v. Daryl Atkins

May 22, 1944
Casablanca, Morocco

Twenty-year-old Army private Albert Trop was being held in the base stockade for having been away without leave (AWOL). He found the conditions at the base intolerable. On this day in May, he managed to walk away from the stockade and the base itself with the idea of never coming back. He wanted to join up with his former unit in Italy, where life, he assumed, might be better. But it was cold and rainy, and he had no money, and he was hungry. His escapade lasted less than twenty-four hours. The next afternoon, he hopped an Army truck and returned to base. But he had been gone again, and this time there would be a higher price to pay.

Desertion in a time of war is a serious offense, even a technical desertion like Trop's. Although the government never suggested Trop was going over to the other side or refuted his claim that he wanted to reconnect with a former unit, he was still court-martialed, sentenced to three years at hard labor and loss of all pay, and given a dishonorable discharge. Eight years later, Trop applied for a passport and learned he had also lost his U.S. citizenship, a sanction authorized by Congress for desertion during wartime under Section 401(g) of the 1940 Nationality Act. His application for a passport was denied.

Trop didn't murder anyone and nobody murdered him. So, one might reasonably ask, why is his case in this book? Trop's subsequent appeal may have had as great of an impact—or greater—on capital punishment in the United States than most of the murder cases that *have* reached the Supreme Court. And it has contributed significantly to the debate and criticism over how the Court does, or should do, its work.

Trop argued that to deprive him of his U.S. citizenship, essentially leaving him a man without a country, was cruel and unusual punishment beyond the authority of Congress. The U.S. Supreme Court agreed, finding that the involuntary taking away of citizenship amounted to "the total destruction of the individual's status in organized society" and was in violation of the Eighth Amendment.[1]

The 1954 case of *Albert Trop v. Secretary of State John Foster Dulles* divided the Court, and it has, to some extent, divided every Supreme Court since. The vote was 5–4. The dissenters were led by an incredulous Justice Felix Frankfuter who—after pointing out that desertion from the military in wartime was punishable by death—asked rhetorically, "Is constitutional dialectic so empty of reason that it can be seriously urged that loss of citizenship is a fate worse than death?"

"At the outset, let us put to one side the death penalty as an index of the constitutional limit on punishment," responded Chief Justice Earl Warren, adding that "the existence of the death penalty is not a license to the Government to devise any punishment short of death within the limit of its imagination."

Figure 5.1. Earl Warren, Chief Justice of the United States from 1953–1969.

Warren went on to describe the history and meaning of the ban against cruel and unusual punishment with words that have reverberated through generations of Eighth Amendment cases, particularly those involving the death penalty:

> The exact scope of the constitutional phrase "cruel and unusual" has not been detailed by this Court. But the basic policy reflected in these words is firmly established in the Anglo-American tradition of criminal justice. The phrase in our Constitution was taken directly from the English Declaration of Rights of 1688, and the principle it represents can be traced back to the Magna Carta. The basic concept underlying the Eighth Amendment is nothing less than the dignity of man. While the State has the power to punish, the Amendment stands to assure that this power be exercised within the limits of civilized standards. Fines, imprisonment and even execution may be imposed depending upon the enormity of the crime, but any technique outside the bounds of these traditional penalties is constitutionally suspect. This Court has had little occasion to give precise content to the Eighth Amendment, and, in an enlightened democracy such as ours, this is not surprising. But when the Court was confronted with a punishment of 12 years in irons at hard and painful labor imposed for the crime of falsifying public records, it did not hesitate to declare that the penalty was cruel in its excessiveness and unusual in its character. The Court recognized in that case that the words of the Amendment are not precise, and that their scope is not static. *The Amendment must draw its meaning from the evolving standards of decency that mark the progress of a maturing society.*[2] (emphasis added)

The Court clearly has the authority to draw some bright lines. Few would complain, for example, were it to prohibit the execution of an infant or of one who met the clinical definition of an idiot. But what about a defendant who is only mildly retarded, or a juvenile just shy of his eighteenth birthday but who has still shown himself to be a cold-blooded killer? In these gray zones, addressed in this and the subsequent chapter, the words of Chief Justice Earl Warren about "evolving standards of decency" echo loudly.

August 17, 1996
Hampton, Virginia

Thirty-two-year-old Garland Clay, the foreman for a plumbing and mechanical contractor, had had a long day. It was hot, and he was tired . . . and it was getting late. Clay was ready to join his coworkers for some billiards and a brew or two at their regular hangout, Petro's Tavern in Hampton. He got there around 9:00 p.m. and hung around until closing. He had consumed at least a six-pack of beer before heading home in the wee hours of the morning. On the way home, all that beer was starting to drain through his body. Clay got off of I-64 at the Lee Hall exit in hopes of finding a little wilderness—what hikers call "the green door"—to relieve himself.

It was now about 3:45 in the morning. As he turned off the road, Clay's headlights shined through some low-lying fog revealing what appeared to be a body stretched out alongside the road. Clay picks up the story in a crowded courtroom in Yorktown, Virginia, a few years later.

> *Virginia Commonwealth's Attorney Eileen Addison:* Did you see anything unusual during those early morning hours?
> *Clay:* You could say that. I came across some guy who appeared to be sleeping on the side of the road. And I stopped immediately, rolled my window down, and yelled twice and blew the horn and yelled a third time; and I got no response from him. And from what I could see, I didn't think I was going to.[3]

Upon closer examination, Clay saw the bullet-riddled body of a very young man. He drove to the first house he could find, woke the person who was living there, and had them call the police. Deputy Troy Lyons of the Major Crimes Unit of the York County Sheriff's Department said he got the call shortly before five in the morning and "was directed to the intersection of Crafford Road and Tower Road, where a body had been found."[4] Lyons would be the lead investigator of the case.

The victim's wallet was missing, leading Lyons to assume robbery was the motive. It had rained that night yet the victim's clothing was still relatively dry. This had just happened, he thought, and the pool of blood surrounding the body told him that it had happened right there, on the spot he was standing, not at some distant venue. Lyons also found a pay stub in the victim's pocket from Advance Auto Parts in Hampton that led to the identification of twenty-one-year-old Eric Nesbitt who worked at the store part-time. Apparently he was also an airman first class at the nearby Langley Air Force Base.

Figure 5.2. Eric Nesbitt.

An important break in Nesbitt's murder case came three days after his body was found, when Lyons got a call from the local branch of Crestar Bank saying they had a video tape of Nesbitt making a $200 withdrawal from a local ATM on the night he was killed. In the video, Nesbitt can be seen seated in his pickup truck between two men, one of them holding a gun to his head.

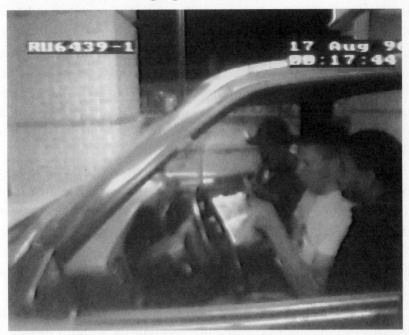

Figure 5.3. Eric Nesbitt *(middle)*, shortly before being shot to death by his captors, William Jones *(foreground)* and Daryl Atkins *(background)*.

Photographs made from the video were distributed to local newspapers and television stations, and it wasn't long before deputies received a number of "Crimeline" telephone tips that one "William Jones" appeared to match the man in the driver's seat in Nesbitt's truck. The truck itself turned up at a motel in Newport News, Virginia. Police maintained surveillance of the motel area, and when Jones returned, they promptly arrested him.

No one other than William Jones and the second man, subsequently identified as Daryl Atkins, can say what actually happened that night, but prosecutors—and apparently the jury—believed Jones's version, which was offered in exchange for leniency. The following story is now part of the official record in the lower courts and in the U.S. Supreme Court.[5]

Jones and Atkins were "drinking fruit juice and gin and smoking weed" at the home Atkins shared with his father. It continued late into the evening; friends came and went. One friend of Atkins's, Mark Dallas, showed up around 10:30 at night with a handgun. He gave it to Atkins, who said "that he wanted to use it and would bring it back in the morning." An hour later, Atkins and Jones made one of several walks that day down to the 7-Eleven to buy some beer. Atkins told Jones he didn't have enough money and was going to panhandle to get what he needed, with the gun tucked behind the waistband of his pants, partially concealed by his belt buckle.

While Jones waited, Atkins approached several people to ask for money and collected a bit from one or two customers. Nesbitt arrived at the store in his 1995 Nissan pickup truck at around 11:30 p.m. After a brief conversation with Atkins, Nesbitt went into the store. When he came back out and got back in his truck, Atkins whistled at him. Nesbitt stopped and rolled down his window. That turned out to be a fatal mistake.

Atkins then went to the passenger's side of the truck; Jones, to the driver's side. Atkins pointed the handgun at Nesbitt's head and ordered him to "move over, let my friend drive." Both men then entered the truck, and Jones drove off.

Atkins demanded that Nesbitt surrender his wallet. Atkins removed sixty dollars and, as he handed the wallet back, noticed Nesbitt's Crestar ATM card. On Atkins's instruction, Jones drove to a Crestar Bank ATM. Once there, Atkins forced Nesbitt to withdraw another $200. The security camera in this automatic teller machine recorded the truck arriving at the bank shortly after midnight on August 17, 1996. The videotape produced by the camera showed that Jones was driving, Atkins was in the passenger seat, and Nesbitt was between them. During this entire time, Atkins kept the handgun pointed at Nesbitt.

Figure 5.4.

Jones then drove to the parking lot of a nearby school where he and Atkins discussed what they should do with Nesbitt. Jones urged Atkins to "just tie him up so we can get away." Atkins told Jones he knew of a place near his grandfather's house in Yorktown where they could leave Nesbitt and directed Jones to drive toward Yorktown on Interstate 64. Nesbitt pleaded with them, saying "just don't hurt me" and made no attempt to escape.

Upon arriving in a secluded area off of I-64, Atkins exited the truck and ordered Nesbitt to do the same. "Nesbitt stepped out of the vehicle and probably took two steps" when Atkins began shooting him. Jones jumped out of the truck and tried to wrestle the gun from Atkins. In the ensuing struggle, Atkins was shot in the leg. Jones, now in control, drove Atkins to the emergency room of a local hospital, leaving Nesbitt's dead body at the scene of the shooting. Outside the emergency room, Jones asked Atkins for some of the money that had been taken from Nesbitt and then drove away, alone in Nesbitt's truck.

Jones then drove to the King James Motel in Newport News where he abandoned the truck. He spent the next several days moving from motel to motel. He cut his hair in an attempt to disguise his appearance. He subsequently returned to the first motel, where police were waiting and arrested him. The handgun was not found in the truck and was never recovered.

One of the "Crimeline" tipsters that turned police on to Jones reported that "a person that Mr. Jones runs with was a Daryl Atkins."[6] Jones's father confirmed to Deputy Lyons that Atkins was with his son on the night of the murder, and he provided Atkins's address. Lyons then went to Atkins's home, saw that Atkins matched the security camera photographs, and placed him under arrest.

Figure 5.5. Nesbitt's body at the crime scene.

An autopsy revealed that Nesbitt had sustained eight separate gunshot wounds to the thorax, chest, abdomen, arms, and legs. Several of the bullets exited and reentered the body. Three of the gunshot wounds were lethal. However, the coroner concluded that Nesbitt could have lived for several minutes before "the bleeding was to the point where his blood pressure would not support consciousness and life."[7] Three bullets were recovered during the autopsy.

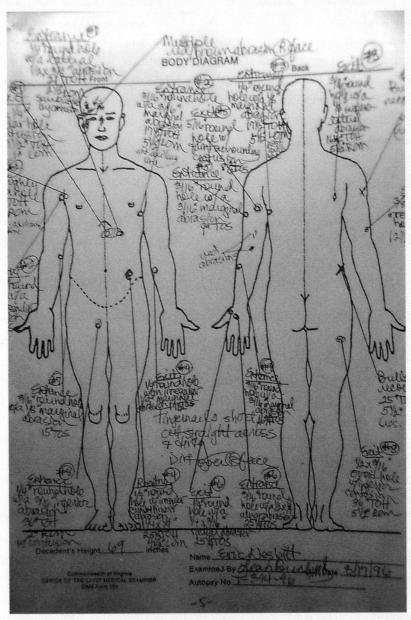

Figure 5.6. Autopsy sketch.

The gruesome details of the crime began to filter in. Although only eighteen years old at the time of the offense, Atkins had more than twenty felonies under his belt, including a burglary when he was only thirteen. Atkins was the only defense witness at the guilt phase of his trial, and his testimony sharply contradicted that of Jones. It was Jones who initiated the contact with the victim, insisted Atkins. It was Jones who forced his way into Nesbitt's truck. And it was Jones who fired the fatal shots. The jury, however, believed Jones, convicting Atkins of capital murder. Under Jones's agreement with the government, he pled guilty and was sentenced to life in prison.

The prosecution made clear that it would be seeking the death penalty for Atkins, citing both the "vileness" of the crime and Atkins's "future dangerousness" as the aggravating factors. Prosecutor Eileen Addison told the jury: "He could have simply pushed Eric Nesbitt out of that truck and left him stranded in the woods. He could have knocked him unconscious, he could have shot him in the leg so that he would have trouble getting to a house to get help. But that wasn't enough for Daryl Atkins. It wasn't enough to shoot Eric once or twice. He shot him eight times. Eighteen bullet holes where the bullets went in . . . and passed out . . . and back in again. The evidence of Daryl Atkins's crime is horrifying. It is vile."[8]

The jury also heard from Nesbitt's friends and relatives. Nesbitt's coworkers recalled the squadron picnic the afternoon of the murder and remembered Nesbitt as being "light-hearted" and "fun-loving," "a guy who liked to joke around," and the "life of the party." But now he was "gone." Mark Armitage, an Air Force buddy who claimed to be Nesbitt's best friend, said he was devastated. "It hurt really bad. My wife was nine months pregnant and I had to tell her he was dead. She didn't stop crying for four days. She gave birth four days later. Eric was supposed to be my son's godfather."

But the most wrenching testimony came from Nesbitt's mother, Mary Sloan, who told of the pride she had in her son, an Eagle scout who aspired to have a career in the Air Force. "I had a little counseling after Eric had died but it didn't seem to do any good. I just sat there and cried. I don't know how you can counsel for something like this."

The jury recommended the death penalty for Atkins, and the presiding judge, Prentiss Smiley, agreed. In Virginia, as in most states, all death sentences go to the state supreme court for automatic review. The Virginia Supreme Court upheld the guilty verdict, but in an opinion by Justice Lawrence Koontz, it found a procedural flaw in the sentencing part of the trial. On retrial before an entirely different jury, the defense pressed its claim that Atkins should be spared because he was mentally retarded.

Virginia, like many states, left it to jurors to assess how mentally impaired a defendant may be and to weigh the testimony of competing forensic psychiatrists (and in this case psychologists) whose expertise far exceeds their own. The bible of the psychiatric community is the *Diagnostic and Statistical Manual of Mental Disorders*, published by the American Psychiatric Association. Version Four (DSM-IV) was in use at the time, which defined the essential feature of mental retardation as "significantly sub-average general intellectual functioning (Criterion A) that is accompanied by significant limitations in adaptive functioning in at least two of the following skill areas: communication, self-care, home living, social/interpersonal skills, use of community resources, self-direction, functional academic skills, work, leisure, health, and safety (Criterion B). The onset must occur before age 18 years (Criterion C)."

"Mild" mental retardation is typically used to describe people with an IQ level of 50–55 to approximately 70.[9] Dr. Evan Nelson, a forensic psychologist, testified that Atkins's IQ was 59, suggesting a mental age of from nine to twelve. Atkins's "adaptive functioning" was quite awful. In addition to his various felonies, Atkins never held a job and was an abject failure in the Hampton public schools. He had failed the second grade. He had received failing grades in all his classes when in the eighth grade and had scored in the fifteenth percentile on standardized achievements tests. It was further downhill from there. When he reached the tenth grade, which he also failed, he scored in the sixth percentile. With a cumulative high school grade point average of 1.26 out of a possible 4.0, he dropped out of school. Nelson diagnosed Atkins as "mildly retarded" with an antisocial personality disorder.

The Commonwealth of Virginia countered with its own forensic psychologist, Dr. Stanton Samenow, who never administered any IQ tests to Atkins but interviewed him twice and concluded that he was not at all retarded. When Atkins's lawyer, George Rogers, asked, "Do you have an expert opinion as to the Defendant's intellect?" Samenow answered, "He is of average intelligence, at least." When asked to explain how he came to this conclusion, Samenow said it was through "the vocabulary and syntax that he used in talking with me." Samenow was also impressed that Atkins was able to name the governor of Virginia and knew that the son of former president John F. Kennedy had died in a plane crash.[10]

Whatever weight the jury applied to the defense's claims of mental retardation, it wasn't enough. After deliberating for thirteen hours, the jury recommended death and Judge Prentiss Smiley again complied. The Virginia Supreme Court affirmed the death sentence, rejecting a claim that sentencing a mentally retarded offender to death violates the Eighth Amendment prohibition of cruel and unusual punishment.

The Virginia Supreme Court decision could hardly have come as any surprise. On matters of federal constitutional law, state courts and lower federal courts are all bound by the interpretations of the U.S. Supreme Court. And the U.S. Supreme Court had ruled only seven years earlier, in 1989, that mental retardation was not an automatic bar to a death sentence, although it was a factor a jury could and should consider.[11] That case involved Johnny Paul Penry, convicted of the brutal rape and murder of Pamela Mosely Carpenter, sister of the Washington Redskins' star placekicker Mark Mosely. Although Penry was said to have had the mental age of only a seven year old, the Court ruled he could still be a candidate for the death penalty. The Court noted that the abilities of mentally retarded individuals vary and that many may still "act with the degree of culpability associated with the death penalty." The Court also rejected the use of a presumed "mental age" as an excuse for criminal conduct, finding it susceptible to being feigned and inherently unreliable.[12]

Significantly, however, the Virginia Supreme Court was not unanimous; two justices dissented. Lawrence Koontz—the same judge who had written the earlier decision upholding Atkins's guilt—wrote a bold and passionate dissent that seemed to repudiate everything the U.S. Supreme Court had said in its *Penry* decision years earlier. "It is indefensible," admonished Justice Koontz, "to conclude that individuals who are mentally retarded are not to some degree less culpable for their criminal acts. By definition, such individuals have substantial limitations not shared by the general population. A moral and civilized society diminishes itself if its system of justice does not afford recognition and consideration of those limitations in a meaningful way."[13]

Justice Leroy Hassell joined Koontz's dissent but also wrote separately about the commonwealth's claim that Atkins was at least of average intelligence: "I simply place no credence whatsoever in Dr. Samenow's opinion that the defendant possesses at least average intelligence. I would hold that Dr. Samenow's opinion that the defendant possesses average intelligence is incredulous as a matter of law." As you will see, the words Justices Koontz and Hassell chose would have a subsequent impact even they could not have foreseen.

Watching these proceedings carefully from the sidelines was a law professor in Albuquerque, New Mexico, named Jim Ellis. In addition to teaching constitutional law at the University of New Mexico Law School, Ellis had devoted most of his adult life to working on behalf of people with mental disabilities. A conscientious objector during the Vietnam War, Ellis agreed to alternate service as an orderly at the Yale Psychiatric Institute. The experience changed him forever. At the time, he was changing bedpans. But in the years that followed, he would be changing lives.[14]

After his time at the psychiatric institute, Ellis went to law school, became a lawyer, and channeled his skills to advance the cause of

America's less fortunate. He rose to become the president of the American Association on Mental Retardation (AAMR); he had filed more than a dozen legal briefs on behalf of the association in various court cases, including one in the landmark case of *Penry v. Lynaugh* discussed earlier The decision against Penry was a huge disappointment for Ellis. At the time the *Penry* case was decided, only two of the thirty-eight states that authorized capital punishment had made an exception for offenders with mental disabilities—which was hardly a national consensus. Drawing on the Court's 1958 decision in *Trop v. Dulles*, Justice Sandra Day O'Connor wrote for the majority: "While a national consensus against execution of the mentally retarded may someday emerge reflecting the 'evolving standards of decency that mark the progress of a maturing society,' there is insufficient evidence of such a consensus today."[15]

Ellis took the *Penry v. Lynaugh* decision personally, and he *personally* traveled the country to change the legislative landscape, to create the national consensus that Justice O'Connor found lacking. He appeared before dozens of legislative committees arguing for the rights of people with disabilities. And it appeared to have worked. In the next thirteen years, another sixteen death-penalty states joined the ranks of Georgia and Maryland in prohibiting the execution of such individuals, in no small measure due to the efforts of Jim Ellis.

While Ellis was watching the Atkins case rebound up and down the courts of Virginia, the Virginia Resource Center, which was handling Atkins's defense, had *its* eyes on Ellis. And when the U.S. Supreme Court announced it would take up the Atkins case, the center tapped Ellis to argue it. It was a daring gamble. Ellis had never argued a court case in his life, not even for a traffic ticket. Now he would be in the highest court in the land arguing an issue that had, for decades, been the closest to his heart. It would be the challenge, and the opportunity, of a lifetime.

The Atkins case was now national news. The Supreme Court's argument, set for February 20, 2002, had drawn much more attention than either the trial or the crime itself. It was one of those special cases in which even a reporter regularly assigned to cover the Court had to make a reservation to be assured a seat.

As the Petitioner in the case challenging the Virginia Supreme Court's decision, Ellis was first up. He began by declaring, "the evidence is now clear that the American people in every region of the country have reached a consensus" against the execution of mentally retarded people.[16]

Less than a minute into his argument, Chief Justice William Rehnquist interrupted, "What is your definition of a consensus, Mr. Ellis?" Ellis replied: "It's when the American people have reached a settled judgment based on a—" Rehnquist again interrupted, "That's a perfectly sound phrase, but how do we go about figuring out when that occurs?" Defining just what constitutes a consensus would dominate most of the hour-long hearing.

Ellis emphasized how the number of death-penalty states prohibiting the death penalty for mentally retarded individuals had grown from only two in 1989 to eighteen in 2002. The question then arose how the Court is to count the twelve states that don't have capital punishment at all. If we were to add them in, we would have thirty states opposed to such executions. That would constitute a clear majority and further evidence of an evolving consensus.

At this point, Justice Antonin Scalia broke in, saying that "an *evolving* consensus isn't enough, you need a *consensus*."

Rehnquist wanted to know how New Hampshire, where he maintained a summer home, might be counted. The New Hampshire death-penalty law allowed the execution of offenders with mental disabilities, but there hadn't been an execution in the state in sixty years.

Justice John Paul Stevens, one of the four dissenting justices in the *Penry* case and the only Penry dissenter still on the Court, was clearly sympathetic toward Ellis and tossed him a red-letter pitch: "Apart from the consensus arguments, what's really behind your position? What's wrong with executing the mentally retarded?" Ellis answered that "they lack the culpability, the blameworthiness . . . because they lack the full understanding of the consequences of their actions."

Justice David Souter interjected: "They know it's wrong, but they don't appreciate how wrong it is." Ellis: "Yes."

Justice Ruth Bader Ginsburg appeared frustrated that Ellis had failed to address another possible explanation—one Ellis *had* made in his written brief to the Court—as to why mentally impaired offenders should be spared death sentences. "Isn't it true, she asked, "that people in this class of diminished capacity will often respond inappropriately, such as smiling when they should be showing remorse," making it all the more difficult for counsel to effectively represent them?

Ellis agreed, saying the phenomenon presented "a particularly and uncomfortably large possibility of wrongful conviction and thus wrongful execution."

Justice Scalia, who clearly did not believe mentally retarded defendants were entitled to any blanket exception, asked Ellis why the defense can't simply explain the defendant's inappropriate conduct to the jury: "It seems to me . . . the more he'd smile, the more . . . the jury would say, 'Boy, this—this person really shouldn't be executed. He's not playing with a full deck,' or whatever."

Ellis responded with what most criminal-defense lawyers know well. The mental-retardation defense is a double-edged sword. While research shows that mentally impaired individuals are less likely to resort to violence than those in the general population, some juries may be even more disposed to sentence a mentally impaired defendant to death, particularly one who, for whatever reason, might smile when charged with a horrible crime.

When Pamela Rumpz, the assistant attorney general representing the Commonwealth of Virginia, got up to speak, the argument returned to determining what constitutes a "consensus" and how trends of the past thirteen years might bear on the country's "evolving standards of decency." What follows is a summary of the discussion in the Court.

The twelve states that don't even allow capital punishment are not part of the equation, insisted Rumpz. These states had not staked out any position on the mental-retardation issue, and if they were to subsequently change their laws to allow the death penalty, there would be no way of predicting whether mentally retarded offenders would be included.

Rumpz went on to argue that even the eighteen states that Atkins's lawyers said had created a consensus have not entirely abandoned the death penalty for impaired offenders. New York, for example, will still allow the execution of an impaired inmate who commits murder while in prison. And several of the eighteen states do not apply the exception retroactively to offenders sentenced before the changes in the state's laws took place. And even if you do count all eighteen states, pressed Rumpz, that isn't a majority given that twenty other death-penalty states have no such exceptions. If there is any consensus, continued Rumpz, it is to allow the juries to decide.

By now, the U.S. Supreme Court had spent nearly thirty years refining death-penalty procedures. The justices' best efforts, however, left some potholes to traverse in succeeding cases. One of them came up in the Atkins arguments. In *Gregg v. Georgia*, the court insisted that defendants on trial for their lives be given careful, individual-ized consideration, taking into account "their character and record." That command was central to Rumpz's argument: "What is at stake here is this Court's long-established jurisprudence of individualized sentencing in matters of the death penalty. Atkins would have this Court remove from individualized sentencing one whole group of people based upon one mere factor, and that is their alleged mental retardation."

As she pressed the point that a defendant's mental disability is exclusively a matter for the jury, Rumpz found herself wading into treacherous waters. Justice Anthony Kennedy, who has an uncanny talent of being on the winning side in close cases, asked, "So *any* person who has criminal responsibility can be executed, *no matter how retarded they are?* That's your position?" Rumpz: "That is the position of the Commonwealth of Virginia, yes." Justice Scalia threw Rumpz a lifeline: "You would *not* say 'no matter *how* retarded,' I mean, presum-ably, there's some point at which the retardation is so severe that the person does not comprehend what he's doing." Rumpz, reversing ground: "Exactly, Your Honor."

Rumpz's point seemed to be that the state would still have to prove the act was deliberate and carried out with premeditation; after that, anyone would be eligible for society's ultimate sanction. Justice Souter asked how that rationale might be applied to children: "Let's take five year olds. Would you argue that five year olds should be executed if they deliberated on the act and the state can otherwise prove the mental element?" Rumpz responded: "I think that's unlikely to happen, but if a person can deliberate and premeditate, and if a person can commit a brutal, calculated, premeditated murder, and if a person is found competent at the time he commits that murder, and competent to assist his lawyers at the time of the trial, then we're not looking at somebody whose culpability is any less than yours or mine."

The hour-long argument ended with no clear winner. And at no time during the hearing did the actual crime that led to this high-stakes court case ever come up; the name Eric Nesbitt was not uttered a single time.

The case was argued on a Wednesday, so if the Court followed its usual practice, the first tentative vote would have been the following Friday— only two days later. While that tentative vote rarely changes, it still took the justices a full four months to get their decision out. On June 20, 2002, the Court announced its long-awaited ruling. The justices had voted 6–3 to throw out Atkins's death sentence and put an end to the execution of anyone who met their state's definition of mental incapacity.[17]

The decision of the Court was announced by Justice John Paul Stevens, who, after laying out the facts of the case, quoted at length from the dissenting opinions of Justices Koontz and Hassell on the Virginia Supreme Court. "Because of the gravity of the concerns expressed by the dissenters," wrote Stevens, "and in light of the dramatic shift in the state legislative landscape that has occurred in the past 13 years, we granted certiorari to revisit the issue that we first addressed in the *Penry* case."

The Court's majority concluded that executing mentally retarded offenders would serve neither of the two accepted social purposes of the death penalty identified in *Gregg v. Georgia*, that is, retribution and deterrence. "Unless the imposition of the death penalty on a mentally retarded person measurably contributes to one or both of these goals," wrote Stevens, it "'is nothing more than the purposeless and needless imposition of pain and suffering,' and hence an unconstitutional punishment."[18]

The Court reasoned that because those who are mentally impaired have a diminished understanding of the consequences of their actions, they are more likely to act on impulse and are generally incapable of the same premeditation and deliberation as those who are not so afflicted, that they are less culpable and less deserving of the retribution of death. And, for the same reasons, they are also less likely to be deterred by the threat of a death sentence.

The justices also relied on polling data, which Stevens said "shows a widespread consensus among Americans, even those who support the death penalty, that executing the mentally retarded is wrong. Although these factors are by no means dispositive, their consistency with the legislative evidence lends further support to our conclusion that there is a consensus among those who have addressed the issue."[19]

The decision drew a withering dissent from Justice Scalia, who seemed to pick up where the prosecutor left off with dramatic oratory in her closing argument. "Atkins ordered Nesbitt out of the vehicle and, after he had taken only a few steps, shot him one, two, three, four, five, six, seven, eight times in the thorax, chest, abdomen, arms, and legs."

Scalia is a thoughtful justice and a good writer, but he is at his combative and uninhibited best when he writes dissents, which, unlike opinions for the Court, do not need the vote of any other justice. He has been a particularly forceful critic of the Court's death-penalty decisions and his dissent in the *Atkins* case was no exception:

Today's decision is the pinnacle of our *Eighth Amendment* death-is-different jurisprudence. Not only does it, like all of that jurisprudence, find no support in the text or history of the *Eighth Amendment*; it does not even have support in current social attitudes regarding the conditions that render an otherwise just death penalty inappropriate. Seldom has an opinion of this Court rested so obviously upon nothing but the personal views of its members.[20] (italics in the original)

Figure 5.7. Justice Antonin Scalia.

But it was not so much the Court's setting aside Atkins's death sentence that set the Justice off as it was the rationale behind the decision, that the sentence went against "the evolving standards of decency that mark the progress of a maturing society." Scalia has long argued that *Trop v. Dulles* was wrongly decided and that evolution in the Constitution can only be through a constitutional amendment. That is, the words of the Eighth Amendment mean what they say and cannot be changed in any way other than by the rigorous process of amending the Constitution.

Scalia had written previously that "the risk of assessing evolving standards is that it is all too easy to believe that evolution has culminated in one's own views,"[21] precisely what he claimed the Court's majority had now done in the *Atkins* case. He accused the Court's majority of using a "fudged" and "contrived" consensus to reinterpret the meaning of the words "cruel and unusual" in order to impose its own view of what is right for America, adding, "The arrogance of this assumption of power takes one's breath away."[22]

In his opinion and during the oral argument, Scalia did acknowledge that there is some point at which the Court might draw a line on the mental state of a defendant who might be sentenced to death. At the time the Bill of Rights was ratified, observed Scalia, the severely or profoundly retarded would not face execution. But in 1791, it would have been up to the jury to determine how Atkins, who was mildly retarded at worst, should be punished. Given that the words of the Eighth Amendment are precisely the same today as they were then, contended Scalia, the Court does not have the prerogative to take that authority away.

As you have seen in previous chapters and will see in subsequent chapters, this approach to the Constitution has had Scalia voting to uphold death sentences where a majority of his colleagues would not. It has also worked to the benefit of criminal defendants in some noncapital cases. His literal interpretation of the Sixth Amendment is just as strong as it is of the Eighth Amendment. And Scalia has shown no hesitation to set aside the convictions of other murderers,[23] drug dealers,[24] and child molesters[25] where it has been shown that they have been denied the right to confront the witnesses against them face-to-face in court, as the Confrontation Clause of the Sixth Amendment requires.

While the Court declined to ban the execution of mentally impaired offenders in 1989 and imposed just such a ban in 2002, it didn't technically overrule itself. The test the Court applied in each case was the same: whether the practice was consistent with the country's evolving standards of decency. Only the facts had changed from one case to another, with the Court finding a consensus in 2002 that it did not perceive in 1989.

And while the majority did throw out Atkins's death sentence, they left open the possibility that he could still be executed. You will recall there was a difference of opinion during the trial as to whether Atkins was in fact mentally disabled, the forensic psychologist for the defense insisting that he was, but the forensic psychologist for the state insisting that he wasn't. The U.S. Supreme Court did not weigh in on this question but rather remanded the case back to the Virginia courts, where it continued to take some odd, if not bizarre, twists and turns.

The Virginia Supreme Court ordered the Circuit Court for York County to empanel another new jury and conduct yet another sentencing hearing, the third such hearing. It did so, and the new jury concluded that Atkins was not mentally retarded under Virginia law and once again recommended he be put to death. After three trials that produced a cumulative vote of thirty-six to nothing in favor of executing Atkins, Judge Prentiss Smiley again dutifully followed the jury's recommendation. And as Atkins was being led from the courtroom, he fulfilled Justice Ginsburg's apprehensions about mentally impaired defendants by flashing a broad smile and a peace sign to his family in the spectators' gallery. Atkins appeared to be the only person in the courtroom quite unfazed by the outcome.

The case, however, wasn't over yet. Attorneys for Atkins again appealed to the Virginia Supreme Court citing thirty-seven errors in the latest sentencing proceeding, most of which went nowhere. But the Court *did find* two of the alleged errors persuasive. The Court agreed with the defense that one of the state's witnesses should not have been allowed to testify as a so-called expert. The Court also ruled that prosecutors should not have told the new jury that a previous jury had already sentenced Atkins to death and that doing so was unduly prejudicial. The Court ordered the Circuit Court to try again with yet another, fourth jury, solely to determine whether Atkins was mentally impaired under Virginia law.

What followed was a twist that no one could have anticipated. One of the central issues during the initial trial back in 1998 was who had actually shot Eric Nesbitt. Was it Daryl Atkins? Or was it his codefendant, William Jones? Each had accused the other, and Jones had agreed to testify against Atkins in exchange for a life sentence.

In preparing Jones for his courtroom testimony back in 1998, prosecutors had questioned him for two hours about what he was going to say, which is not at all an unusual practice. The session was tape-recorded. But when Jones's story became what prosecutors later described as "problematic," they shut off the tape recorder. Some of what Jones was saying was inconsistent with the forensic evidence. While the recorder was off, prosecutors staged a reenactment of the crime to help Jones get his story straight. And when they turned the recorder back on sixteen minutes later, Jones's story had changed somewhat.

The defense never learned about the unrecorded break in the interview until Jones's lawyers came forward with the story many years later. Atkins's lawyers seized the new information to accuse prosecutors of suborning perjury in the coaching of their witness and of failing to disclose to the defense Jones's uncertainty, in violation of *Brady v. Maryland*, the landmark 1963 decision requiring prosecutors to turn over all relevant exculpatory evidence.[26] After all of this, could it be that they had the wrong man? Was it possible that Jones was the killer and not Atkins after all?

Probably not. The chief investigator for the case, Troy Lyons, who attended Jones's interview and operated the recorder, told the authors that the change was insignificant, that Jones was merely confused, that he got mixed up over such matters as to whether the gun was in Atkins's left hand or right hand.[27] But Judge Prentiss Smiley saw that mix-up as significant, believing it might cast doubt on Jones's credibility, that it might provide just enough doubt in the jury's mind about who pulled the trigger to make a death sentence inappropriate. Judge Smiley had already sentenced Atkins to death three times. He had had enough. Following two days of hearings, he commuted Atkins's sentence to life in prison.

This time, it was the Commonwealth of Virginia who appealed to the state supreme court arguing, among other things, that Judge Smiley had been directed only to determine whether Atkins was so mentally impaired that his execution could not proceed under the U.S. Supreme Court's decision in his case. Throwing out the death sentence on unrelated grounds, the commonwealth argued, exceeded his authority. Dividing 4–3, the Virginia Supreme Court disagreed and upheld Judge Smiley.[28] The decision was announced by Justice Leroy Hassell, the same justice who felt early on that Atkins was not an appropriate candidate for the death penalty and who had dissented so passionately from the Virginia Supreme Court's initial decision holding otherwise.

Ten years after the trial and seven years after the Supreme Court's precedent-setting decision in the now-famous case of *Atkins v. Virginia*, it was finally over. And despite all the wrangling over the punishment for mentally retarded defendants, Atkins's own punishment wound up turning on a completely unrelated matter.

Atkins is now serving out his life sentence at the Wallens Ridge State Prison in Big Stone Gap, Virginia. Jones is serving his life term at the Nottoway Correctional Center near Burkeville, Virginia. Under Virginia law, neither will ever be eligible for parole.

Judge Prentiss Smiley never did learn how his case ended. He passed away after a long bout with cancer, two months before the Virginia Supreme Court affirmed his decision to commute Atkins's death sentence to life in prison.

In a recent interview with the authors, Eric Nesbitt's mother, Mary

Sloan, expressed neither anger nor indignation at the case's outcome. But Sloan told us she believed "Atkins knew what he was doing. I felt the jury did a good job. It was an intelligent, well-picked jury and they [the courts] should have listened to them. We miss Eric. He's still a member of the family, even though he's not here." And she added, she has adapted to the loss: "You have to adapt. You have no choice. You can't let someone like Daryl Atkins take your life away."[29]

Figure 5.8. Daryl Atkins.

Figure 5.9. William A. Jones.

Figure 5.10. Ellis turned the country around and then turned the U.S. Supreme Court around.

The Virginia State Bar dismissed misconduct charges against commonwealth attorney Eileen Addison for her handling of the Atkins prosecution. In August 2011, however, Addison was cited for misconduct for withholding exculpatory evidence in another, unrelated murder case.[30] Two weeks later, she lost her bid for reelection in the Republican primary election, defeated by a former deputy.

Jim Ellis, who played such a large part in turning the country around along with the Supreme Court, continues to be a very popular law professor at the University of New Mexico Law School. Following his landmark Supreme Court victory, the American Bar Association presented Ellis with its prestigious Paul Hearne Award for Disability Advocacy. He received the Champion of Justice Award from the National Association of Criminal Defense Lawyers. And, although he had only one actual court appearance under his belt, the *National Law Journal,* one of the country's most respected legal periodicals, named Ellis its 2002 Lawyer of the Year.

6

JUVENILE KILLERS—
SHOULD THEY DIE?

. . . because the bitch seen my face.
—Christopher Simmons, age seventeen,
on why he murdered Shirley Crook,
944 S.W.2d 165, 170

S hirley Crook was forty-six years old. She had two grown children and a loving husband named Steven. The couple had a modest home in Fenton, Missouri, about sixty miles southwest of St. Louis, and they lived a tough life. They both drove tractor trailers for a living. They took their work seriously and were grateful for the little income it produced. They dreamed of the day when they might have an easier life. Dreams may have their own excuse for being.

For Shirley and Steven Crook, a dream would be as close as it would come. On a September morning in 1993, two bass fishermen found Shirley's battered and bloated body floating in the Meramec River, which winds its way through scenic wilderness in central Missouri. With her hands tied behind her back and duct tape over her eyes and mouth, it was instantly clear that this was no accident. She had bruises all over her body and broken ribs. An autopsy subsequently revealed the cause of death to have been drowning. Veteran cops and prosecutors can get accustomed to gruesome crimes, but the identities of the perpetrators of this crime and their motives caught officials off guard.

Two teenage boys, seventeen-year-old Chris Simmons and fifteen-year-old Charlie Benjamin, had murdered Shirley Crook. Incredibly, the idea of a murder, and just how it would go down, had been discussed and reasonably well thought out. Who would be the victim, however, was another matter. That would be pure happenstance. The evidence showed it was Simmons's idea. He had discussed with Charlie and another young friend, sixteen-year-old John Tessmer, how "cool it would be" to murder someone, anyone. It was lame talk at first. Simmons's idea was to rob the victim first. It would start maybe with a burglary, but it would end with a murder. Perhaps pushing someone off of a bridge.

Figure 6.1. Shirley Crook in a family photograph.

How do such thoughts enter the mind of a child? Simmons later told authorities that his home life had never been happy, that his father left home just before he was born and that his stepfather, Robert Hayes, had physically abused him. One of Simmons's classmates later testified that she saw Hayes punch Simmons so hard in the ear that he punctured the young man's eardrum and blood was streaming down his neck. Simmons said the abuse was painful and, when it happened in front of his friends, he was very embarrassed. Hayes had a drinking issue and a bad temper. Simmons's mother, Cheryl Hayes, told the authors that her husband was rough on Chris but denies that he had ever physically abused him.[1] Although only seventeen, Simmons admitted that he would drink a lot, smoke a lot of pot, and often miss school.[2]

Figure 6.2. The crime scene.

Chris's life began to resemble a modern version of Charles Dickens's *Oliver Twist*. He would stay for weeks at a time at the home of a convicted felon, thirty-seven-year-old Brian Moomey, who had guided Chris, Charlie, and a handful of other neighborhood kids into Moomey's own world of drugs, booze, and petty crime. In exchange for Moomey's place to "hang out," they would do favors and odd jobs for him, sometimes even breaking into cars or mobile homes for quick cash, which they would all share. They never got caught. If the two youngsters had gotten mixed up with a bad crowd, they seemed to fit in quite well.[3]

Simmons's burglary-murder plan was beginning to take shape. Where would they start? An odd character they had referred to as the "voodoo man" would be an easy mark. He lived a few blocks away and they thought he had money, that he owned a chain of hotels or something like that. The anomaly of anyone with any money living in a ratty mobile home in a rundown trailer park apparently did not occur to them. The three boys had their plan and agreed to meet later that night—2:00 a.m. at Moomey's place—to carry it out.

Tessmer showed up, but then had second thoughts. Simmons assured him they had nothing to worry about. They would never get caught and, even if they did, being just kids there was little the authorities could do to them. But Tessmer would have no part of it and went home.

It was September 9, 1993. Charlie Benjamin and Chris Simmons would begin a course of action that would change their lives and the death penalty in the United States forever. Chris and Charlie knew they would start with their voodoo man, but they were not sure where or how their escapade might end. Talk is one thing, especially among rebellious young boys. But were they really prepared to take another human life? Moomey had supposedly advised them, "If they recognize you, you can't leave 'em alive." The guidance turned out to be useless in the case of the voodoo man. He wasn't even home, and his place was locked up tight.

Simmons and Benjamin then wandered aimlessly through the neighborhood. Perhaps they could find some other trailer, or maybe they would just go home. Then they stumbled onto a new opportunity: another mobile home, only this one with an open window in the back. Simmons was able to reach through and unlock the back door. Once inside, Simmons turned on a hallway light. A woman's voice cried out, "Who's there?" They were not strangers. In a most unfortunate coincidence, Mrs. Crook and Simmons had been involved in a minor traffic accident, a fender bender, only a few weeks earlier. Shirley Crook was home alone, her husband away for the night on a business trip. Simmons entered her bedroom and recognized Mrs. Crook. She apparently recognized Simmons as well.

Simmons ordered Mrs. Crook out of bed and when she resisted, they forced her to the floor and proceeded to kick and beat her, fracturing several of her ribs. The boys were unarmed and as Benjamin held Mrs. Crook down, Simmons went rifling through the house to find a weapon. There was none. He did find a brand new roll of duct tape, which he used to tie Mrs. Crook's hands behind her back. She was in effect hog-tied and when she began to cry, Simmons covered her mouth and eyes with additional duct tape. They then forced her into the back of her minivan, the same vehicle Simmons had crashed into, and took her for a drive. Shirley Crook's fate had been sealed, at least in the mind of Chris Simmons.

They drove around for over an hour and ended up at Castlewood State Park in neighboring St. Louis County. Simmons had been there before with his friends to drink and get high. In the early 1900s, the park was a mecca for St. Louis young people wanting to party. In 1993, as is the case today, it is known for its hiking and biking trails, broad meadows filled with wildlife, and good fishing.

Simmons parked the van near a towering railroad trestle that spanned the Meramec River. When he and Benjamin began to unload Mrs. Crook, they discovered that she had freed her hands and had removed some of the duct tape from her face. Using Mrs. Crook's purse strap, the belt from her bathrobe, a towel from the back of the minivan, and some electrical wire found on the trestle, Simmons and Benjamin bound Mrs. Crook again, restraining her hands behind her back and covering her head with a towel. Simmons and Benjamin walked Mrs. Crook to the railroad trestle. "Take my van, take anything you want . . . just let me go," she pleaded.

The trestle stood about sixty feet above the water and although it may have been solid enough to hold a train, it seemed rickety when one walked along the narrow tracks. The boys marched this terrified woman to the middle of the trestle and then Simmons calmly pushed her off, down into the river below. She survived the fall. She was alive and conscious after hitting the water. But badly hurt and with her hands tied behind her, she would drown within a few minutes.

Simmons and Benjamin then threw Mrs. Crook's purse into the woods and drove the van back to the mobile home park across from the subdivision in which Mrs. Crook lived. Later that day, Simmons returned to Moomey's home and bragged to Moomey and others that he had killed a woman "because the bitch seen my face."[4]

Figure 6.3. The railroad trestle.

Meanwhile, Mrs. Crook's husband, Steven, had returned home to find his house in disarray and his wife nowhere around. He found the couple's poodle wrapped in duct tape, whimpering on the bed in the master bedroom. He called police and learned a short while later that the body of a woman matching his wife's description had been pulled from the Meramec River earlier in the day.

The next afternoon, police showed up at Fenton High School and took Simmons and Benjamin into custody.[5] Police reports do not reveal what turned them on to the two boys, but it's not hard to imagine. They had boasted to a number of friends about what they had done, and any one of them could have called in a tip. In the interview room at the Jefferson County sheriff's office, Simmons didn't look very tough at all in a videotaped confession. Holding back tears as best he could, he looked more like the young boy he was rather than a cold-blooded killer. "Who pushed her off?" asked Detective Shane Knoll. Simmons whispered, "I did." He would cooperate fully with police, even taking them to the scene for a reenactment that would also be videotaped.

Figure 6.4. Simmons arrested at Fenton High School.

Figure 6.5. Within hours of his arrest, Simmons confesses to police.

The sheer brutality of the crime had stunned the community. Missouri law defined a juvenile defendant as anyone sixteen years of age or under. But the law also allowed them to be tried as adults for particularly heinous crimes. Benjamin, although only fifteen, was charged as an adult, eventually pleaded guilty, and was sentenced to life in prison. Simmons, however, was seventeen; prosecutors made it clear that they would be seeking the death penalty.

 To see the police videotape of Simmons's confession, go to: http://murderatthesupremecourt.com/simmons

When the U.S. Supreme Court reinstated capital punishment in *Gregg v. Georgia* in 1976, opponents redirected their campaign to at least limit its use wherever possible. If they couldn't do away with capital punishment in one fell swoop, perhaps they could accomplish the same goal through a piecemeal approach, chipping away at it case by case. Sparing those who were sixteen or seventeen at the time of their crimes would become a large part of that effort. Most would agree there must be some minimum age at which the death penalty would be inapplicable, but there has long been disagreement over what that age might be and who should be drawing the line. In 1885, a Cherokee Indian named James Arcene was hanged for a robbery and a murder he had committed when only ten years old.[6]

In 1944, South Carolina executed fourteen-year-old George Stinney, who had been convicted in a quick and questionable trial of the murder of two young white girls.[7] At five feet one and only ninety pounds, Stinney's feet didn't even reach the floor when he was strapped into the electric chair. The odds of a death sentence increase proportionately with the age of the defendant. In the post-*Gregg* era, the debate turned to whether states might execute those aged between fifteen and eighteen. The justices took their first crack at determining a minimum age for death-penalty eligibility in 1988, rejecting the death penalty for Wayne Thompson who, at fifteen, had

murdered his brother-in-law.[8] Dividing 5–3,[9] the Court concluded
that executing anyone that young at the time of the offense would
violate the Eighth Amendment prohibition of cruel and unusual
punishment. (This decision, made five years prior to the murder
of Cheryl Hayes, caused Benjamin to be ineligible for a death sentence.) The decision, however, left open the more difficult question
of whether juveniles just one or two years older at the time of their
crimes must also be spared.

 For a video report on the *Thompson* case, go to:
http://murderatthesupremecourt.com/thompson

    That question reached the Supreme Court the following term
in *Stanford v. Kentucky*,[10] with the Court allowing such executions
and finding no national consensus against it. On the day the high
Court ruled in the *Stanford* case, thirty-seven states allowed the death
penalty and fewer than half of them—fifteen, exactly—prohibited
the execution of sixteen-year-old offenders. Fewer than one-third
of them—twelve—prohibited the execution of offenders who were
seventeen at the time of their crimes. The *Stanford* decision was 5–4.
Justice Antonin Scalia, writing for the Court, said that federal courts
must show deference to the will of the states in these matters, and
he suggested the dissenters would have the Court play the role of
"philosopher-kings" rather than guardians of the Constitution.
    Decisions of the U.S. Supreme Court on the meaning and scope
of the Bill of Rights are binding on the states. While Simmons's
youth and troubled childhood might have been considered by the
jury as mitigating factors in his defense, they would not comprise an
automatic bar to a death sentence. The Court's decision in *Stanford v.*

Kentucky meant Simmons would be eligible for a death sentence. And when compared with the viciousness and heartlessness of his crime, Simmons's youth and childhood misfortunes didn't seem to help his case very much.

At the trial, Jefferson County prosecutor John Appelbaum told the jury how Simmons had carefully planned the chain of events that would end in Shirley Crook's death and how he had even tried to get others to go along: "He used his age as a sword, saying 'Kids, you can get away with this because nobody will think we're capable of doing this.'"[11] Appelbaum found Simmons to be an eminently good candidate for the death penalty. He still does, telling the authors that Simmons "was talking to people, trying to incorporate them into his plot. It doesn't necessarily have to be Shirley Crook that night. That's what's so scary about this case. It could have been anybody."[12]

In court, Appelbaum called Moomey and other associates of Simmons who all testified how Simmons had talked about burglarizing the home of the voodoo man and then taking his life. John Tessmer, the sixteen-year-old who had backed out of the plan, testified that Simmons talked about a plan to murder someone because "he wanted a bunch of money." Tessmer said that on three to five occasions Simmons had told him he would throw the victim off a bridge and that he had the voodoo man in mind.

Steven Crook testified about his loss and how his wife was the center of the family, a loving person who "accepted everyone because she knew everyone made mistakes." He said he could not go back to the couple's home in Fenton because it so reminded him of her. Detective Steven Knoll testified that although Simmons cried during his confession, he never once said he was sorry. The jury also heard from Pertie Mitchell, Shirley Crook's sister, who described in agonizing detail the pain Simmons's action had caused loved ones left behind.

Shirley Crook's children had not gotten over the death of their mother, and they never would. Nor do they speak publicly about it. Shirley Crook's husband passed away one year after the murder.

Friends said he was grieving to the end. In an interview with the authors in 2004, Mrs. Mitchell was particularly embittered by Simmons's lack of any semblance of remorse: "These boys went to school the next day and they were bragging about what they had done. They said, 'Guess what we did last night. We beat up an old lady. And we took her out to the trestle and we pushed her off. And guess what *she* did. She went bubble, bubble.' You think that didn't hurt us?"[13]

Figure 6.6. Pertie Mitchell, the victim's sister.

To put it mildly, the trial was not going well. Simmons's court-appointed lawyer, David Crosby, pleaded with prosecutors to spare his client. And, in midtrial, they agreed: life in prison with no parole if Simmons would plead guilty. Simmons wouldn't hear of it, still believing no jury would convict him. He would agree to ten years, but nothing more. Crosby was exasperated with his stubborn client, the determination of the state to execute him, and his own inability to strike an acceptable deal. And Crosby was also struck by the irony of it all: "Here's a child that in Missouri couldn't buy a car because he's under age to contract, and yet he makes life and death decisions."[14]

Figure 6.7. Simmons in court.

It was an open-and-shut case. The jury found Simmons guilty of first-degree murder and recommended a penalty of death. Circuit court judge Timothy Patterson agreed. Death would be by lethal injection. Simmons's mother and brothers wept as the jury delivered its decision. Steven Crook expressed neither joy nor sorrow, saying he was prepared to accept the jury's verdict, whatever it was.

A number of appeals followed, but Simmons had received a fair trial and claims that he hadn't went nowhere. He complained about the conduct of his arresting officers who had told him that cooperating would be in his best interests. But it was his own cooperation that ultimately sealed his fate at trial. He also complained about the presence of television cameras at his trial, which, his attorneys argued, may have led prosecution witnesses to embellish their testimony. But there was no evidence that it actually did. He claimed that, given that he was charged with first-degree murder, he should have been tried in St. Louis County, where Shirley Crook's death occurred, rather than in Jefferson County, where the burglary and abduction occurred. That didn't work either.[15]

That Simmons *must* be spared the death penalty because of his youth at the time of the offense was never part of the equation since the U.S. Supreme Court had appeared to have resolved that question five years earlier in the *Stanford* case. The age of fifteen would be the cutoff for executions, not seventeen. After the Missouri Supreme Court upheld Simmons's conviction and death sentence without dissent on April 29, 1997, his attorneys took their appeals to the federal courts, which also rejected them. The U.S. Supreme Court declined to review the case. All reasonable avenues for appeal had been exhausted. The stage had been set for an execution.

A new development was taking shape in the nation's capital, however, that offered Simmons at least a glimmer of hope. On the same day in 1989 that the Court had announced its decision in *Stanford v. Kentucky*, it also ruled in another important death-penalty case, *Penry v. Lynagh*[16] (discussed more fully in the preceding chapter) and concluded that it did not violate the Eighth Amendment ban against cruel and unusual punishment to execute a murderer who was mildly retarded at the time of his crime.

But that was a dozen years ago, and times had changed. It was now October 1, 2001, and the Supreme Court announced it would reconsider its *Penry* decision in a new case involving Daryl Atkins, in light of the changing times.

If the Court were to overrule its *Penry* decision and find that "evolving standards of decency" now forbid the execution of mentally impaired inmates, perhaps the same argument could be made to overrule *Stanford v. Kentucky* and bar forever the execution of juvenile offenders like Chris Simmons. It was a long shot to be sure. At this juncture, it was the only shot Simmons had.

Chris Simmons had been sitting on death row at Missouri's Potosi Correctional Center for eight years. He'd seen a dozen or so new inmates come in and a handful of them walk out to meet the executioner. He had befriended inmates on death row over the years and could not help but think of their last walk to a small room where they would be put to death by lethal injection. "Every night you think about the steps they took and what may happen to you."[17] Now, his own date with death was drawing near. His original execution date was set for May 5, 2002, though the state supreme court suddenly—and apparently on its own—moved the date back a month to June 5. He was now twenty-six years old, and his execution was only nine days away when another one-sentence order came from the Missouri Supreme Court. Simmons execution would be put off again, indefinitely and without explanation.[18]

Although there were no dissents in the earlier decision by the Missouri Supreme Court to uphold Simmons's death sentence, the composition of the court had changed in the intervening years and some of the new state justices were having second thoughts about the ruling. The court's one-sentence stay on the eve of Simmons's execution didn't need much of an explanation. The Missouri Supreme Court was awaiting a decision from the U.S. Supreme Court in the Atkins case. As with mentally impaired inmates, a growing number of states had passed laws against executing anyone under eighteen. Was it a sufficient trend? A decision in Atkins's favor would effectively pave the way for a new appeal by Simmons's attorneys to challenge the Supreme Court's decision in *Stanford v. Kentucky* on the consensus arguments similar to those raised in Atkins's case. It would also provide an opportunity for the Missouri high court to reconsider whether the execution of one so young may violate "the evolving standards of decency that mark the progress of a maturing society."

Three weeks later, the U.S. Supreme Court announced its decision in *Atkins.* As seen in the preceding chapter, the case bitterly divided the Court with a five-justice majority rejecting the death penalty for mentally retarded offenders.

Lawyers for Simmons took the cue and filed for a writ of habeas corpus on the ground that in contemporary America, the execution of one so young at the time of the crime had similarly become cruel and unusual punishment in violation of the Eighth Amendment. For many, it was a hard sell. Certainly it was true that the trend among the states against executing mentally impaired offenders was unmistakable, from two states in 1989 to eighteen states in 2002. But while there may have been a trend against executing juvenile offenders, it was not nearly so dramatic. Of the thirty-five states that allowed the death penalty in 1989, twelve prohibited the execution of offenders who were under eighteen.

When the Simmons case came back to the Missouri Supreme Court fourteen years later, only six additional states had joined the list. If that's a trend, it is a modest one. And there was another problem. Decisions of the U.S. Supreme Court are the law of the land, and all other courts—state and federal—are considered duty-bound to follow the Supreme Court's edicts on matters of U.S. constitutional law. If for some reason a lower court were to conclude that a Supreme Court decision for whatever reason has lost its validity, the lower court can say so in its opinion, but it is most unusual for a state court to discard a U.S. Supreme Court decision and substitute its own judgment on contemporary values. In a word, it might be called *chutzpah*.[19] It is also, however, a very effective way to get the attention of the nation's highest judicial tribunal.

And that is precisely what happened here. The Missouri Supreme Court effectively overruled the U.S. Supreme Court's decision in *Stanford v. Kentucky* and commuted Simmons's death penalty to life in prison.[20] The decision was 4–3, with Justice Laura Denvir Stith writing for the majority:

> Applying the approach taken in Atkins, this Court finds that, in the fourteen years since *Stanford* was decided, a national consensus has developed against the execution of juvenile offenders, as demonstrated by the fact that eighteen states now bar such executions for juveniles, that twelve other states bar executions altogether, that no state has lowered its age of execution below 18 since *Stanford*, that five states have legislatively or by case law raised or established the minimum age at 18, and that the imposition of the juvenile death penalty has become truly unusual over the last decade. Accordingly, this Court finds the Supreme Court would today hold such executions are prohibited by the Eighth and Fourteenth Amendments. It therefore sets aside Mr. Simmons' death sentence and re-sentences him to life imprisonment without eligibility for probation, parole, or release except by act of the Governor.

The three dissenting judges observed that if the U.S. Supreme Court had any doubts about the viability of its decision in *Stanford*, it had numerous opportunities for reconsideration and had passed them up. Dissenting Judge William Ray Price added:

> This Court's solemn duty to abide by decisions of the Supreme Court of the United States is not abridged simply because we disagree with that Court's decision or even if it appears that a decision was clearly in error. Neither can this Court imply or anticipate the overruling of a decision of the United Sates Supreme Court. . . .
>
> It is the prerogative of the Supreme Court of the United States, and it alone to overrule one of its decisions. The proper venue for Simmons to seek relief on this issue is in the Supreme Court of the United States. I would deny the writ.[21]

State supreme courts ordinarily do not—and ordinarily should not—disregard or disobey decisions of the nation's highest court. There are, however, practical consequences of such an action beyond offending the sensibilities of individual Supreme Court justices or the Supreme Court itself.

The justices exercise great care in deciding what cases they will hear. In their Friday conferences, they cull through lists of hundreds of cases to find just the right case to precisely address an issue. One of the most important rules at the Supreme Court is the unwritten "Rule of Four." It takes four justices to agree to hear a case before the full Court will take it up.[22] Of the thousands of cases submitted to the Court each year, only about seventy or eighty are scheduled for oral argument in the Court's august chamber. Had the Missouri Supreme Court merely expressed its misgivings about the continuing vitality of *Stanford v. Kentucky* but upheld Simmons's death sentence, the U.S. Supreme Court could have easily denied review. But it's not quite so easy when a state supreme court calls into question the wisdom of a decision of the U.S. Supreme Court. Rather, it is quite remarkable.

Whatever characterization one might give to the Missouri Supreme Court's decision, it was all but certain that Judge Stith and her colleagues had forced the Supreme Court's hand. On January 26, 2004, the U.S. Supreme Court announced it would review the Missouri Court's decision in *Roper v. Simmons*. It would be among the first cases the justices would hear in the new term that started the following October. The fate of Simmons and nearly eighty other juvenile offenders around the country who also faced the death penalty would be riding on the Court's decision.

At the time the case reached the U.S. Supreme Court, the United States was the only country in the world to give official sanction to the juvenile death penalty, and the decision of the justices to reconsider the issue drew worldwide attention from humanitarian groups as well as other groups. And the international community was united in support of Simmons.

The decision of the jury in rural Fenton, Missouri, was being second-guessed and criticized by eighteen recipients of the Nobel Peace Prize. In an *amicus* or "friend of the Court" brief, they told the Court: "The death penalty for child offenders is contrary to internationally accepted standards of human rights." Signatories to the brief included former U.S. president Jimmy Carter, Soviet president Mikhail Gorbachev, Poland's Lech Walesa, President Oscar Arias Sanchez of Costa Rica, William de Klerk and Desmond Tutu of South Africa, and the Dalai Lama. Ten former U.S. diplomats also submitted a joint brief urging that Simmons be spared, arguing, among other things, that Simmons's execution was "inconsistent with minimum standards of decency shared by nearly all nations of the world" and that the practice "strains diplomatic relations with close American allies, increases America's diplomatic isolation and impairs important U.S. foreign policy interests at a critical time."[23]

In the United States, it came as no surprise that the leading civil rights groups would also oppose Simmons's execution.[24] More mainstream groups also rallied to the Simmons cause, including the American Bar Association, the American Medical Association, the American Psychological Association, and the American Psychiatric Association. "Friend of the Court" briefs were also submitted in support of Missouri, although they were fewer and mostly from other states that also allowed the execution of youthful offenders. Briefs supporting Missouri focused on the idea that, in a democracy, the decision of where to draw the line on the minimum age for execution was a "policy judgment" that should be made by the people through their elected representatives and not by judges, and certainly not by federal judges who serve for life and cannot be held accountable for their decisions. Also, allowing an execution is not tantamount to requiring it; Missouri and other states argued that juries should have the discretion to impose death in extreme cases.[25]

Interest groups spend thousands of dollars preparing "friend of the Court" briefs that are seldom actually read by the justices or even their clerks.[26] The justices ordinarily have more than ample material on which to form their opinions. The lower-court opinion and the briefs of the actual parties are the starting point and are often sufficient. When lower courts have disagreed on how to interpret a point of constitutional law, the justices will ordinarily review these conflicting opinions.

The "friend of the Court" briefs filed by special-interest groups, however, are often a consummate waste of money. But not always. A handful of organizations are so widely respected at the Court that their briefs also get attention. A brief bearing the name of a respected Supreme Court advocate or any former U.S. solicitor general will usually get the justices' attention. Perhaps no single legal organization is held in higher esteem at the Court than the U.S. Solicitor General's Office, and even when the office is not directly involved in a case, its views are often sought and always considered when offered.

When a party to a Supreme Court case specifically refers to the support of a respected professional organization, that organization's amicus brief is apt to be reviewed. The amicus brief filed by the American Psychiatric Association (APA) in support of Simmons got considerable attention from the media, if not from the Court. Simplified, the APA brief explained what every parent already knows: teenagers can be difficult, much more so than preteens or postteens.

What made the brief important, however, was that it claimed medical research now had empirical evidence as to *why* teenagers act impulsively and often don't consider the consequences of their actions.

The APA brief makes the case that scientists can demonstrate that adolescents are immature not only to the naked eye but also in the very fibers of their brain. Magnetic resonance imaging (MRI) research "shows that adolescent brains are more active in regions related to aggression, anger and fear and less active in regions related to impulse control, risk assessment, and moral reasoning than adult brains."[27] The frontal lobe of the brain, associated with reasoning, is not fully developed in many people until their early twenties.

Some of these briefs (particularly one filed by the APA) did get the attention of Justice Scalia and drew a mocking rebuke. Scalia noted that the same groups claiming that those under eighteen years of age lack the maturity to take responsibility for their crimes also claim that they did have the maturity to obtain abortions without parental involvement.[28]

The timing of all of this could also have been a factor working against Simmons. In October 2002, one year before the Simmons case went to the Supreme Court, snipers John Allen Muhammad and Lee Boyd Malvo went on a three-week random shooting spree terrorizing the Washington, DC, metropolitan area. They shot ten people to death from the back of their car—one by one—and they wounded three others. The rampage was preceded by a series of murders and robberies in Louisiana and Alabama. There was no apparent reason, although there was speculation that Muhammad wanted to include his ex-wife among the victims.[29] The thought was that with so many random victims, he would not be such an obvious suspect. Muhammad was sentenced to death and executed by lethal injection in November 2009.

Malvo, however, was only seventeen at the time of the killing spree. Even so, the commonwealth's attorney in Prince William County (Virginia), Paul Ebert, had no apprehensions about seeking the death penalty. "I'm going to take a shot at him," he told the authors in 2004 on the eve of the arguments in the Simmons case at the U.S. Supreme Court. No prosecutor in Virginia has sent more men to death row than Ebert, who acknowledged that in some cases a defendant's youth might weigh against the death penalty. But not in this one. "Yeah, we've pretty much made the decision to go after him. I just don't see how you can say someone who is eighteen and one month should be treated differently from someone who is seventeen and nine or ten months."[30]

James Layton, Missouri state solicitor, would press that same argument to the U.S. Supreme Court on the morning of October 13, 2004, in Simmons's case. The initial questioning would be led by two justices who had long been close friends, although they sat on the opposite ends of the ideological spectrum. Justices Antonin Scalia and Ruth Bader Ginsburg, along with their respective spouses, had celebrated New Year's Eve together almost every year since they served together on the U.S. Court of Appeals for the District of Columbia a decade earlier. They are both opera lovers and sometimes attend together, and they have, on a few occasions even played bit parts in operas. As close as they are off the bench, when it comes to ideological issues before the Court, they are often light-years apart. Scalia wrote the dissent in *Atkins*, denouncing the majority opinion banning the execution of mentally retarded offenders, and he was anxious to see that his majority opinion in *Stanford* involving juveniles was preserved.

Barely a minute into Layton's argument, Scalia asked sarcastically: "Why pick on the death penalty? I mean, if you're going to say that somehow people under 18 are juveniles for all purposes, why just pick on the death penalty? Why not say they're immune from *any* criminal penalty."

Ginsburg, on the other hand, noted that society does make important distinctions based on youth affecting both rights and privileges:

> *Layton:* There are seventeen-year-olds who are equally culpable with those who are eighteen, twenty, twenty-five or some other age.

Ginsburg: But the age eighteen is set even for such things as buying tobacco. The dividing line between people who are members of the community, the adult community, is pervasively eighteen—to vote, to sit on juries, to serve in the military. Why should it be that someone is death-eligible under the age of eighteen but not eligible to be an adult member of the community?

Simmons was represented by Seth Waxman, a highly regarded Supreme Court advocate, solicitor general in the Clinton administration, and frequently mentioned as a potential Supreme Court nominee himself. Waxman argued that not only was the execution of defendants as young as Simmons exceedingly rare but that medical research demonstrated that it was disproportionate to the culpability of a child. Drawing on the APA brief, Waxman pressed the point that seventeen-year-olds were *biologically* more likely to act irrationally than adults, and that they were less likely to appreciate the consequences of what they do and thus are less culpable.

Scalia wasn't buying: "If all this is so clear, why can't the legislature take it into account? All you have to do is bring these facts to the attention of the legislature."

Four justices—John Paul Stevens, David Souter, Stephen Breyer, and Ruth Bader Ginsburg—had previously staked out positions against executing juveniles: a "relic of the past" they had called it in another case two years earlier.[31] So all eyes were fixed on Justice Anthony Kennedy, who in so many cases and on so many diverse issues would provide the fifth and deciding vote. And Kennedy seemed troubled, wondering out loud if fixing the minimum age for the death penalty at eighteen might encourage street gangs to designate sixteen- and seventeen-year-olds as their "hit men." Kennedy appeared shocked by a brief filed by the state of Alabama in support of Missouri that described in detail a number of grisly crimes committed by children. At one point, Kennedy offered that those justices who signed on to accept Simmons's petition for

Supreme Court review should have read Alabama's gruesome brief before doing so.

Simmons's legal team was dismayed. They felt they needed Kennedy's vote, although Justice Sandra Day O'Connor might also provide the crucial fifth vote. Both Kennedy and O'Connor had joined the majority in *Atkins*. But Kennedy had a peculiar habit of always being on the winning side in 5–4 cases. He had been crucial on a wide range of issues, and his ascension to the high Court over defeated nominee Robert Bork has had significant implications for American society as well as its jurisprudence. The Bork-Kennedy scenario is also a striking illustration of the impact a president can have on the country with a single Supreme Court appointment.

To the surprise and dismay of the administration that had appointed him, Kennedy had provided the critical fifth vote to uphold a woman's right to choose abortion in *Planned Parenthood v. Casey*,[32] the fifth vote for holding that desecrating the American flag constitutes protected "speech" under the First Amendment in *Johnson v. Texas*,[33] wrote the 6–3 majority decision striking down the Texas antisodomy law thereby invalidating similar laws throughout the United States that criminalized sodomy between consenting same-sex adults,[34] and he also wrote the 6–3 majority decision banning invocations to God at public school commencement ceremonies, finding it a violation of the First Amendment's Establishment Clause.[35]

Robert Bork, the judge originally picked to fill the vacancy on the Court left by the retirement of Justice Lewis Powell (ultimately filled by Kennedy), had publicly denounced each of these decisions, and the outcome of each would surely have been different had Bork been confirmed.[36] And these are only the cases we know about. There presumably are scores of other cases in which Bork's defeat and Kennedy's elevation have had just as significant although perhaps not as obvious an impact on the law and American society.

Anthony Kennedy is a thoughtful, pleasant, and caring judge; he is a good writer, he makes those around him feel comfortable, and he is comfortable himself in just about any surrounding. Shortly after his appointment to the Court, Kennedy was invited to make some informal remarks following a dinner hosted by a Washington Shakespeare Society and held at the Supreme Court. Guests were invited into the majestic courtroom after dinner, where Kennedy regaled them with anecdotes about the common law. And then he went on to discuss the role of the U.S. Supreme Court in late twentieth-century America. "It's not just our job to say what the law is," intoned Kennedy. "It's also our job to say what the law was and what *it ought to be.*"[37] (emphasis added)

Figure 6.8. President Reagan names Anthony Kennedy to the U.S. Supreme Court, November 30, 1987.

A collective gasp passed across the faces of the conservatives in the group who knew instantly that this man would be no Robert Bork. It had been the mantra of President Ronald Reagan's inner circle that the job of federal judges was exclusively to say what the law is. What it *ought to be* is the business of others in the American tripartite system of government, namely the elected branches of Congress and the White House.

To say that Kennedy has been a disappointment to conservatives, particularly those who had adored Robert Bork and crusaded to save his doomed nomination, is something of an understatement. Unlike Bork, Kennedy could not be counted on. Yet on many issues—particularly those involving Federalism and the balance of power between the states and the federal government—Kennedy remains a faithful ally of conservatives. And on some criminal-law issues, too—just not this one.

If Kennedy seemed on the fence during the oral arguments in the Simmons case, his mind was made up two days later when the justices took up the matter at their regular Friday conference. Kennedy not only provided the fifth vote for a majority, Justice John Paul Stevens—the senior justice in the majority—assigned Kennedy to write the opinion of the Court. Kennedy had decided that executing juvenile offenders, much like executing mentally impaired offenders, violated the country's evolving standards of decency and, thus, the Eighth Amendment's prohibition of cruel and unusual punishment.

Kennedy, joined by the predictable other four justices—Stevens, Souter, Ginsburg, and Breyer—concluded that the evidence of a national consensus against the death penalty for juveniles was similar to and in some respects parallel to the evidence against executing offenders who were mentally retarded. Kennedy also noted that juveniles had been specifically excluded from the new Federal Death Penalty Act of 1994[38] and that society had come to view juveniles as "categorically less culpable" than the average criminal. A final, subsidiary argument would come under immediate attack. Kennedy wrote that the United States was the only country in the world that continued to give official sanction to the juvenile death penalty. He emphasized that while the practices of the rest of the world can hardly be controlling, "it is proper that we acknowledge the overwhelming weight of international opinion against the juvenile death penalty."[39]

The allusions to the practices and opinions in other parts of the world drew instant criticism from those who felt such references had no place in either interpreting or applying provisions of constitutional law. The critics had a point. The "Bill of Rights" is actually a misnomer. The document, modeled after the French Declaration of the Rights of Man,[40] is actually a bill of prohibitions, not rights; it's a list of practices that the government is prohibited from engaging in. And it reflects the outer limits of what the government *may* do; it was never intended to be a guide to what the government *should* do.

The Court has said repeatedly that it is not its job to judge the fairness or wisdom of any government practice or statute, only whether it exceeds the outer limits defined by the Constitution.[41] As a result, many unfair and even ridiculous statutes have been upheld. Federal judges, perhaps more than any other public servants in America, must sometimes hold their noses if they are faithfully to perform their duties.

While practices in the rest of the world are surely relevant to governors, presidents, and legislatures in their policy-making roles, the critics are correct that these considerations should have no bearing on defining the wide latitude that the Constitution gives to federal, state, and local governments. The critics are incorrect, however, when they claim the *Simmons* decision rested largely on notions of what the rest of the world thinks. The decision in *Roper v. Simmons* relies more on legitimate constitutional concerns, although many Americans, including the four dissenting justices, have reasonably concluded that those concerns are insufficient.

Justice O'Connor, in dissent, wrote that the majority (and Simmons's lawyers) had failed to demonstrate that any national consensus had actually developed against executing seventeen-year-olds in the brief time since the Court's decision in *Stanford v. Kentucky*. O'Connor also complained that the Court had failed to show that juries were not capable of assessing a youthful defendant's maturity or of giving due weight to the mitigating characteristics associated with youth.[42]

The sharpest criticism, however, came from Justice Scalia, whose majority opinion in *Stanford* had just been eviscerated. Scalia scoffed that the Court's majority had proclaimed itself "the sole arbiter of the nation's moral standards" and that the meaning of the Eighth

Amendment "ought not be determined by the subjective views of five members of the Supreme Court and like-minded foreigners."[43]

The Court's decision meant that, in addition to Chris Simmons, scores of other sixteen- and seventeen-year-olds sentenced to death would have their sentences commuted to life in prison. Immediately following the ruling and as a natural result of it, prosecutors in Prince William County, Virginia, abandoned their plans to seek the death penalty against Lee Boyd Malvo in the sniper shootings. He eventually pleaded guilty and is now serving six consecutive life terms in prison with no chance for parole.

Since the Court's decision, there also have been advances in medicine and science. A team of physicians and scientists at Washington University's School of Medicine in St. Louis, Missouri, claim they can now predict how mature a person is using a five-minute brain scan. Researchers say new MRIs can determine with 92 percent accuracy whether a brain is that of an adult over twenty-five or that of a child.[44] Lawyers may someday be offering a defense of immaturity based on the defendant's brain scan.

The Court's landmark decision in the *Simmons* case has also been extended to other situations involving juveniles. In May 2010, the Court—again dividing 5–4—ruled that juveniles who commit crimes in which no one is killed may not be sentenced to life in prison without parole.[45] Again it was Justice Kennedy who wrote the decision of the Court, relying in part on his own decision in the *Simmons* case to find that the practice violated both U.S. and international moral standards and that "a national consensus has developed against it." Two years later, the Court went even further, requiring judges to consider a defendant's youth (defined as anyone under eighteen) before issuing a sentence of life in prison without parole.[46]

Looking back, Simmons's mother, Cheryl Hayes, says she failed her son. When the *Simmons* case was pending before the Supreme Court, she told the authors that she would gladly give her life, if she could, if that would bring Shirley Crook back, and that Christopher would as well. Her eyes welled up with tears as she told us that she did the best she could, but her life was a mess at the time, "and they just don't teach you in school how to be a good parent."[47]

Figure 6.9. Cheryl Hayes, Chris Simmons's mother.

Chris Simmons today is serving his life sentence at Missouri's Southeast Correctional Center in Charleston, Missouri. He says prison has given him the discipline he never had at home, that he's matured and would like someday to get out and have a normal life and family.[48] Prosecutors and prison officials say it will never happen. That's not to say Simmons hasn't truly changed. Seventeen-year-olds, even in prison, usually do. He's become a Christian, has finished his high school education, and counsels young people about the consequences of crime and drugs. And he is most emphatic about the remorse he feels for his crime, telling a reporter for the *Kansas City Star*, "In a way, I've killed myself."[49]

Where to draw the bright line between what age is acceptable for an execution or what level of intellectual capacity should be required cuts to the heart of modern-day Supreme Court decision making. There are those who, we all might agree, are either too young or too mentally impaired to be executed. The difficulty lies in that gray area: What is the appropriate punishment for the mildly retarded killer or the cold-blooded seventeen-year-old just shy of his eighteenth birthday? And even then, the larger question is not what the right answer is, but rather who has the right to decide. Should these questions be decided by juries with the guided discretion of a state legislature? Or are they so "implicit in the concept of ordered liberty" that the U.S. Supreme Court—the ultimate arbiter of what the Constitution means—must decide?[50]

For Justice Scalia, this is a simple matter. If the practice wasn't cruel and unusual in 1791 when the Bill of Rights was ratified, then it isn't cruel and unusual today. And it is a "two-way street," he told the authors shortly before this book went to print. Should the American people for whatever reason decide to begin punishing its criminals with thumbscrews to the point where it ceased to be "unusual," it still would not be permitted because it was considered both cruel and unusual in 1791. There are, however, other practices acceptable in 1791 that most Americans would find unacceptable today. Scalia's response to that is that "you can always find some extreme case, but the more extreme it is, the less likely it is to really happen.[51]

The arguments advanced on behalf of Christopher Simmons, like those advanced on behalf of Daryl Atkins (Chapter 5), failed to win a majority of the Court only a few years earlier and likely would not have won a majority vote at the time the Bill of Rights was adopted. In 1791, there was no movement against the execution of middle-teenagers or those modestly retarded. Justice John Paul Stevens—who got the reversals rolling with his opinion for the Court in *Atkins*—wrote a simple, one-paragraph concurrence in the *Simmons* case that underscores how the Court's death-penalty jurisprudence has largely been shaped by the Court's landmark decision in a non-death case, *Trop v. Dulles*. Stevens suggested those who drafted our Constitution would have wanted today's Court to take note of changing times and standards, and that the majority's recognition of that may be the single most important feature of its decision in *Roper v. Simmons*:

Perhaps even more important than our specific holding today is our reaffirmation of the basic principle that informs the Court's interpretation of the *Eighth Amendment*. If the meaning of that Amendment had been frozen when it was originally drafted, it would impose no impediment to the execution of 7-year-old children today. The evolving standards of decency that have driven our construction of this critically important part of the *Bill of Rights* foreclose any such reading of the Amendment. In the best tradition of the common law, the pace of that evolution is a matter for continuing debate; but that our understanding of the Constitution does change from time to time has been settled since John Marshall breathed life into its text. If great lawyers of his day—Alexander Hamilton, for example—were sitting with us today, I would expect them to join Justice Kennedy's opinion for the Court. In all events, I do so without hesitation.[52] (italics in the original)

The ruling, and Justice Stevens's thoughtful discussion of the country's "evolving standards of decency," would be of little comfort to Shirley Crook's sister, Pertie Mitchell. Years after the murder, Simmons sent Mitchell a letter from the penitentiary in which he tried to express his regrets for what he had done. But the letter was not accepted. "I don't want anything from Christopher Simmons besides his death," said Mitchell. "And I would love to see him suffer the way Shirley did. I will never change my mind."[53]

7
MEDICATE TO EXECUTE?

The question before the Court today is whether or not the State of Louisiana may, for the sole purpose of executing an inmate, forcibly medicate a mentally ill inmate with psychotropic drugs.

—Keith B. Nordyre,
arguing *Louisiana v. Perry* before the
U.S. Supreme Court on October 2, 1990

I n 1983, singer Olivia Newton-John, then thirty-five years old, was riding a huge crest of popularity following a successful world tour. Newton-John's "Physical Live" tour had begun the previous year and had brought her renewed fame and more fortune—as well as a determined stalker named Michael Perry. Times were desperate enough for her to call upon a private security service for help.

"[Perry] developed an obsession involving my client's eyes and was convinced they had changed colors as a signal to him," said Gavin de Becker, head of the security service Newton-John hired. Perry, an escapee from a mental institution, camped out near Newton-John's Malibu home and sent her letters saying he wanted to prove to himself she was "real," rather than a "Disneyland mirror image."[1] Perry came from a small Louisiana town some forty miles from the Gulf Coast and had written her, "The voices I hear tell me that you are locked up beneath this town of Lake Arthur and were really a muse who was granted everlasting life."[2]

"Somehow he convinced himself that she was responsible for dead bodies rising through the floor of his home," de Becker said.

His firm's employees turned Perry away from Newton-John's estate twice. Perry eventually returned to Louisiana, where his fantasies escalated into violence.[3]

Figure 7.1. Downtown Lake Arthur, Louisiana, circa 1989.

Perry's hometown of Lake Arthur was a sleepy community of about 3,500 people in 1983, though economic changes have since shrunk the population to about 3,000. The principal sources of livelihood were family farms and the oil fields—Louisiana's first producing well was drilled fewer than twenty miles away, in Evangeline, at the turn of the century. Whether you approached from the north on Highway 26 or from the south on Highway 14, you were greeted by a roadside sign announcing, "Lake Arthur—A Good Place to Live."[4] The biggest attraction in town was the high school football team, the Tigers.

While in school, Michael Perry was lead trumpet in the band that played at the Tigers' home games. Pookie Marceaux, who lived across the street and was a year behind him at school, said Michael was a good student—"His IQ was higher than some bowler's average"— and he was more inclined to books than athletics.[5]

Perry's father worked on oil rigs; his mother was a "tireless home-maker," said Marceaux, "with a warm smile, a generous box of spattered recipe cards, and a talent for making them a reality." Michael was the middle child of three in a church-going family.

Figure 7.2. Chester and Grace Perry, parents of Michael Perry.

Marceaux said Perry seemed to lose his way after graduation; he was accident prone and kept getting into minor scrapes with the law. "He constantly attracted attention to himself by doing weird things," said Marceaux.[6] But Marceaux and the entire community were shocked to the core by the way Perry imploded after his return from one of his California stalking trips in the summer of 1983.

On the afternoon of July 17, armed with a 16-gauge shotgun, a 12-gauge shotgun, a .357 Magnum, and a Beretta pistol, Perry set off on a shooting spree in which he killed his parents and three other relatives. The victims were Chester Perry, forty-eight; Grace Perry, forty-seven; cousins Randy Perry, nineteen, and Brian LeBlanc, twenty-two; and his nephew Anthony "Tony" Bonin—just two years old. Perry shot his parents through the eyes.

Figure 7.3. Randy Perry and Brian LeBlanc.

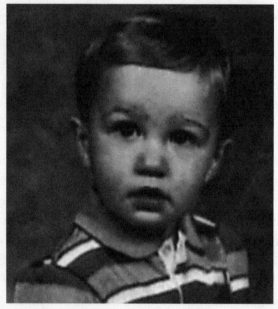

Figure 7.4. Anthony Bonin.

Perry confessed the murders to his uncle and aunt after he was taken into custody several weeks after the murder. "He told me the scene was like a battle in Vietnam . . . because there was blood everywhere," Zula Lyon, Grace Perry's sister, would later testify. "He said not to worry about it, those people meant nothing to him," she said.[7]

"I killed the five people," Perry told Jefferson Davis Parish jailers Herbert Durkes Jr. and Robert Lee. Durkes testified that Perry asked to see the two jailers because he wanted to confess. It was an unusual request, but Perry refused their suggestion that he talk to police detectives instead. Durkes and Lee went to his cell and squatted down in the corridor so they could talk through the small opening in the cell's steel door normally used to pass food. From that position, they were each able to see Perry's head and shoulders and watch his facial expressions.[8]

Durkes read Perry his Miranda rights, and Perry said he understood them. Durkes asked if Perry wanted a lawyer present; Perry said, "No." The surreal preliminaries out of the way, the two jail guards listened intently as Michael Perry recounted his shooting rampage. He first shot his two cousins with a pistol, Perry told the two jailers, then finished them off with the 16-gauge shotgun. Then he crossed the yard to his parents' empty home and broke in. His mother and father were expected back shortly from an out-of-town trip with their young grandson, Tony. While he waited, Perry passed the time by listening to music.

When his parents arrived home, "I blew my father's brains out," Perry said. He told the jailers he then walked up to his mother with a pistol and "shot her head off."[9]

Durkes said he asked Perry why he killed the child and quoted Perry as saying, "I had to be sure the little witch was dead. The kid was evil, some sort of a devil, a witch." Durkes said Perry told him that the Bonin child "was a very smart kid, too smart for his age."[10]

Following the murders, Perry removed $3,000 from his father's wallet, took his parents' car, and drove more than 1,200 miles to Washington, DC, where he registered at a motel near the Supreme Court. The proximity of the Court would take on new relevance later, when investigators unearthed an additional list of Perry's potential new victims.

Two weeks after his arrival, Perry was accused of stealing a radio from another motel guest. Metropolitan police officers who responded to the complaint ran a routine check of Perry's name, turning up five murder warrants from Louisiana.

After his arrest and return to Louisiana, Perry told authorities where to find two of the guns, which he had dumped into a canal. The admission took place as Sheriff Dallas Cormier and Deputy Ervin Trahan were driving Perry to a psychiatric evaluation at the Feliciana Forensics Facility, 130 miles away in Jackson, Louisiana. His lawyers would later argue that the statement was inadmissible because of their client's mental condition. The Louisiana Supreme Court ruling on that issue was explicit and in keeping with the odd nature of the case:

> Even were we to agree with this medical conclusion, the diagnosing doctors testified defendant lost contact with reality when the trigger words, "Olivia Newton-John," were used. Otherwise, defendant remained in contact with reality. We note Deputy Trahan testified those trigger words were not brought up during the trip to Feliciana.[11]

The peculiarities of *Perry v. Louisiana* would continue to unravel. Perry initially confessed to the murders and then recanted. He pleaded innocent by reason of insanity, then dropped that plea over the objections of his lawyers, entering a simple "Not guilty." "He told me, 'I killed those people, but the judge doesn't want me to plead guilty because the case is so serious,'" one of Perry's aunts, Zula Lyon, testified. Perry's delusions and disorientation spilled over into the courtroom.

Although a team of psychiatrists had found Perry competent to stand trial and to assist in his own defense, Perry's demeanor was erratic.[12] During his preliminary hearing, Perry interrupted witnesses, spit from the defense table, gestured to relatives, and stuck out his tongue at them.[13]

As his jury was being selected, Perry loudly challenged one prospect who stated he preferred life imprisonment as the punishment for murder. "Sir, are you aware that people get killed in a penitentiary?" Perry called out. Judge Cecil Cutrer told Perry to stop talking. "It's my life, it's my life," Perry replied. "I'll protect it the best I can. Now shut up," Cutrer said.

Figure 7.5. Michael Perry in Fulton County courtroom.

Perry recognized the mother of one of the victims in the courtroom, and he repeatedly gestured at her and made faces until the woman left the room in tears. He removed his shoes and socks while seated at the defense table, and he tied a string and rubber bands around his toes. He also wrapped a white bandanna around his head.

During a break in proceedings, Perry told a television reporter he was doing these things because "it's the lifestyle of the Mafia. You got to keep moving." He also told the reporter that he was arrested by "a top-secret agent," and that if the state didn't kill him in the electric chair, then he would be killed in prison. "You remember that; you remember that," Perry told the reporter.[14]

By contrast, Perry showed no emotion during testimony or the introduction of exhibits that elicited gasps and expressions of shock from others in the courtroom. Among the exhibits shown to the jury were a bloodstained sofa cushion where cousin Randy Perry's body was found; a bloody, light-blue pillowcase with hair and skull fragments from cousin Brian LeBlanc; an almost completely blood-stained printed pillowcase; and a stained sheet and pink bedspread also from LeBlanc's bed. Some jurors blanched, but Perry did not visibly react.[15]

Although they had been warned that the photographs would be explicit and gruesome, many of the jurors appeared shaken when they viewed the pictures; several of them openly wept. The pictures, visible at times from the audience, showed the victims and the locations where they were discovered. Large pools of dried blood surrounded the bodies of two-year-old Tony and Michael's mother, Grace Perry. The photos of these two victims appeared to be especially disturbing to the jurors.[16]

After six days of testimony, Assistant Attorney General Rene Saloman used photographs again in summing up the prosecution's case. He showed the jury pictures of the victims alive and well, then as they appeared after being shotgunned to death. Saloman said they died "by hatred, by design, by purpose of mind."[17]

"If you should ever say a prayer, say it for each one of these victims," the prosecutor said. "If you should ever shed a tear, shed it for these victims. Michael Perry killed out of hate, greed and avarice to put them out of his way."

Defense Attorney Mark Romero cited "shoddy" police work in his closing argument, saying there were serious flaws in the state's case, especially concerning Perry's alleged confessions, that presented the jury with reasonable doubt. "There's too much doubt, too much doubt," he said. The jury apparently had few doubts. After just one hour of deliberation—an hour Michael Perry spent eating lunch in his cell—the panel of nine men and three women found him guilty of five counts of first-degree murder. Perry heard the verdict impassively; the mother and grandmother of victim Randy Perry clutched shaking hands as it was read, then collapsed into each other's arms.

Under Louisiana law at the time, it was the jury's obligation to decide on a sentence of life or death; its recommendation would be binding on the judge. In the penalty phase of the trial, conducted on the same Halloween afternoon on which the original verdict was delivered, the defense called two doctors who had examined Perry after his arrest. Dr. Louis Shirley, a family practitioner who was the first to see him in jail, said Perry showed "definite signs of schizophrenia, paranoia" and that he recommended Perry for further evaluation. Dr. Harold Sabatier, a veteran of Louisiana sanity commissions, said his later diagnosis was "chronic schizophrenia."

Dr. Sabatier testified that schizophrenic tendencies had been diagnosed in Perry's family—the defense indicated that a sister, cousins, aunts, and uncles suffered from mental illness—and that schizophrenic tendencies can be genetic. He said Perry might not have been able to resist the "inner voices" commanding him to commit violent acts. Dr. Sabatier said that a paranoid person had the capacity to plan a crime, such as the ambush of Perry's parents, "ingeniously, and wait for them with unlimited patience."[18]

Defense Attorney Romero told the jury that Perry was suffering from mental problems when he committed the five murders and "he's still suffering from mental problems." "You've seen the way he looks, the way he's acted, what he's done," Romero told the jury, referring to his client's erratic actions in the courtroom. He asked for a sentence of life without parole, saying, "I don't think taking one life will bring back five other lives."

Arguing for the death penalty, Assistant Prosecutor Steve Laiche said Perry deserved no mercy. "Where was that mercy for the victims?" he asked. "We should say to Michael Perry that life is precious to us, and if you violate the law, then you have to pay the penalty."

That's what the jury said. It took them twice as long as the original verdict, almost two hours this time, to decide that Perry had committed the murders "with an intent to inflict great bodily harm," and in an "especially heinous, atrocious, or cruel manner"—two elements required to return a death sentence and reserve Perry a seat in Louisiana's electric chair.[19]

As the clerk read the verdict, Perry cupped his hand under his chin, his elbow pressing against the defense table, his face showing no visible emotion. Randy Perry's mother, Gwen Walker, jumped up and wrapped her arms around prosecutor Rene Saloman to thank him for his role in convicting her son's killer.

"The chair is too good for him," Mrs. Walker told reporters moments later. She held her mother's arm as they stood on the courthouse steps in a chilly breeze, her hands quivering and tears streaming down her face. "It's not going to bring Randy back, or any of them back, but he thought he could get away with it," she said. "He should be killed just like he killed all of them."[20]

Death verdicts in Louisiana are automatically appealed to the state supreme court, which, a year after the trial, unanimously upheld Perry's conviction. The court noted that although Perry had "a history of emotional or mental disorders" predating the murders, three physicians making up a court-appointed sanity commission "were unanimous in their conclusions that the defendant was able to proceed with trial."[21]

Perry had killed the victims "in a violent, bloody encounter which was deliberately planned," wrote Associate Justice Luther F. Cole for the court. "The death penalty in such a case is proportionate to the offenses and to this particular defendant."[22] The Louisiana Supreme Court ruling was definitive in its appraisal of Perry's sanity through the time of his trial, but it left a legal door open to the defense on the issue of the condemned man's state of mind following the jury's verdict. If Perry had become insane *after* his trial, the court indicated, and no longer understood the death penalty or that it was a punishment for his crime, he might not be competent enough to be executed. In the words of the ruling, "The State will not impose the death penalty on Michael Owen Perry if a court determines he has become insane subsequent to his conviction."[23]

The court practically invited Perry's lawyers to seek another sanity hearing. Judge L. J. Hymel, who had inherited the case from Judge Cutrer, granted a new sanity hearing in April of 1988, at which he had a question for the defendant: "What do you want me to do for you, Michael?" Replied Perry: "Well, I know you're the most fierce judge in the world and the whole world knows it. . . . I want to be found innocent and give me all the money in the world."

In frequently rambling testimony, Perry said, "I did it. I was tattooed. I was paid $9 million. I did it for you." Perry also told the court, "I was God when I was 7 years old. And I'm innocent. I didn't do it." But in response to questions, Perry said he knew the location of the electric chair, the State Penitentiary at Angola, and that it killed people "dead like a doornail, the end of the world." These statements seemed to indicate that Perry understood the death penalty and its punishment.

Three psychiatrists and a psychologist testified that Perry suffered from psychotic and paranoid delusions, showed a loose association with reality, and was "a moving target" when it came to competency. "He's not in the same place all the time," Dr. Aris Cox testified. "Sometimes he is competent, sometimes he's not."[24]

As Dr. Cox told us in an interview for ABC's *World News Tonight,* "When he's been off medication, I have him tell me he does not believe that the process of electrocution will kill him. He has a lot of ideas that he's some sort of religious figure who's immortal."[25]

At the trial, the experts agreed that Perry's condition improved with medication—and they said that was their dilemma. "I certainly have problems with giving someone medication so that they can get better and be executed," Dr. Cox told the judge.

That was the central issue: Was it legal for Perry to be medicated against his will to make him well enough to be electrocuted? Judge Hymel said yes, and the Louisiana Supreme Court agreed. Michael Perry's fate would now depend upon an appeal to the U.S. Supreme Court.

Figure 7.6. Dr. Aris Cox.

The Court had already refused to consider an appeal filed by Perry's lawyers in 1987. No reason for that rejection was cited. But this latest appeal raised an issue that apparently intrigued the justices.

The justices of the Supreme Court had decided in 1986 that prisoners could not be executed while insane. The case of *Ford v. Wainright* involved a murderer who was apparently both sane and competent when he was tried in Florida and sentenced to death for killing a police officer during a restaurant robbery. But Alvin Bernard Ford deteriorated on death row: he began hearing voices and suffering delusions; he became convinced he was "Pope John Paul III." A panel of three psychiatrists appointed by the governor could not agree on a diagnosis, but they did agree that Ford understood why the death penalty had been imposed and what it meant. That was enough for Governor Bob Graham. He signed the death warrant.

Ford was within fourteen hours of execution in December of

1981 when a federal appeals court granted a stay, starting his case on the long road to the U.S. Supreme Court. The justices heard the case on April 22, 1986, and Ford's lawyers made two arguments: that there was a common law tradition, dating back to the thirteenth century, prohibiting the execution of the insane; and that Florida had no clearly established procedures for determining the sanity of the condemned.

In death penalty appeals, lawyers generally keep their clients away from the press, concerned about negative images. Ford's defense team used a reverse strategy: they had him hold a press conference so that everyone could see how unbalanced he was. The strategy worked; the hoped-for negative image reverberated from coast to coast.

 For a video report on the *Ford* arguments before the Supreme Court, go to: http://murderatthesupremecourt.com/ford

The Court agreed with the Ford team's arguments, ruling 5–4 that states may not execute prisoners who have become insane and that only an independent panel of doctors or a court may decide questions of sanity.[26] There were two further, unusual twists to the *Ford* case, one of them tragic. In 1989, a federal judge ruled that Ford had become sane and was eligible for execution. Ford's lawyers launched an appeal, but before the case could be heard, Alvin Ford was found unconscious in his cell on Florida's death row. He died two days later at the age of thirty-seven; the death was determined to be from natural causes.

The Supreme Court dealt with the issue of forced medication in 1992 when it ruled in favor of David Riggins, a Nevada prisoner who had been given antipsychotic drugs against his will in order to make him competent to stand trial for murder. Riggins was convicted, but the Court set the conviction aside, ruling that his Sixth Amendment right to a fair trial had been violated by the forceful administration of the drugs before and during his trial.[27] The legal stage was set for the Perry appeal. The Supreme Court had resolved the issues of executing the insane and of medicating the insane before trial. But the issue of "forced sanity" to enable an execution was novel enough that the Court agreed to hear Perry's case. And even as lawyers for the opposing sides prepared their arguments, the question spurred furious debate outside the legal community.

Many doctors were particularly incensed. Relations between the medical community and the officials charged with carrying out executions had long been strained: physicians and other medical practitioners felt barred by the canons of their profession from taking an active part in executions. Doctors would agree to pronounce death, but not to assist in it. Medical professionals might help a condemned person prepare for an execution, even to the extent of prescribing tranquilizers, but they drew the line at helping executioners inject lethal chemicals. Now they were being asked to make mentally ill prisoners well enough so that they could be put to death; for many, there was no way to reconcile such treatment with their Hippocratic commitment to "do no harm."[28]

"If Michael Owen Perry takes anti-psychotic drugs, he may no longer imagine Olivia Newton-John is a Greek demigoddess beneath a lake," began an editorial in *U.S.A Today*, "but then Michael Owen Perry will be put to death." Medicating Perry in order to execute him was "an insane idea," the newspaper said. "You cure people to help them, not to kill them. To do otherwise replaces justice with vindictiveness."[29]

That editorial stirred up so much reaction that two days later, the paper ran a slew of Letters to the Editor containing such opposing comments as:

—"I think insane inmates should be cured so they can be executed. There are enough murderers in this world." (Springfield, Missouri)

—"They should be brought to a clarified state of mind, then executed. . . . Through various psychotropic medications, their level of consciousness may be raised so they can realize the consequences of their action." (Beaumont, Texas)

—"I think they should be executed whether they're sane or insane. If they're sane enough to obtain a weapon and ammunition and drive down to someone's house and take their life, then they're eligible." (Crossville, Tennessee)[30]

A *St. Louis Post-Dispatch* editorial bore the mocking headline "First Cure Him; Then Kill Him." "If it weren't true," the editorial read, "the latest capital punishment case before the U.S. Supreme Court would sound like some kind of sick joke."[31]

The pro-execution argument was perhaps most trenchantly summed up by Linda Chavez, a former Reagan administration official writing as a syndicated columnist: "Justice would not be served by allowing a man who has slaughtered five members of his own family to avoid a lawfully imposed punishment. Perry should take his medicine."[32]

Figure 7.7. The Supreme Court of the United States.

"The question before the Court today is whether or not the State of Louisiana may, for the sole purpose of executing an inmate, forcibly medicate a mentally ill inmate with psychotropic drugs," Defense Attorney Keith Nordyke said on the morning of October 2, 1990, setting the stage for his life-or-death argument before the Supreme Court. He argued that involuntary medication of Perry would be a violation of the Eighth Amendment's prohibition against "cruel and unusual punishment," and it would also violate Perry's Fourteenth Amendment guarantee to "due process under the law."[33]

Appearing against Nordyke and speaking from the same lectern in the Court's splendid chamber, Louisiana's assistant attorney general Rene Salomon responded: "We submit that if Louisiana can establish competency for a defendant to go to trial when that individual's presumption of innocence and other rights are at its zenith, then the State of Louisiana should be allowed to establish competency in order to carry out its sentence in this particular case." It was reasonable, he argued, for the state to require medication that produced sanity for both trial and execution.

In questioning Nordyke, Justice Antonin Scalia noted that people lose many ordinary rights when convicted of crimes and that they also lose the "luxury" of many choices, including medical choices. "I guess the issue is whether someone who's been condemned to death," asked Scalia, "continues to have that luxury?"

Before Nordyke could answer, Justice John Paul Stevens interrupted, asking the defense lawyer, "Do you agree that's a luxury?"

"Do I agree it's a luxury to be able to refuse medication?" responded Nordyke. "No, Your Honor, I believe it's an absolute, fundamental right that bottoms out in human decency."

At one point, Salomon referred to the medication as "treatment," and Justice Thurgood Marshall interrupted to ask, "But the primary purpose is to kill him?"

"I would say, yes sir, that's correct," Salomon replied. "It is basically to execute him, in this case because the State has an interest."

Later in the argument, as Salomon continued to press the state's

right to inject Perry with psychotropic drugs, Marshall again interrupted to ask sarcastically, "Well, if all you say is true in the interest of
Louisiana, while you're giving him the injection, why don't you give
him enough to kill him then? It would be cheaper for the State."

The arguments lasted fifty-five minutes, after which Chief Justice
William Rehnquist thanked the lawyers and routinely announced,
"The case is now submitted." With those words, he effectively drew
the curtain over a legal mystery that persists to this day.

The Supreme Court never decided the thorny question that
prompted it to accept the Perry case for review; that is, whether a
condemned prisoner could be forced to accept medication that
would restore his sanity to the point where the state could execute
him. The Court did spare Perry's life, but it punted. The constitutional issue would live to be fought another day.

Rather than issue a ruling in the case, the justices issued an
unsigned order directing the Louisiana courts to reconsider the
mandate that Perry be medicated. The Supreme Court said it wanted
Louisiana to look at the issue again, in light of a case that it had
decided *before* it even accepted the Perry case for argument. In that
case, *Washington v. Harper*, the Court found that inmates had a limited
right to refuse unwanted drugs.

It was a puzzling dismissal of the *Perry* issue. First, the *Harper* case
was not a death-penalty case; Walter Harper was a disturbed prisoner
serving a long sentence for robbery in Washington State. He was
manic-depressive and prone to violence, but he felt he had a legal
right to refuse psychotropic medication. Second, *Harper* provided no
clear-cut guidance to the Louisiana courts.

In *Harper*, all nine justices agreed that the Fourteenth Amendment's guarantee of due process gives inmates what the justices called
"a significant liberty interest" in avoiding unwanted mind-altering
medication. But by a 6–3 vote, the Court ruled that a state can nonetheless "treat a prison inmate who has a serious mental illness with anti-
psychotic drugs against his will, if the inmate is dangerous to himself
or others and the treatment is in the inmate's medical interest."

Why did the Supreme Court avoid the issue it had committed itself to resolve by accepting *Perry*? An empty seat on its bench at the time might provide a clue. Justice William Brennan had retired from the Court after thirty-four years, and his replacement, David Souter, was awaiting Senate confirmation when the *Perry* case was argued. He did not participate in the deliberations, and it is conceivable that the Court's remaining justices could have cast a tie vote of 4–4 in Conference. As the knowledgeable court observer Linda Greenhouse noted in the *New York Times*, a tie would have upheld the Louisiana Supreme Court decision that Michael Perry be medicated and executed; remanding the case to the state court for reconsideration on the basis of *Harper*, instead, insured that both Perry and the constitutional issue would survive the justices' order.[34]

There is another eerie ingredient to this Supreme Court mystery. Michael Perry was arrested in Washington, DC, just a mile from the Court's steps. And at the scene of his murders, investigators found what they believed to be a Perry "hit list" naming other potential victims, including Justice Sandra Day O'Connor.[35]

Gavin de Becker, the security expert who had been tracking Perry since his stalking of Olivia Newton-John, told us that he believed Perry went to Washington, DC, to kill Justice O'Connor. "Michael Perry had said that he believed that no woman should be in a place that high and that he pursued her for that reason," according to de Becker.[36] There is also an ethical component to this mystery. If a justice is aware that his or her life may have been endangered by a convicted murderer, should he or she be deciding whether that murderer goes to the electric chair? Justice O'Connor participated fully in the Court's consideration of Michael Perry's case. When the authors inquired about the possible conflict at the time of the Court's ruling in 1990, the justice issued a statement saying she was "unaware" of any threat posed by Mr. Perry.

That's understandable, given the fact that threats against the Supreme Court justices are received with such frequency so as to be unremarkable. But she did thank de Becker for the warning, at the time, in a letter he shared with us. "Unfortunately there are people in our country who are sufficiently unstable to constitute genuine threats to the safety of others," Justice O'Connor wrote. "I am very grateful for the information you shared concerning Michael Perry. You have helped to prevent what could have been a serious problem."[37]

Supreme Court of the United States
Washington, D. C. 20543

CHAMBERS OF
JUSTICE SANDRA DAY O'CONNOR

September 22, 1983

Mr. Gavin de Becker
8951 St. Ives Drive
Los Angeles, California 90069

Dear Mr. deBecker,

Dr. Mark Cannon has informed me of the work you have done in connection with your investigation of Michael Perry.

Unfortunately, there are people in our country who are sufficiently unstable to constitute genuine threats to the safety of others.

I am very grateful for the information you shared with Dr. Cannon concerning Michael Perry. You have helped to prevent what could have been a serious problem.

Sincerely,

Sandra D. O'Connor

SO'C/lab

Figure 7.8. Letter from Justice Sandra Day O'Connor.

By order of the United States Supreme Court, the decision on the fate of Michael Perry would move far away from Foggy Bottom and the hazy memories of Washington, DC, back to a boxlike building just off Interstate 12 in Baton Rouge—the courtroom of Judge L. J. Hymel.

Hymel, a lifelong Baton Rouge resident with a background as a prosecutor at both the state and the city levels, had been elected to a state district court bench in 1983. He would later be appointed a U.S. attorney by President Bill Clinton. It was Hymel's court order to medicate and execute Michael Perry that the U.S. Supreme Court had "vacated and remanded" five months before Hymel again gaveled his court to order on April 25, 1991.

Figure 7.9. The Honorable L. J. Hymel.

The session was short. There were no arguments; each side had submitted briefs and the judge was prepared to rule. "I have essentially done what the U.S. Supreme Court ordered me to do," Hymel announced. "It's my opinion that *Washington v. Harper* doesn't change any of the conclusions I reached on Oct. 22, 1988." He then reissued his original order that Michael Perry be forcibly medicated to allow his execution. "There is no question that Louisiana's interest in carrying out the verdict overrides Mr. Perry's rights," Hymel said.[38] Hymel decried what he viewed as a lack of guidance in the Supreme Court's order. "I call upon the U.S. Supreme Court to answer this question forthrightly," Hymel said. "We're not dealing with some penological requirement. This is a case dealing with mental competence to proceed."[39]

"I was frustrated," Hymel told the authors almost twenty years later. Looking back, he felt the Supreme Court had failed to deal with the central issue of medication *after* a verdict: "The jury determined the defendant's guilt and decided on the death penalty," Hymel said, "and I thought the verdict should be given effect. A defendant should not be able to escape the verdict of a jury by refusing medication."[40]

Hymel was not alone in his frustration. In the interim between the Supreme Court finding and Hymel's hearing, Assistant Attorney General Salomon had filed another appeal to the high Court imploring the justices to decide the underlying issue of medication to enable execution; his petition was denied without explanation.[41] The justices remained mute.

Keith Nordyke then unleashed a new assault upon the Louisiana Supreme Court, hoping that the remand from Washington might carry more weight with the state's highest court than it did with Hymel. He was right; the state supreme court essentially reversed itself on the same set of facts—and the identical Hymel order—after reexamining the case in light of *Harper*. The court's decision read:

> The trial court's determination that Perry is not competent for execution without the influence of antipsychotic drugs is affirmed. The court's order requiring the state to medicate Perry with antipsychotic drugs without his consent is reversed. The execution of the death sentence is stayed.[42]

The Louisiana high court interpreted the remand order very differently from Judge Hymel. "As the Supreme Court has recognized," the 5–2 state supreme court decision read, "the forcible injection of antipsychotic drugs into a nonconsenting person's body, even when done in his medical interest with medical appropriateness, represents a particularly severe interference with that person's liberty."

The scholarly decision, written by Justice James Dennis, analyzed the way the U.S. Supreme Court had dealt with the concept of "cruel and unusual punishment" through a variety of cases—from the abortive electrocution of Willie Francis through the more contemporary legal travails of Troy Gregg, William Henry Furman, Alvin Ford, David Riggins, and Walter Harper. It dissected Louisiana law on the issues of punishment and personal freedoms. In thirty-nine painstaking pages, the court artfully reversed its conclusions of 1986.[43]

Michael Perry's life was spared; he did not have to take the state's medicine. "Carrying out this punitive scheme would add severity and indignity to the prisoner's punishment beyond that required for the mere extinguishment of life," Justice Dennis wrote.

And the court stuck by its guns: less than two months after the ruling, the state attorney general's office filed another appeal, labeling as "ridiculous" the court's conclusion that the state's interest in carrying out the death penalty was not sufficient to override Perry's interest in refusing medication. The court ruled, again by a vote of 5–2, that it was dead serious about its conclusion.

Michael Perry, who is not eligible for parole, is serving his life sentence as Inmate number 111850 at Angola State Prison, a forbidding eighteen-thousand-acre penitentiary that is the largest in the United States. He will presumably die there, and, if his body is unclaimed by relatives, he will be buried in Angola's Point Lookout Cemetery.

The case of *Perry v. Louisiana* is closed. But the question of medicating to execute is still open, waiting to be addressed again by the United States Supreme Court.

Figure 7.10. Point Lookout Cemetery.

 For a video report on the *Perry* Supreme Court case, go to:
http://murderatthesupremecourt.com/perry

8

GETTINGEVEN

RETRIBUTION AND THE DEATH PENALTY

I'm in my eighteenth year as Sheriff and I've seen a lot
of bad things happen, and this is probably the worst.
—Jefferson Parish (LA)
Sheriff Harry Lee, March 2, 1998

Longtime Jefferson Parish sheriff Harry Lee had indeed seen his
share of "bad things happen," but this was different and his statements on the local TV news that March night in 1998 captured the
sentiments of a stunned New Orleans community.

Eight-year-old Dawn Leval (a pseudonym; her real name has been
kept secret by the courts and the media) had been brutally raped while
selling Girl Scout cookies near her home in the quiet Woodmere subdivision of Harvey, Louisiana, just across the Mississippi River from
New Orleans. When emergency technicians arrived at her home, they
found her bleeding so profusely that her life was in danger. While in
shock from blood loss, she had passed out.

Dawn was rushed by ambulance to Children's Hospital in Gretna
for emergency surgery, leaving behind a neighborhood in fear and
disbelief that something so grotesque could happen in their quiet
little enclave. Their children were no longer safe. "There's gotta be
some maniac running around out here," as one local resident—the
father of two young girls—told a local TV reporter.[1] And Sheriff
Lee put up five thousand dollars of his own money for information
leading to the arrest of the person or persons responsible.

Lee, the pear-shaped sheriff who walked with a jiggle, was easy-going but not to be taken lightly on this or any case. His whole life had been devoted to solving crime, and the rape of this small child in Woodmere would be getting his undivided attention. Over the years, Lee had become a colorful and controversial local celebrity.

Figure 8.1. Jefferson Parish sheriff Harry Lee.

One of his more notorious assaults on good sense came in the wake of a suburban crime spree in 1986. Lee ordered all his deputies to stop black men for no reason other than driving "rinky-dink cars" in predominantly white neighborhoods. The order led to calls for his immediate resignation, but Lee survived.[2] Years later, he said he didn't really understand what all the fuss was about; he blamed the news media for blowing his transparently racist order out of proportion. To Sheriff Lee, it was simply another example of "good police practice."

The events of that morning in Woodmere would dominate the news in New Orleans for several days, and Sheriff Lee and his policies would be in the middle of it. Investigators were able to piece together a detailed timeline of what had occurred and a profile of who might have been responsible.[3]

It was March 2 at 9:18 in the morning. The little girl's stepfather, Patrick Kennedy, said he was preparing Dawn's younger brother for school when he heard screaming coming from the garage. Kennedy said he ran outside and found Dawn lying in the side yard between their house and an empty lot next door. Kennedy called 9-1-1. In the dispatcher's recording, he is heard telling the operator that two boys had grabbed his stepdaughter, pushed her down, pulled her to the side yard, and raped her.

"Were they white males or black males?" the operator inquired. "She said they was black boys." Kennedy went on to tell the operator that he had seen one of the boys "walking through the neighborhood all the time," and described him as "about eighteen years old, wearing a black shirt and blue jeans and riding a ten-speed bike."

Figure 8.2. Patrick Kennedy, Dawn's stepfather.

Jefferson Parish sheriff's deputy Mike Burgess was in the neighborhood at the time and arrived at the Kennedy home within minutes. Kennedy was still on the phone talking to 9-1-1. Burgess felt he was so close that he might even catch the perpetrator running away from the scene. It was not going to be so easy.

Officers wanted to know why Dawn wasn't at school at 9:00 a.m.—and where was her mother during all of this? Carol Kennedy, who had married Patrick only one year earlier, had left for work at 5:30 in the morning. Patrick said he had fixed Dawn breakfast but that she had not been feeling well. She vomited in the bathroom. After she threw up a second time, Kennedy said he gave her some orange juice mixed with Tylenol and then called her school to report that she would be absent.

Dawn confirmed to Deputy Burgess what her stepfather had told the 9-1-1 operator in all pertinent respects: She was selling Girl Scout cookies in the garage with her brother when two boys dragged her into the yard and that one of them raped her. Kennedy later told Detective Mike Hullihan that when he found his daughter in the yard, he also may have seen the attacker fleeing. He provided a description similar to the one he had given earlier to the 9-1-1 operator: a black male, about 250 to 270 pounds, wearing blue jeans and a black T-shirt, a gold earring on his left ear, racing away on a light-blue, ten-speed bicycle, with the handlebars turned down. It wasn't long before thirty more deputies would be canvassing the neighborhood for possible suspects . . . in vain.

The rape continued to dominate the news in the days that followed, but the true extent of Dawn's injuries either was withheld from the media or was too extensive and disturbing for the evening news or the morning papers. She had been raped with such force that the injuries extended through the vaginal area into the rectum. The pain was intense. As news spread (sanitized though it was) about her precarious medical condition and her mounting medical bills, the New Orleans community rallied. Civic groups organized fund-raising drives. Even the New Orleans Saints football team spearheaded a fund-raising effort. Saints linebacker Richard Harvey, himself the father of three, went on the local TV channels to empathize with Dawn and her family.[4]

The media, for their part, acted responsibly in not identifying Dawn by name or even her family. Her stepfather, however, did give occasional interviews to TV reporters who would show up unexpectedly on the family's doorstep. At six feet four inches and 375 pounds, Patrick Kennedy was an imposing man who professed an abiding faith in Jesus. He sang in the church choir and would frequently send religious notes to Dawn and her two younger brothers. With his face either shaded out or otherwise electronically distorted, Kennedy told reporters he was cooperating with authorities to the best of his abilities and was hopeful there would be a prompt arrest. He even accompanied police to a nearby K-Mart in an effort to better identify the kind of bicycle Dawn's assailant might have used for his getaway.

In the ensuing days, the media attention only intensified. Anything new, anything at all, was deemed important. One local television station led its broadcast with news that hospital officials now say the little girl, still unidentified, had smiled. But there were still no hard leads. The Jefferson Parish sheriff's office was under growing pressure to break the case. Who would or could have done such a thing? And until there was a break in the investigation, no one felt safe.

With reporters grasping for any little straw that might advance their stories, it should not be surprising that not all the straws they found were well founded. Word had leaked out that deputies were now looking for only one suspect, not two as had been originally reported. Sheriff Lee had personally taken over the case, directing every aspect of it, including the media coverage. He would be holding news conferences or granting interviews outside the victim's home, outside the hospital where she was being cared for, and (on those occasions when the photo op did not appear to matter), from his office in Gretna, across the river from New Orleans and slightly downriver from Dawn's home in Harvey.

Sheriff Lee reminded reporters and their audiences that the

victim had said there were two teenagers involved but that she then revealed that one of them might have been an unwitting, if not an unwilling, accomplice. She had said that one of the two had encouraged the other not to do it and wanted to leave. Lee reported that the victim had quoted the second teen as saying, "C'mon. Let's go." The sheriff then broadcast a plea to the second teenager: "Come forward and tell all you know and we will not prosecute you. Not only that, you will be eligible to share in the reward money." But no one came forward.[5]

Acting on the stepfather's information that he had seen the potential assailant fleeing on a bicycle, the sheriff's office began stopping all young black men in the neighborhood, asking them questions, and, in some cases, even conducting pat-down searches. If you were black, male, and under twenty, you were a suspect.

The new push not only failed to turn up any solid leads, but it also exacerbated racial tensions in the community. Black leaders again accused Sheriff Lee of "racial profiling." To Lee, of Chinese descent and a minority himself, it was much ado about nothing. "I'm going to catch that bastard," Lee said at the time, "and when I catch him, he is going to be black. I just don't give a damn what people think of me anymore. If that was their daughter and we weren't doing that, they would be on our ass."[6]

If investigators were becoming frustrated by all the dead ends they appeared to be pursuing, they didn't show it. They did keep much to themselves, however, as might be expected of those who spend most of their waking hours scrutinizing crimes of unspeakable violence such as the Woodmere rape. Privately, however, they were concerned that pieces of this puzzle were just not coming together. Not at all.

Patrick Kennedy had described the bike on which the possible assailant had fled as being a light-blue ten-speed with handles turned down. But on the visit with police to the nearby K-Mart, Kennedy picked a regular bike with the handles straight out as the one matching the bike he had seen earlier. Still later, Kennedy positively identified another bike found in a field a few blocks from his home as the one he had seen on the morning of the attack. The bike was blue, but it had no gears at all, was covered with rust and spider webs, had a flat tire, and was generally inoperable. The grass underneath the bike had been dead and pressed to the ground, suggesting the bike had been abandoned and hadn't been ridden for quite some time.

Kennedy had been mistaken about the bike, which was perhaps understandable given the traumatic events of that morning. But the contradictions did not end there. Kennedy had told police that he found his stepdaughter lying in the yard bleeding, that he had wrapped her in a blanket and carried her to an upstairs bedroom. There was a circle of coagulated blood in the yard and a few drops on the stairs, but there was no blood trail from the backyard to the bedroom even though the victim had been bleeding profusely. Nor did Kennedy have any blood stains on his clothing.

Stephen Brown, emergency medical services field supervisor for West Jefferson Medical Center, was in the ambulance that responded to the 9-1-1 call. He too found contradictions. In assessing the victim's blood loss, Brown noticed that the blood appeared to be more coagulated than it should have been if the time of the rape was reported accurately. Brown suspected the rape must have occurred earlier. The Jefferson Parish sheriff's office also brought in a nationally recognized forensic expert, Dr. Henry Lee from the Connecticut State Police Forensic Science Lab, to assist in the case. After examining crime-scene photographs, Dr. Lee (not related to Sheriff Lee) reported that there was nothing to indicate any kind of a struggle, since there were no depressions in the grass. Furthermore, the small amount of blood sitting on top of the grass indicated, at least in Dr. Lee's mind, a "low velocity dripping," suggesting the blood had been planted there.[7]

The media began running stories that an arrest was imminent, but what was supposed to be "imminent" continued to stretch out for days. Sheriff Lee eventually disclosed to reporters that investigators had developed misgivings about the victim's story. Lee went so far as to allow that during his many years in law enforcement, when something like this happens, "it has not been unusual for some family member to have been involved." Despite the fact that Dawn, from her hospital bed, continued to cling to her story that the attackers were two black neighborhood men, suspicion began to turn toward her stepfather. Investigators were closing in.

Stephen Brown and Detective Mike Burgess (the first officer on the scene) shared with one another that they had found Kennedy's behavior atypical and suspicious. For one, whenever they tried to interview the victim, Kennedy was there offering answers and suggesting what Dawn was to say.[8]

Figure 8.3. Newspaper clippings.

A case against the stepfather was quickly building. A check of Kennedy's phone records indicated a call to his employer, the A. Arpet Moving Company, had been made hours before the 9-1-1 call. Alvin Arguello, the chief dispatcher for the moving company, told police that when he arrived for work at around 6:15 a.m. on March 2, there was a recorded message from Kennedy indicating he would not be available to work that day. Kennedy called Arguello again between

6:30 and 7:00 a.m., sounding nervous. Arguello said Kennedy had inquired on how to get blood out of a white carpet because his stepdaughter "had just become a young lady." Another call was made to the B&B Carpet Cleaning Company at 7:37 the same morning. The company owner, Rodney Madere, said Kennedy had called him to schedule an urgent carpet-cleaning job to remove bloodstains.[9]

The telephone conversations tended to support the theory that the rape had occurred earlier than initially reported and suggested the delay may have been to give Kennedy the time he needed to clean up the evidence. Detectives obtained search warrants that would allow luminol blood testing[10] of areas in the victim's home. The tests revealed the presence of blood in a large area of the carpet at the foot of the victim's bed, on the carpet pad, and on the subfloor beneath. The police also found a one-gallon-jug container labeled "SEC Seam Low Foam Extraction Cleaner" in the garage. An examination of carpet samples showed that someone had attempted to clean bloodstains from the carpet.

Confident they had their perpetrator, Kennedy was read his Miranda rights and charged with the aggravated rape of his stepdaughter. Jefferson Parish sheriff Harry Lee was there to personally make the arrest.

Although confident they had the right man, prosecutors knew the case could be problematic. No semen was found at the crime scene that would enable police to perform DNA testing that might positively—and conclusively—link Kennedy to the crime. And even more troublesome, Dawn continued to insist that two young men had pulled her from the garage and that one of them had raped her in the yard while the other watched. Hospital personnel reported that Dawn had been consistent, telling them the same story she had given the police.

Within a week, Dawn was released from the hospital and went home to be with her mother, Carol Kennedy. Still frightened, she slept in the same bed with her mom. In a few days, a substantially different story began to emerge.

Mrs. Kennedy told police that Dawn began crying uncontrollably, more than she had ever seen her daughter cry before. She said she could not hold it in any longer and that it was her stepfather—Carol's husband, Patrick—who had raped her.

Louisiana, wisely recognizing that children can be easily influenced by the adults around them, has a system in place to minimize the impact of family members and police. Child-abuse victims are interviewed by independent social workers outside the presence of both parents and police. Dawn's videotaped interview more than a year and a half after the incident was conducted by Amalee Gordon of the Louisiana Child Advocacy Center.

Figure 8.4. Amalee Gordon of the Louisiana Child Advocacy Center interviews Dawn Leval outside the presence of parents and police.

Dawn, now nine years old and fully healed of any physical injuries, explained in the taped interview how she woke up that March morning to find Kennedy on top of her, with his hand over her eyes and mouth, having sex with her. Gordon asked if this was the first time Kennedy had violated her; Dawn shook her head and, holding up five fingers, said, "I think five."

With a large sketch pad and crayons, Dawn drew pictures of her stepfather, herself, and their "private parts" and explained, as best she could, what had happened. Gordon held her breath and did all she could to make Dawn feel comfortable, to make the conversation seem like an ordinary conversation that two girls might have with one another. It was anything but. And one cannot help but wonder what this poor little child might dream about at night. Sugar plum fairies and handsome princes? Probably not.

Dawn also told Gordon, as she had told her mother, that it was Kennedy who had made up the story about the two youths on a bicycle. "He told me that he gonna make up a story and I better say it." The bit about the Girl Scout cookies was also Kennedy's fabrication. Dawn wasn't even a Girl Scout. It turns out that Kennedy had stolen the cookies and had given them to Dawn. She was to sell them for whatever she could and turn over the proceeds to him.

Three years before Dawn was attacked, in 1995, Louisiana made the rape of a child under the age of twelve a capital offense—punishable by death. It was the first state to do so since the U.S. Supreme Court reinstated capital punishment in 1976 in *Gregg v. Georgia* (Chapter 2). To be sure, not all child rapes would bring the death penalty; equally certain under the Louisiana law is that any rape of a child would be enough to put the death penalty in play. Rape a child, and the prosecutor had the discretion to seek the death penalty, the jury had the discretion to recommend it, and the judge had the authority to impose it.

The driving force behind the Louisiana law was state representative Pete Schneider. Schneider is smart, pleasant, and patrician; his family has owned the St. Joe Brick Works in Slidell, Louisiana, for more than a hundred years. At the time he introduced Louisiana's death penalty for rape law, he was the company's president and general manager, a post he had held for more than thirty years. Among the company's claims to fame, it has laid most of the bricks on the streets of the New Orleans French Quarter. Schneider also prides himself on his conservative bona fides: He was named Conservative of the Year by the Conservative Political Action Committee of St. Tammany.[11]

Figure 8.5. Former Louisiana state representative Pete Schneider.

Schneider says his research showed that 29 percent of the rape cases in this country are committed against children eleven years old and younger and "they're horrendous crimes. You steal their childhood, you steal their soul. You hurt the world when you do something like that to a child." Schneider, grimacing, told the authors that the child molester is essentially incurable. "Child molesters, by the research that I've done, and by their own convictions, are incurable . . . so you have monsters and predators out there all the time."[12]

Criminologists, scholars, and legal philosophers point to four classical purposes or goals of punishment: (1) Deterring others from committing similar crimes. (2) Preventing the specific offender from repeating his offense. (3) Rehabilitating the offender. (4) Retribution, which has a variety of synonyms—popular among them, *vengeance* and its euphemism *justice.* If child molesters are in fact incurable, as Schneider and many sociologists believe, then the following question arises: "What purpose of punishment is served by executing them?" It wouldn't be deterrence. Preventing specific offenders from reoffending can be accomplished by sentencing them to life in prison, in solitary confinement if necessary, rather than executing them. Offenders are hardly rehabilitated by being put to death. Which leaves only retribution.

Although it might appear contradictory to Schneider's premise for the law, he says he believes, and hopes, the Louisiana law might still deter child rape. And if it doesn't? Is the state's interest in retribution by itself sufficient to justify the death penalty? Schneider says yes. Would he have pushed for this law had he been presented irrefutable evidence that it would deter no one? "Without question." Retribution alone is enough? "Retribution alone is enough."

Indeed, retribution, not deterrence, may now be the leading justification for capital punishment. A 2003 Justice Department study found that 37 percent of death-penalty supporters cited "an eye for an eye/they took a life/fits the crime" as their reason for supporting capital punishment. Another 13 percent cited, "They deserve it." Deterrence was cited by only 11 percent of supporters.[13]

There are some sociologists who believe that sex offenders are not as incorrigible as popularly believed, particularly when treated early. But because of their generally high recidivism rate and because their crimes against children are particularly offensive, society's interest in "retribution," rightly or wrongly, would seem to apply with special force.

Retribution has long figured into our laws, particularly in death-penalty cases. As Justice Potter Stewart wrote in his concurring opinion in *Furman v. Georgia,* rejecting capital punishment as then applied, "The instinct for retribution is part of the nature of man, and channeling that instinct in the administration of criminal justice serves an important purpose in promoting the stability of a society governed by law. When people begin to believe that organized society is unwilling or unable to impose upon criminal offenders the punishment they 'deserve,' then there are sown the seeds of anarchy—of self-help, vigilante justice, and lynch law."[14]

Other justices, however, have scoffed at such reasoning. Justice William Brennan, arguably the Court's most influential jurist of the twentieth century, wrote in rebuttal to Justice Stewart, "There is no evidence whatever that utilization of imprisonment rather than death encourages private blood feuds and other disorders. It simply defies belief to suggest that the death penalty is necessary to prevent the American people from taking the law into their own hands." As we have seen, Brennan opposed the death penalty in all cases and for any reason, referring to death, at least privately, as "God's work, not man's."[15]

Justice Thurgood Marshall, another consistently passionate opponent of capital punishment, also rejected retribution as a justification. In his dissenting opinion in *Gregg*, Marshall wrote:

> There remains for consideration what might be termed the purely retributive justification for the death penalty—that the death penalty is appropriate not because of its beneficial effect on society, but because the taking of the murderer's life is itself morally good. Some of the language of the opinion of my Brothers . . . appears positively to embrace this notion of retribution for its own sake as a justification for capital punishment. . . . The mere fact that the community demands the murderer's life in return for the evil he has done cannot sustain the death penalty. . . . To be sustained under the Eighth Amendment [which forbids the infliction of cruel or unusual punishment], the death penalty must "comport with the basic concept of human dignity at the core of the Amendment; the objective in imposing it must be consistent with our respect for the dignity of men." Under these standards, the taking of life because the wrongdoer "deserves it" surely must fall, for such a punishment has as its very basis the total denial of the wrongdoer's dignity and worth.[16]

Classical theorists such as John Stuart Mill also rejected retribution in favor of more utilitarian goals. According to Mill, "there are two ends which . . . are sufficient to justify punishment: the benefit of the offender himself and the protection of others."[17]

Mill also suggests that retribution is irrational:

> If anyone thinks that there is justice in the infliction of purpose-less suffering; that there is a natural affinity between the two ideas of guilt and punishment, which makes it intrinsically fitting that whenever there has been guilt, pain should be inflicted by way of retribution; I acknowledge that I can find no argument to justify punishment inflicted on that principle.[18]

A number of states have even passed laws or amended their constitutions to state that the purposes of criminal penalties shall be rehabilitation and deterrence, specifically rejecting retribution. Defendants in those states, however, have had a difficult time getting clearly punitive sentences reversed; the courts have tended to find the directives against retribution aimed more at the legislature in drafting its criminal laws than at judges in applying them.

Schneider's colleagues in Baton Rouge were on board. The Louisiana Senate gave his bill final approval by a vote of 34–1, notwithstanding strong opposition from the state's Catholic bishops. Others had objected that extending the death penalty might cause legal problems. For one, almost thirty years earlier, the U.S. Supreme Court had rejected the death penalty for rape. Without giving short shrift to the horrors of the crime, the Court had concluded that death was so disproportionate a punishment for the crime as to be unconstitutional. That case, however, involved a sixteen-year-old married woman. Louisiana felt the Court's decision would not apply to the rape of a small child, which its citizens would find so much more offensive. The constitutional question, however, never made it to the House or Senate floor for debate. There was no debate at all in either chamber.

The men and women who make the laws in Louisiana appeared

to have no difficulty at all with retribution, the thirst for "justice," as sufficient justification by itself for executing child molesters. Asked if Patrick Kennedy was the kind of person the legislature had in mind when it passed its death-penalty law, Pete Schneider said, "Absolutely. Someone who would brutally rape a child—and rape is wrong no matter whom it is done to—but, in a situation like this, I believe the death penalty *is* the appropriate punishment for the crime."[19]

On May 7, 1998, Patrick Kennedy was indicted by a grand jury for the rape of his eight-year-old stepdaughter in violation of Louisiana Revised Statute 14:42 (aggravated rape; victim under the age of twelve), and the state subsequently gave notice of its intent to seek the death penalty.

Figure 8.6. Kennedy's mug shot.

The district court found that Kennedy was indigent and appointed counsel to represent him. After a vigorous pretrial period, during which the defense counsel filed approximately fifty substantive motions, a jury was finally selected in August 2003, more than five years after the offense.

There was never much question as to who the state's star witness would be. Dawn Leval, now nearly fourteen, took the stand on the fifth day of the trial. There was a brief delay at the beginning of the trial during which one of the prosecuting attorneys stepped out of the room. While waiting to begin her testimony, Dawn, only about twenty feet from the man who had raped her and whom she could send to death row, began to cry. The defense moved for a mistrial. It was denied. After she regained her composure, the trial resumed with prosecutors asking Dawn some preliminary questions: Where did she live? How old was she? The prosecutor then asked, "Do you remember what happened to you in 1998?" Answer, "Yes."

When asked to relate what had occurred, Dawn said, "I woke up one morning and Patrick was on top of me and . . ." She was unable to continue. With this still-small child trembling and weeping, the Court ordered a recess. The defense again moved for a mistrial. It was again denied.

Given the witness's inability to testify while in Kennedy's presence about what had occurred, the court allowed the state to introduce the videotaped interview Dawn had given Amalee Gordon of the Louisiana Child Advocacy Center four years earlier. On the tape, Dawn is seen and heard telling Gordon the details of what had happened. When Gordon probes for additional details, Dawn says that it happened in her room, on the bed, with Kennedy's hand covering her eyes, while her shorts were off and Kennedy was naked. She says that after seeing that she was bleeding, Kennedy called 9-1-1. And that's all she could remember.

As the tape was playing, Dawn remained seated at the witness stand—teary eyed and shaken. The defense again moved for a mistrial. Denied. After hearing all the evidence, the jury returned a verdict of guilty of aggravated rape. As in all death-penalty cases, the defendant is entitled to a second hearing to determine the penalty— life in prison or death. At the penalty phase of a capital case, the jury hears evidence that might be too prejudicial to be allowed at the guilt stage. Sometimes this new round of evidence is favorable to the defense, but usually it is not. And it wasn't in Kennedy's case.

The state presented the testimony of Sue Ann Lawson (a pseud-onym, she is identified in court records only as SL). Sue Ann's cousin had been married to Kennedy. Sue Ann testified that when she was only eight or nine years old, Kennedy had sexually molested her on three separate occasions, the first involving inappropriate touching and the last involving intercourse. Sue Ann said she was embarrassed and ashamed and had kept it to herself for two years. When she finally shared her secret with family members, they urged her not to pursue any legal action, and she did not. It turned out that Kennedy had also been accused of sexually molesting four young foster chil-dren in his care. Although he was never charged, the children were subsequently removed and placed elsewhere.

At the conclusion of the penalty phase, the jury unanimously determined that Kennedy should be sentenced to death. Kennedy's court-appointed lawyers filed motions for a new trial on a variety of grounds including that Louisiana's death-penalty law was uncon-stitutional, that it conflicted with the Supreme Court's 1977 land-mark decision in *Coker v. Georgia* in which the death penalty was ruled unconstitutional for the crime of rape. The *Coker* case would be central to Kennedy's appeal. Given the historical reluctance of the U.S. Supreme Court to overrule itself, prosecutors knew they had to distinguish what had happened to Dawn Leval from what had occurred in the *Coker* case.

Erlich Coker had been serving a number of consecutive life sen-tences for murder, rape, kidnapping, and aggravated assault when he escaped from the Ware State Prison near Waycross, Georgia, in 1972. Later that same evening, at approximately 11:00 p.m., he entered the home of Allen and Elnita Carver through an unlocked kitchen door. Threatening the couple with a "board," he tied up Mr. Carver in the bathroom, obtained a knife from the kitchen, and took Mr. Carver's money and the keys to the family car. Brandishing the knife and saying "you know what's going to happen to you if you try anything," Coker then raped Mrs. Carver. Soon thereafter, he drove away in the Carver car, taking Mrs. Carver with him. Mr. Carver, freeing himself, notified the police and not long thereafter Coker was apprehended. Mrs. Carver had not been further harmed. Given Coker's criminal record, the jury sentenced Coker to death in Georgia's electric chair. He had already been sentenced to life in prison at the time of his escape, and jurors were persuaded that anything less than the death penalty would be all but a free pass for the rape of Mrs. Carver. Five years later, however, the U.S. Supreme Court found that death was so disproportionate to the crime of rape as to violate the Eighth Amendment guarantee against "cruel and unusual punishment." Coker's death sentence was commuted to life in prison.[20]

It had been almost forty years since anyone in the United States was sentenced to death for the crime of rape. The last was Ronald Wolfe in Missouri in 1964. Although rape was punishable by death throughout most of American history, the penalty has been applied mostly against blacks and mostly in the South. Here, Coker, a white man, was convicted of raping a white woman and, unlike most rape cases that bring death sentences, race was not an issue. By 1954, rape was punishable by death in eighteen states, sixteen of them in the South. Louisiana executed fourteen rapists between 1930 and 1967, its last such execution. All fourteen of the condemned were black, as would be the state's newest candidate, Patrick Kennedy. Nationally, in this same time frame, 90 percent of those sentenced to death for rape had been black men convicted of raping or attempting to rape white women. The race issue may have complicated the proportionality question, which some of the justices appeared to be itching to address. There were other cases in Georgia that would have allowed the Court to address both race and proportionality. Opponents of capital punishment saw either issue, disproportionality and the role of race in death penalty sentencing, as a possible avenue for doing away with the death penalty altogether.

The *Coker* decision, at first blush, would appear to spare Kennedy the death sentence in Louisiana. But legislators in Baton Rouge saw their statute as quite different from the Georgia law that the U.S. Supreme Court had rejected, and the Louisiana Supreme Court had agreed in an unrelated case.[21] The Louisiana court essentially signed on to Representative Schneider's contention that the rape of a small child is demonstrably worse than the rape of a sixteen-year-old married woman and thus could be treated differently. The Louisiana Supreme Court held that "given the appalling nature of the crime, the severity of harm inflicted on the victim, and the harm imposed on society, the death penalty is not an excessive penalty when the victim is a child under the age of twelve years old."[22] Following the recommendation of the jury, Kennedy was sentenced to death by lethal injection.

In Louisiana, as in all states, those sentenced to death are entitled to have their sentences reviewed by the state supreme court (in many states, the review is automatic, even if the condemned prisoner doesn't want it). And when Kennedy's case reached the Louisiana Supreme Court, his lawyers had made sixty-nine "assignments of error" by the trial judge, mistakes that they would argue denied Kennedy the fair trial guaranteed all criminal defendants by the Sixth Amendment to the U.S. Constitution.[23]

Among other things, the defense argued that the videotape in which Dawn tells Amalee Gordon that it was her stepfather who had raped her was highly prejudicial and should not have been shown to the jury. After all, they argued, the victim was available in court. She should have been required to testify in person so that the defendant could confront her and challenge her testimony.

The Louisiana Supreme Court disagreed, noting that states have some leeway to protect child-abuse victims who are asked to confront in court the adult who had abused them, and, more importantly, Dawn had been available in court for cross-examination even after the tape had been played.

The heart of the defense case, however, remained that Kennedy's death sentence was inconsistent with—and barred by—the U.S. Supreme Court's 1977 decision in the *Coker* case. The vote in *Coker* was 7–2, but there was no majority opinion. Justice Byron White wrote the Court's main opinion. Speaking for himself and three other justices, White summed up what the decision meant: "We have the abiding conviction that the death penalty, which is unique in its severity and irrevocability, is an excessive penalty for the rapist who, as such, does not take human life."[24]

But the Louisiana Supreme Court was not persuaded. It had, after all, already ruled that the rape of a small child was quite different from the situation in *Coker* in Georgia (a sixteen-year-old married woman) and that all states had a special obligation to protect their children, who are their future. Justice White's opinion in *Coker* referred to the victim as an adult on fourteen occasions. The Louisiana Supreme Court found those references to be further evidence that the U.S. Supreme Court's *Coker* decision should not extend to an eight-year-old. In addition, since Louisiana enacted it's death-penalty law, five other states had followed suit, providing the death penalty for those who would rape a child.[25] Also, by this time, the Court's most forceful opponents of capital punishment, Justices Brennan and Marshall, were now gone, having been replaced by justices decidedly more sympathetic to the right of a state to adopt is own principles on criminal sentencing.

"Oyez, Oyez. Oyez. . . . All persons having business before the Honorable, the Supreme Court of the United States, are admonished to draw near and give their attention, for the Court is now sitting. God save the United States and this Honorable Court."

Thus it began on April 16, 2008, more than ten years after Patrick Kennedy had raped his stepdaughter. If the crime was now only a distant memory for the citizens of metropolitan New Orleans, the attorney for Jefferson Parish had little difficulty bringing the horrors of the morning of March 2 to life before the nine justices. Perhaps appreciating that the passions of Supreme Court justices can be inflamed just as those of anyone else, attorney Juliet Clark did not hold back. She began her argument,[26] "Mr. Chief Justice, and may it please the Court: This case involves the very savage rape of an eight-year-old child by her stepfather. He raped her so brutally that he tore her entire perineal opening from her vaginal opening to her anal opening. He tore her vagina on the interior such that it separated partially from her cervix and to allow her rectum to protrude into her vagina. Invasive emergency surgery was required to repair these injuries. It is Louisiana's position that the cruel and unusual punishment clause of the Eighth Amendment does not preclude the State of Louisiana from—"

Figure 8.7. Seal of the U.S. Supreme Court.

Justice John Paul Stevens had heard enough and interrupted: "Could you just clarify about the—were those injuries permanent?"

"Your Honor, those injuries, after surgery they did heal. So the surgery was required to repair them."

Stevens: "They were not permanent injuries."

Clark, again: "In the sense that they healed, that's correct, Your Honor. But I think that was an injury inflicted upon a child, psychologically and mentally as well as physically."

Moments before the argument for the *Kennedy* case began, the Supreme Court had announced a decision in another important death-penalty case, *Baze v. Rees*. By a 7–2 vote, the Court had upheld the current practice of using lethal injections for executions against claims that the procedure posed an unnecessary and unconstitutional risk of excruciating pain. Stevens joined the majority but, in an extraordinary concurring opinion, wrote that while allegiance to precedent compelled his vote, he had strong misgivings about the constitutionality of the death penalty itself and he called on state legislatures and his own colleagues to reconsider banning it altogether. Borrowing language from Justice Byron White's 1972 opinion in *Furman v. Georgia* (finding that the death penalty had been implemented arbitrarily), Stevens wrote, "I have relied on my own experience in reaching the conclusion that the imposition of the death penalty represents 'the pointless and needless extinction of life with only marginal contributions to any discernible social or public purposes. A penalty with such negligible returns to the State is patently excessive and cruel and unusual punishment violative of the Eighth Amendment.'"[27]

Typically, the author of the Court's majority decision summarizes the ruling in open court. Justices who file concurring or dissenting opinions have the liberty of summarizing their views as well. Stevens, however, chose not to do so with his concurring opinion in the *Baze* case. Reporters in the press room one floor below the courtroom were well aware of the position Stevens had just taken and were busy telling the world about it. But neither the lawyers arguing the *Kennedy* case nor anyone else in the courtroom other than the other justices could have had any clue about Justice Stevens's remarkable about-face. After thirty-two years on the Supreme Court bench in which he had consistently upheld the death penalty, the Court's senior justice had had a change of heart.

In the Supreme Court chamber, attorney Juliet Clark pressed on: "As an initial matter, I would like to address the *Coker* question. I think that it is quite clear that *Coker* was limited to the rape of an 'adult woman.' There are at least fourteen separate references in the opinion to an adult woman or to an 'adult female.'" Clark argued that the country was becoming increasingly hostile to sexual predators who would rape small children and that this hostility is reflected in the growing number of states that had adopted similar laws to that of Louisiana. In addition to the five other states that had such laws, a number of states filed briefs with the Court in support of Louisiana, indicating they might also adopt an identical statute if the Supreme Court would give the green light by affirming Patrick Kennedy's sentence.

Justice Anthony Kennedy saw a contradiction in Louisiana's argument. If other states needed a "green light" from the Court to follow Louisiana's lead, then maybe the *Coker* decision was the "red light" and other states actually did see it as applicable to all rape, even those involving children. Kennedy would be the key. With the departure from the Court of the more moderate justice Sandra Day O'Connor and the conservative chief justice William Rehnquist two years earlier, Kennedy had become the swing vote on those emotionally charged issues that have historically divided the Court much as they have the nation. That was particularly true in all the recent death-penalty cases. While not all of those cases were decided by 5–4 votes, Kennedy was always on the winning side. Each side knew that without Kennedy, it would probably lose.

Justice Steven Breyer worried aloud about where allowing the death penalty for rape might lead. "My problem is I can think of many, many awful, truly horrible circumstances that are categorized under many different criminal statutes; I'm not a moralist. I'm a judge. As a judge, I look at the law. It seems for forty-three years, no one has been executed but for murder." And Breyer wondered what horrible crime—short of murder—would be next to bring the death penalty, should the Louisiana law be upheld.

Justice Antonin Scalia was a clear vote for upholding Kennedy's death sentence. Scalia, the Court's most forceful conservative, calls himself an "originalist." That is not to be confused with a jurisprudence based on the original intent of the framers of the Constitution. The framers, after all, did not speak with one voice or mind. And Scalia would be the first to admit that he has no clue, nor concern, about what individual framers may have intended. Rather it's Scalia's view that the words in the Constitution mean today whatever they meant when they were written.[28] Simple as that. The Constitution, ratified in 1789, specifically referred to capital punishment, and capital punishment at the time was regularly imposed for crimes that had not resulted in death. End of case, at least for this justice.

The argument lasted precisely sixty minutes. Patrick Kennedy's life was hanging in the balance. Although it would be months before the public would learn the outcome, the case was actually decided two days later at the Court's super-confidential, regularly scheduled Friday conference. And the justices were every bit as divided in their Conference as they appeared to be in Court. The vote was 5–4, with Justices John Paul Stevens, Anthony Kennedy, David Souter, Ruth Bader Ginsburg, and Stephen Breyer voting to reverse Kennedy's death sentence. Chief Justice John Roberts, joined by Justices Antonin Scalia, Clarence Thomas, and Samuel Alito, voted to affirm. Justice Stevens, as the senior justice in the majority, had the power to assign the writing of the opinion of the Court. Stevens would have liked to have assigned the opinion to himself, but he knew that would be problematic given his disclosure on the very morning of the *Kennedy* argument of his deep misgivings about the constitutionality of the death penalty itself. Stevens also knew that Justice Kennedy's vote was not only critical but, perhaps more than that of any other justice, also had the potential to disappear. Kennedy might change his mind. It had happened before. As the surest bet to prevent that, Stevens assigned the majority opinion to Kennedy.

The Kennedy majority agreed with Louisiana that the *Coker* decision applied only to the specific facts of that case, the rape of an adult woman. All nine justices agreed that the rape of a child was different and that *Coker* left open whether it could still be punished by death. The majority then went on to answer that question in the negative. Justice Kennedy, writing for the Court, flatly rejected Louisiana's contention that any national consensus had been developing in favor of allowing the death penalty for the rape of a child. Six states, in Kennedy's view, could hardly be deemed a "consensus" and, more importantly, Louisiana stood alone as the only state since 1964 to sentence anyone to death for the crime of rape.

If there was any popular consensus on the question, Kennedy found it would be *against* the death penalty in such cases, not in favor. Kennedy and his colleagues in the majority went further, writing that whether the death penalty is disproportionate to the crime also depends "on the standards elaborated by controlling precedents and on the Court's own understanding and interpretation of the Eighth Amendment's text, history, meaning and purpose."[29]

Justice Kennedy, however, did not minimize the magnitude of the crime.

> Here the victim's fright, the sense of betrayal, and the nature of her injuries caused more prolonged physical and mental suffering than, say, a sudden killing by an unseen assassin. The attack was not just on her but on her childhood. For this reason, we should be most reluctant to rely upon the language of the plurality in *Coker*, which posited that, for the victim of rape, "life may not be nearly so happy as it was" but it is not beyond repair. Rape has a permanent psychological, emotional, and sometimes physical impact on the child. We cannot dismiss the years of long anguish that must be endured by the victim of child rape. It does not follow, though, that capital punishment is a proportionate penalty for the crime. The constitutional prohibition against excessive or cruel and unusual punishments mandates that the State's power to punish "be exercised within the limits of civilized standards."[30]

A number of child advocacy groups had urged the Court to side with the defendant in this case, not out of any concern for child molesters but rather in the belief that allowing the death penalty could be harmful to children. The Louisiana Foundation against Sexual Assault filed a "friend of the Court" brief, noting that the perpetrators of child rape are often relatives or individuals known to the victim. Allowing the death penalty for the molester, someone the child may know or even love, might make the victim less likely to come forward and report the abuse.

Judy Benitez, the Foundation's executive director, wrote that making child rape punishable by death might also help persuade the rapist to murder his victim, having nothing more to lose if caught.[31]

Figure 8.8. Judy Benitez, from the Louisiana Foundation against Sexual Assault.

The National Association of Criminal Defense Lawyers also urged the Court to reject the Louisiana law on the ground that child-rape cases usually turn on the testimony of the child victim, testimony that is often far from reliable. The risk of error, the association argued, is particularly great.[32] While these are all policy considerations ordinarily left for state legislatures, the Supreme Court majority embraced all of them in finding the Louisiana law, like the Georgia law it had invalidated in *Coker*, unconstitutional. The punishment, the Court found, remained so disproportionate to the crime as to be "cruel and unusual."

Patrick Kennedy now must serve the rest of his life in prison with no possibility of parole. The community is safe from Kennedy, safer, it would appear, than the company Kennedy now keeps at Angola State Penitentiary just north of Baton Rouge. According to records on file at the U.S. Supreme Court, Kennedy has on a number of occasions been accused of sexually molesting other inmates.[33]

It is doubtful after all this time that Kennedy's case will have any deterrent effect on other would-be sex offenders in Louisiana. The offense that so incensed the Woodmere subdivision and much of New Orleans back in 1998 is now but a distant memory. And for those still crying out for retribution, life in prison with no parole will have to be retribution enough.

No one at this point can determine the long-term effects this horrible rape or the subsequent criminal proceedings against her stepfather will have on Dawn. But at last report, she is doing well, attending college in Louisiana, and entertaining thoughts of going to law school. She has never taken a public position in her stepfather's case and, through her lawyer, has asked to be left alone. We have honored that request.

Jefferson Parish's pit bull sheriff Harry Lee had the satisfaction of personally arresting Kennedy and seeing him go to prison, but he never got to see the final dramatic chapter unfold in the U.S. Supreme Court. In October 2007, Lee died of leukemia after having served Jefferson Parish, Louisiana, as its sheriff for twenty-seven years—three weeks away from being elected to an all-but-certain, and unprecedented, eighth consecutive term.[34]

For a video report on the *Kennedy* Supreme Court case, go to:
http://murderatthesupremecourt.com/kennedy

POSTSCRIPT NO.1

Dwight Sullivan, a colonel in the Marine Corps Reserve, was on a plane reading a newspaper story about the Supreme Court's decision and noticed what he considered a serious omission. In finding a national consensus against imposing the death penalty for the crime of rape, the Court failed to even mention that Congress, only a year earlier, had reauthorized the death penalty for members of the military convicted of raping a child.[35] Sullivan was in a position to know an important fact that had eluded lawyers for the state of Louisiana, for Kennedy, for all the groups filing "friend of the Court" briefs, and most important, for the Office of the Solicitor General (which is charged with defending federal statutes in court). Sullivan was a civilian lawyer working for the Air Force, specializing in death-penalty appeals. From 2005 to 2007, he served as the chief defense counsel for the Office of Military Commissions. Sullivan found the oversight offensive and said so on his Internet blog, which he titled, "The Supremes Dis the Military Justice System." Writing for the majority in a 5–4 decision, Justice Anthony Kennedy had specifically mentioned that the federal government had declined to allow the death penalty for rape. Sullivan wrote in his blog, "If the Kennedy Court's apparent unawareness of the military justice system is any guide, military justice remains the Rodney Dangerfield of legal systems."[36]

The blog got a wide range of responses, including one suggesting that "what we need is a Constitutional Amendment adding blogs to the [system] of checks and balances." It also caught the attention of Linda Greenhouse, the Pulitzer Prize–winning Supreme Court correspondent for the *New York Times*, who would write about it a few days later.[37] It is safe to say that at this point all hell broke loose. At the White House, press secretary Dana Perino told reporters that the administration "was disturbed by the *New York Times* report that the court's decision might be based on a mistake" and that the Justice Department would be looking into what had happened and what to do next.

The Justice Department also issued a statement. In a rare admission of error, it conceded that the Solicitor General's Office—so highly regarded at the Supreme Court—should have known about the federal law and informed the Court. "It's true that the parties to the case missed it, but it is our responsibility. We regret that the Department didn't catch the 2006 law when the case of *Kennedy v. Louisiana* was briefed."[38]

The attorneys for the state of Louisiana saw an opening and asked the Court to rehear the case. Rehearings are often requested but rarely granted. Rehearings are so unusual as to defy meaningful statistics, perhaps one in a thousand. But this case was different. The Court's decision appeared to have been premised on some incorrect assumptions. Eighty-five members of Congress signed on to a letter pointing out that the bill providing the death penalty for child rape passed by overwhelming vote, 95–0 in the Senate and 374–41 in the House. The circumstances were sufficiently extraordinary that the Court issued an order inviting the attorneys for Louisiana, Kennedy, and the U.S. government to weigh in on whether the case should be reconsidered.[39]

Attorneys for Patrick Kennedy of course argued the original decision should stand. Their client had narrowly escaped a death sentence; besides, he had no connection to the military. Justice Department lawyers, however, saw the matter differently. For one, they had a duty to defend federal laws in court that is "a deeply valued tradition, not to be tossed aside lightly."[40] Second, the Court's assumptions about a national consensus might not have been as strong as Justice Kennedy and his colleagues in the majority had thought. There were already four votes to uphold Patrick Kennedy's death sentence. There was at least a chance that the awareness of the federal statute might turn one justice—and thus the majority—around.

That was not to be. On October 1, 2007, at the start of the Court's new term, the justices announced that Louisiana's request for a rehearing would be denied.[41] Justice Kennedy, author of the Court's decision, issued a statement that was joined by the four other justices in the majority. Kennedy pointed out that the death penalty had not been carried out against a military offender for almost fifty years and that "authorization of the death penalty in the military sphere does not indicate that the penalty is constitutional in the civilian context." Kennedy concluded that the mere fact that the United States retains the death penalty for members of the military convicted of rape "does not draw into question our conclusions that there is a consensus against the death penalty for the crime in the civilian context."

The vote was 7–2, with only Justices Thomas and Alito indicating, without explanation, that they would rehear the case. Chief Justice Roberts and Justice Scalia, who had dissented in the Kennedy decision, voted not to rehear the case, saying it wouldn't make any difference. Scalia used the opportunity to take yet another swipe at his colleagues for their initial resolution of the Kennedy case and, by inference, their resolution of death cases generally:

> I am voting against the petition for rehearing because the views of the American people on the death penalty for child rape were, to tell the truth, irrelevant to the majority's decision in this case. The majority opinion, after an unpersuasive attempt to show that a consensus against the death penalty existed, in the end came down to this: "The Constitution contemplates that in the end our own judgment will be brought to bear on the question of the acceptability of the death penalty under the Eighth Amendment." Of course, the Constitution contemplates no such thing; the proposed Eighth

Amendment would have been laughed to scorn if it had read "no criminal penalty shall be imposed which the Supreme Court deems unacceptable." But that is what the majority opinion said, and there is no reason to believe that absence of a national consensus would provoke second thoughts.

Kennedy's language could come back to dog the Court in another important respect. His statement, joined by four other justices, at least suggests that the Eighth Amendment prohibition of cruel and unusual punishment may not apply with the same force to members of the military as it does to other citizens. That is certainly true with respect to other guarantees in the Bill of Rights. The First Amendment guarantee of free speech, for example, is not going to apply to a soldier in formation in the same way that it might apply to a citizen on a bus. But it has always been assumed that the Court's death-penalty jurisprudence—including the cases recounted in this book—would apply to all Americans equally. Patrick Kennedy was not associated with the military, and Justice Kennedy was quick to point out that the Court was not deciding whether members of the military have less protection. His statement however raises that very question, a question most observers had thought settled.

POSTSCRIPT NO. 2

Erlich Coker, the central figure in the case of *Coker v. Georgia*, remains incarcerated at the Phillips State Prison at Buford, Georgia, as of this writing. While the authors make no pretense of any genetic predisposition for criminal behavior, Coker's bad habits do appear to run in the family. His thirty-four-year-old son, Eric, was arrested in North Carolina in 2007 for repeatedly sexually molesting a fourteen-year-old niece and then attempting to hire someone to murder the child as well as his wife, who had discovered the abuse and reported it to police.[42] Coker, who was born after his father had entered prison and spent precious little time with him, pleaded guilty to all charges: two counts of statutory sex offense, one count of statutory rape, three counts of taking indecent liberties with a child, and two counts of solicitation to commit first-degree murder. He is now serving a twenty-one-to-twenty-seven-year prison term.

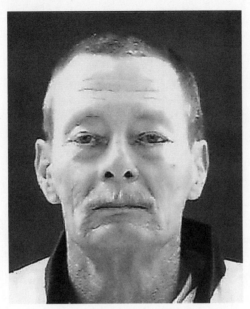

Figure 8.9. Erlich Coker.

9

NON-TRIGGERMEN

JUST AS GUILTY?

Execution is an excessive and disproportionate pun-
ishment, in violation of the Eighth and Fourteenth
Amendments, for one who did not himself take life,
attempt or assist in taking life, and for one who did not
intend that life be taken by another.

—Attorney James S. Liebman, arguing in
Enmund v. Florida, 458 U.S. 782 (1982)

If Tom Kersey had it, he flaunted it. "He had a bad habit of flashing his money," said Perry Knight, "the kind of thing that can lead to trouble." Knight, who would later become the mayor of Bowling Green, Florida, was reflecting on the 1975 murders of Kersey and his wife, Eunice, just outside of town.[1] Kersey's family viewed his bankroll habit as a harmless eccentricity—but it would prove fatal.

The Kerseys—he was eighty-six and she was seventy-four—cultivated vegetables and raised pigs and cattle on their small farm in the rural, central Florida community. Tom Kersey would preach at a small country church on Sundays and tend to his farming chores during the week. The farm had been home to their four children, who were now grown and on their own. The story of the bloodbath on that farm begins with a routine event in the Kersey's life: the sale of a cow.

In negotiating the sale with Earl "Dewey" Enmund, Kersey maintained that he didn't need Enmund's money, that he wasn't anxious enough to accept less than he was asking. "See, I ain't broke," he said, pulling a fat wad of bills out of his pocket. The argument worked; Edmund paid cash for the cow.[2] "Daddy didn't believe in banks," Mary Lee Albritton, Kersey's only surviving daughter, told us.[3] "He loved to flash his money," repeated Perry Knight, who recalled being in a little country store when Kersey pulled out a huge roll of bills and made a production out of slowly counting off five one-dollar bills. "He liked to play with it," said Knight.[4]

The image of Kersey's bankroll stayed with Enmund, age forty-two. He told the story to his twenty-three-year-old son-in-law, Sampson Armstrong, and Armstrong's nineteen-year-old wife, Jeanette. The three of them concocted a scheme to, as Mary Lee Albritton put it, "Get back his money, and then some."[5]

Around 7:30 on the morning of Tuesday, April 1, 1975, Sampson and Jeanette Armstrong knocked on the Kerseys' front door; Sampson had a .22 caliber pistol in his pocket. Earl Enmund waited on the road in a yellow Buick—"He would have been recognized," Jeanette explained later. Enmund was accompanied by his common-law wife, Jean Shaw, who was Jeanette Armstrong's mother.

The Armstrongs asked for water for an "overheated car" and were directed to the rear of the house, where Tom Kersey met them with a jug. Jeanette's confession, recorded on tape, tells what happened next:

> Sampson pulled the gun. The old man said, "Don't kill me. I'll give you the money, but don't shoot." Sampson grabbed him around the neck at the back door and put the gun in his back. The old man was struggling and yelling to the woman. He told her to get the gun.[6]

Eunice Kersey came out of the house shooting. She wounded Jeanette Armstrong with her .38 caliber revolver, but by then Sampson was firing back. Thomas and Eunice Kersey were fatally wounded. The Armstrongs dragged them inside to the kitchen. An autopsy would determine that Thomas had been shot twice; Eunice, six times.

"They bled to death," said Mary Lee Albritton. The bodies were found a short time later by her older sister, Margaret King. "There was a huge pool of blood," recalled longtime Hardee County sheriff Newt "Duke" Murdock, "and that gave us our first clue." A blood sample was found that did not match the Kerseys; it was evidence that Eunice Kersey had wounded one of her killers.[7]

Within a day, investigators got a report of a gunshot victim being treated at Walker Memorial Hospital, about twenty-five miles east of Bowling Green. The victim, Jeanette Armstrong, claimed she had been hit by a stray bullet in a field near the county line. The .38 caliber bullet, which had entered her left breast, was lodged against her spine; doctors could not remove it. "We couldn't make a ballistic comparison" with Mrs. Kersey's gun, Murdock said, "so we couldn't arrest her."

If Tom Kersey's vanity contributed to his death and that of his wife, there is rough justice in the fact that Sampson Armstrong's bragging led to his own arrest and that of his coconspirators.

It started with a rumor. A deputy sheriff in neighboring Highland County heard that someone was claiming knowledge about the Kersey crime. When he tracked the story to its source, a man named J. B. Neil, he hit a dead end. Questioned by the deputy and then by Duke Murdock, Neil claimed he knew nothing. Murdock was determined to break through Neil's stonewalling. He decided to try another tack. "We brought him back in and sat him down," Murdock said. "I pulled out ten one-hundred-dollar bills and told him he'd get five when he gave me the names and five when he testified. He started singing."

Neil said that Armstrong and Enmund had boasted to him about the Kersey robbery-homicide, and Neil provided details to Murdock that had not been released. The information was solid enough to justify arrest warrants for Sampson and Jeanette Armstrong and Earl Enmund. "We got them," said Murdock.[8]

The trial of Sampson Armstrong and Earl Enmund lasted five days; the jury took only four hours to convict them of first-degree murder. A sentencing hearing and the jury's decision to impose the death penalty all took place in an additional hour. Judge William Norris immediately pronounced the death sentences.

Jeanette Armstrong was convicted of second-degree murder in a separate trial and sentenced to life in prison. She served twenty-seven years of that sentence before being released in 2007 at the age of fifty-one. None of the interviews done by the authors long after the crimes, nor any of the surviving records, indicate that race played a part in either the crimes or the punishments. The victims were white; the perpetrators, black. But by all accounts, there were no troubling racial tensions in Hardee County.

The death sentences of "Dewey" Enmund and Sampson Armstrong were handed down in the four-year interval between the Supreme Court's *Furman* and *Gregg* decisions. The death penalty may have been on a legal holiday, but "Old Sparky," the oak electric chair built by prisoners in 1923, was being regularly tested and maintained in a state of readiness at the Florida State Prison in Starke. The death penalty was reinstated in 1976 by *Gregg* while the two men pursued their appeals; their lives were again in jeopardy.

It was Enmund's case that eventually reached the U.S. Supreme Court. "Earl Enmund did not himself take life," attorney James Liebman told the justices in oral argument on the morning of March 23, 1982. He contended that "execution is an excessive and disproportionate punishment," violating the Eighth Amendment, for someone who did not kill or intend to kill. In essence, Liebman was making a distinction that Florida law did not, between a gunman and a getaway driver.

The Court agreed, sparing Enmund's life by a one-vote margin. Justice Byron White wrote for the majority, saying the "cruel and unusual" punishments clause of the Eighth Amendment guards against punishments that, because of their severity, are "greatly disproportioned to the offenses charged." He noted that Enmund was not present at the killings and that there was no proof of a homicidal intent or anticipation of lethal force on his part.[9]

In his writing for the majority, White also referred to the 1977

Coker decision (discussed in the previous chapter). It was in that case that the Court first addressed the issue of proportionality in the application of the death penalty, ruling that a rape not involving murder was not a capital crime.

Figure 9.1. Earl Enmund.

Earl Enmund, prisoner number 049515, is, at this writing, under what the state corrections department terms "close custody" at its prison in Dade County, genteelly called the South Florida Reception Center.

Enmund's son-in-law, Sampson Armstrong, had his sentence reduced on appeal to life in prison. His attorneys successfully argued that the judge's instructions to the jury during the sentencing phase of the trial were faulty; the instructions incorrectly limited the jury's consideration of mitigating circumstances. Armstrong is serving his sentence more than a hundred miles north of Enmund, in a penitentiary at Lake Okeechobee.

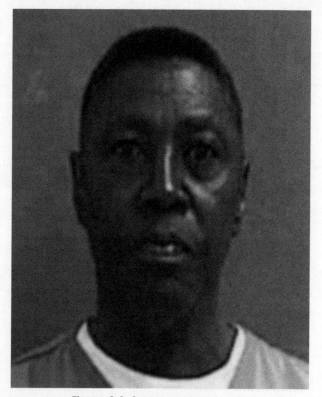

Figure 9.2. Sampson Armstrong.

The *Enmund* case was the first in which the Court determined that the degree of participation in a murder affected the application of the death penalty. Five years later, in 1987, the justices chose to delve even further into the difficult territory of proportionality when they accepted an appeal from Arizona.

From a satellite view, the pavement of Route 95 near Quartzsite, Arizona, looks like it has been photoshopped onto the surface of the moon, a black ribbon cleaving through desolation. In the early-morning hours of August 1, 1978, the silence of the empty desert along the highway was shattered by sixteen blasts from a 20-gauge shotgun. Eleven of them were fired by Gary Tison, a convicted murderer and escaped prisoner; the others were fired by Randy Greenawalt, another murderer who had escaped with Tison from the Arizona State Prison.

The shotgun pellets ended the lives of John and Donna Lyons; their twenty-three-month-old son, Christopher; and a fifteen-year-old niece, Theresa Tyson (whom everyone called Terri Jo). It was point-blank, deliberate murder: the victims were herded into an abandoned car and slaughtered in their seats.[10]

A short distance away, near a car that had been hijacked from the Lyons, the shots were heard by Gary Tison's three sons, ages eighteen, nineteen, and twenty. The three had helped their father and Greenawalt escape from prison. Although they did not pull any triggers that August night, their role would become central in a legal battle that would be decided by the nation's highest court. It was a case in which filial love led to felony murder, and then to death row.

Gary Tison, who first saw the inside of a jail at sixteen, had been serving two consecutive life sentences for the murder of a prison guard. In a walled community riddled with racial and gang tensions, he was known as a tough customer. "Nobody messed with him," said Lieutenant George Goswick of the guard detail, "he was not someone you would want to cross."[11]

"I've never seen a man yet that was too big to tangle with," Gary Tison told a court-appointed psychiatrist in 1961. Dr. William McGrath took him at his word: "Mr. Tison," he wrote, "is impressed with being dangerous." He diagnosed Tison as a sociopathic personality capable of "pronounced moral perversity [and] criminality."[12]

He had a burly, broad-shouldered body and a menacing manner—one convincingly captured by stone-faced actor Robert Mitchum, who played Tison in a 1983 movie. Despite his fearsome reputation, Tison was considered a model prisoner. He was housed in a moderate-security wing of the state penitentiary in Florence, Arizona. The facilities included a grassy area inside the gates, where families were allowed to picnic with prisoners.

On the morning of July 30, 1978, a Sunday, the three Tison boys presented themselves at the visitors' entrance, guns hidden in a cardboard box under a checkered tablecloth. They took over the guard station, aided by Greenawalt, who worked behind the counter as a clerk. He, too, was serving a life term for murder. Tison and Greenawalt changed out of their prison uniforms into western wear brought by the boys, and then the five of them casually strolled out of the prison gates to their car. They pulled away uneventfully, heading out of the prison grounds under the shadow of a silent guard tower.

Tison's sons felt they had been driven by desperation into arranging the escape. Their father had been behind bars most of their lives and was slated to die there. In fact, Gary Tison bitterly joked, with consecutive life sentences, he'd still have time to serve after his death.[13] Donald Tison, the eldest boy, had served two years in the Marine Corps and was taking criminology courses at the local community college; his two brothers had been visiting their father in prison since they were eight and nine years old.

The getaway car, a green Ford Galaxie, pulled into a hospital parking lot where the boys had prepositioned a white 1969 Lincoln Continental. They made the switch and pulled out onto the highway again, undetected and unpursued. That second car would break down near Quartzsite the following night and become an execution chamber for the Lyons family.

John Lyons was a twenty-four-year-old Marine about to finish a two-year assignment to the Marine Air Station in Yuma. He and his family were headed home to Omaha, Nebraska, for a visit with relatives; son Christopher's grandparents were going to meet him for the first time. Lyons spotted a young man waving for help on a dark stretch of Route 95 and pulled to a stop near Ray Tison, the youngest son, and his immobile Continental. While Ray engaged Lyons in conversation, his partners emerged from the darkness with guns in their hands. John Lyons had a loaded Colt .38 in the glove compartment, but he had no opportunity to reach it.

The Tison crew was after the Lyons' new Mazda. They maneuvered the Lincoln off the road into the desert and shepherded their prisoners in its wake. Gary Tison ordered them into the car's back seat and sent his sons back to the Mazda.

Donna cradled Christopher; Terri Jo Tyson held the family's trembling pet Chihuahua in her arms. John Lyons pleaded for their lives. Before the boys left, they heard him say, "Please don't hurt my family. Just leave us out here and you all go home. Jesus, don't kill me."[14]

When the shooting started, Donna tried to shield the baby with her body. There was no protection possible; the shotgun pellets riddled the bodies of all of the victims. The interior of the car was carnage, strewn with fragments of flesh, bone, upholstery, and glass. Unlike her relatives, fifteen-year-old Terri Jo did not die immediately; her body was found a quarter of a mile away from the car. She apparently crawled that far despite mortal bullet wounds to the thigh and abdomen.[15]

A week later, the gang killed again in order to change cars. After crossing into Colorado, Gary Tison and Randy Greenawalt left the boys alone in the woods for a short time and returned driving a new van. The bodies of the van's owners, James and Margene Judge, riddled with gunshot wounds, were later found at their campsite near Pagosa Springs. The Judges, from Amarillo, Texas, had been on their honeymoon. James was twenty-six; Margene, twenty-five.

Gary Tison had hoped to hook up with a friend who owned a small plane that could fly his crew to Mexico. It didn't work out; in fact, the gang narrowly escaped capture. The "friend" tipped off police, who set up an undercover cordon around the airplane. The Tisons spotted the stakeout and hit the road again.

Their luck ran out on Interstate 10 as they returned to Arizona. Police had set up two roadblocks and were on the lookout for the stolen Mazda. They were taken by surprise when the Tisons rolled through the first roadblock in the Judges' van, guns blazing, but they were more prepared at the second location. Deputies from the Pinal County sheriff's office peppered the van with gunfire; it rolled slowly to a stop a short distance away.

The body of twenty-year-old Donald Tison, the eldest brother, was found in the driver's seat. The others had fled—but in the foot chase and search that followed, Randy Greenawalt was captured, as were Ray and Ricky Tison, ages eighteen and nineteen, respectively. Gary Tison escaped the police manhunt, but not the Grim Reaper. He died in the desert of exposure; his body was found eleven days later.

Greenawalt and the surviving Tison brothers were convicted of the murders of the Lyons family and their niece, and the three were sentenced to death. No charges were ever brought in the murder of the Judges: Colorado authorities closed that case believing that an additional trial of the perpetrators, Gary Tison and Randy Greenawalt, was unnecessary.

Before the three defendants went on trial in Arizona for murder, attorneys for Ray and Ricky Tison had negotiated a plea deal that would have taken the death penalty off the table in exchange for their testimony. But in a meeting with Judge Douglas Keddie, the brothers balked when he informed them they would not only have to testify against Greenawalt but also about the prison break. Since that could have put their mother further at risk as a suspected participant in the planning, the two rejected the deal.

"I'm not involving anyone else," Ray said. "I understand we already got our lives in prison. What's it going to hurt?" As author James W. Clarke noted in his classic book about the case: "It was the wrong question, asked in the wrong way, at the wrong time, of the wrong judge."[16]

The three defendants were tried separately before Judge Keddie for the Lyons and Tyson murders and found guilty of first-degree murder. Sentencing for all three was on March 29, 1979, and Judge Keddie had decided their fates identically: death in the gas chamber. Ray's question was answered.

Figure 9.3. Ray and Ricky Tison in custody.

Under Arizona law, it didn't matter whether the Tison brothers had pulled a trigger or had participated in planning a murder. The fact that they were participants in the events leading up to the murders was enough, under state law, to establish criminal intent. This is the so-called principal-accessory rule, on the books in most states. Plainly put, an accessory before the fact is as guilty as the principal. They were also vulnerable to capital-murder charges under Arizona's felony-murder rule. That rule, also common in many jurisdictions, provides that one who participates in a felony is liable for all natural consequences of the felony, including murder. Ricky and Ray Tison were every bit as eligible for the gas chamber as Randy Greenawalt.

As the long pursuit of appeals played out, the Tisons' lawyers saw hope in the Supreme Court's ruling in *Enmund*. The Court agreed to hear their case, and on November 3, 1986, attorney Alan Dershowitz stood at a lectern before the nine justices and declared, "There is no difference between this case and *Enmund*, except that this case is far more compelling."[17]

The justices did not agree about the difference. They did, however, agree that the issues were more compelling—but not the way Dershowitz saw them. In a 5–4 decision, they held that the brothers' actions could be viewed as far more culpable than Earl Enmund's. There was no doubt, as Justice Sandra Day O'Connor said in her majority opinion, that they were "major participants" in the series of crimes that began with the prison break and continued through the murders. The key question, she wrote, was whether they had acted with "reckless indifference to the value of human life." If so, their own lives could be forfeit.[18]

This was a significant expansion of the *Enmund* criteria—and it came about under unusual circumstances. According to the Court historian Edward Lazarus, Justice O'Connor had entered the Conference Room fully prepared to vote to reverse the Tisons' death penalties, based on *Enmund*. He reports that O'Connor was swayed when Justice White, who had written the *Enmund* decision, voted to uphold the death sentences.[19]

The good news for the Tison brothers—the temporarily life-saving news—was that the Court decided to remand the case back to Arizona's trial court to determine whether this newly stated "reckless indifference" standard had been met. The trial court found that it had been met and reaffirmed the death sentences.

It was a legal rollercoaster ride for the Tison brothers, dizzying and nearly fatal, but the Arizona Supreme Court ended it just short of the gas chamber. The justices ruled that because the Tisons were under twenty at the time of the crimes, the death penalty could not be imposed under Arizona law.

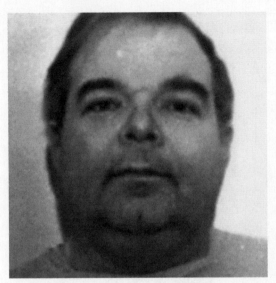

Figure 9.4. Randy Greenawalt.

Randy Greenawalt died where it all began, at the Arizona State Prison in Florence. He was executed on January 23, 1997, by lethal injection. James Clarke was a witness and, although he has reservations about capital punishment, he had no doubts on that day. "Randy Greenawalt," he said, "grew older and died a lot easier than any of his victims."[20]

Figure 9.5. Raymond Tison.

Ray and Ricky Tison now live in the Florence prison. In all likelihood, they will die there.

Figure 9.6. Ricky Tison.

 For a video report on the *Tison* Supreme Court case, go to:
http://murderatthesupremecourt.com/tison

10

THE VICTIMS LEFT BEHIND

DO THEIR OPINIONS COUNT?

It is an affront to the civilized members of the human race to say that at sentencing in a capital case, a parade of witnesses may praise the background, character and good deeds of the Defendant (as was done in this case) without limitation as to relevancy, but nothing may be said that bears upon the character of, or the harm imposed upon the victims.

—Justice William H. D. Fones,
Tennessee Supreme Court, 791 S.W.2d 10 at 28
(criticizing the U.S. Supreme Court's decision
in *Booth v. Maryland*)

Irwin and Rose Bronstein were a loving couple, and all who knew them seemed to be most favorably impressed. He was seventy-eight; she, seventy-five. They had been married for fifty-three years. Irwin had worked hard all his life and was now happily retired. Rose was young at heart and had just taught herself to play bridge. It was Friday, May 18, 1984, and spring was busting out all over. The lawn was manicured and the azaleas were in full bloom at their tidy home in Northwest Baltimore. And that's not all that was in full bloom. Their granddaughter was to be married in four days. Life was good—beautiful, one might even say. The Bronsteins had much to look forward to.

The events that would change everything began with a knock on the door. Irwin answered to find a familiar, friendly face, that of twelve-year-old Daryl Brooks who lived two doors down the street and had occasionally done chores for the Bronsteins. Daryl asked if his uncle could use the phone because their phone was out of order. The uncle, John "Ace" Booth, had been living with Daryl and his mother for several weeks. As Irwin let them in, Willie "Sweetsie" Reid—who had been standing off to the side—burst into the house followed by Booth. Once inside, Booth and Reid tied up the couple and gagged them. The child was left outside. The intent was robbery, but it would become far worse.

A police report indicates that there was no sign of a struggle, and investigators concluded that the Bronsteins did everything they were told to do. Even so, Booth knew the couple could identify them through Daryl. Armed with twelve-inch serrated kitchen knives, Booth and Reid went to work on the elderly couple, stabbing each of them a dozen times in the neck, chest, and side until dead. They took some cash and a few items from the house. They then went back to the apartment of Reid's's girlfriend, Veronda Mazyck, exchanged some of the cash and goods for heroin, and proceeded to "fire up" on the drugs with some friends. Booth invited his girlfriend, Judy Edwards, over to join the party.

During the course of the evening and out of earshot of other guests, Reid confided to one his friends, Eddie Smith, that he "had just killed a couple of mother fuckers."[1] After their visitors had left, Booth and Reid realized that they didn't get everything from the house that they could have, including the Bronstein's Impala, and thought about going back. They would take their lady friends with them. It was late at night on May 18 or early morning on May 19. When Ms. Edwards arrived at the Mazyck apartment, Booth lied and told her he wanted her to drive the car of a friend of his, that he needed someone who had a driver's license in the event the car was stopped by the police. With that, the four of them piled into a taxi and headed over to the Bronstein's home.

Before they entered the house, Booth had a friendly admonition for the ladies: "If you see any dead bodies, pay them no mind."[2] They then entered the house through the rear door, and the two women saw the bound and gagged corpses of Mr. and Mrs. Bronstein in the living room. The group, with large, green plastic trash bags in hand, immediately proceeded to loot everything in sight. They walked out with jewelry, silverware, and two television sets, among other things; loaded it all into the Bronsteins' car; and, with Edwards at the wheel, drove off into the night.

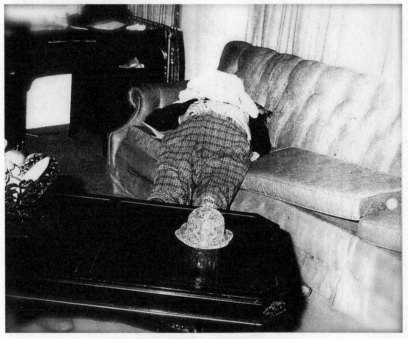

Figure 10.1. Body of Irwin Bronstein.

Back at the Mazyck apartment, they took some heroin and went to bed, Booth and Edwards sleeping on the sofa in the living room. Edwards later recalled that before dozing off, she repeatedly questioned Booth about the couple at the house. Were they really dead? And who had killed them? "I kept asking him over and over to tell me the truth. Then he said, 'Yeah, sure. Sweetsie killed the woman and I killed the man. I took care of the man.' He told me I should have known better than to ask."

Figure 10.2. Body of Rose Bronstein.

Figure 10.3. John Booth: "If you see any dead bodies, pay them no mind."

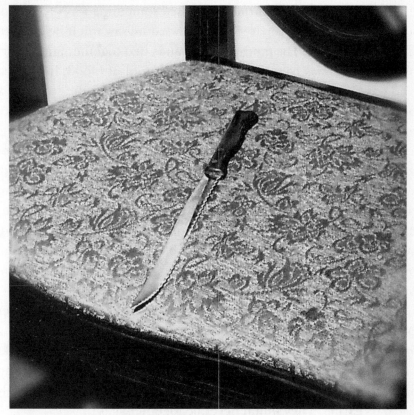

Figure 10.4. The murder weapon.

As her parents lay dead in their living room, the Bronsteins' daughter, Phyllis Bricker, and husband, Bill, were getting ready for their own daughter's wedding. Phyllis had called her parents the night before, but there was no answer. Her brother, Barry Bronstein, had also called his parents on the night of the murders with the same result. Barry and his father were to be ushers at the wedding, and he had been with both his parents earlier in the day. They had a tentative plan for Barry to pick his father up on May 20 so that they might get fitted for their tuxedos. All seemed to be proceeding as planned, however, and there was little concern.

Barry Bronstein showed up dutifully at 4:00 p.m. on May 20 as planned and noticed that the car was gone and the front door was unlocked. The younger Bronstein sensed something was wrong, but nothing could have prepared him for what he saw when he entered his parents' home. His mother, with hands tied together and a scarf over her face, was lying on the floor in a pool of blood; his father, who was also tied up and gagged, was slouched over the sofa with a plastic bag over his head. His clothing was drenched in blood. They had been dead for two days.

Bronstein called 9-1-1, wept, and then called Phyllis. He told her to come to the house at once, that something terrible had occurred. When Mrs. Bricker got there, she found her parents' home surrounded by police and television camera crews. She called her daughter to share the news. Surely it must have entered her mind: What about the wedding? It was just two days away. Barry's children, on the other hand, first learned of their grandparents' death from news bulletins on Baltimore television stations.

The case was a top priority for Baltimore police. The elder Bronstein's 1972 Impala turned up partially stripped in the parking lot of a public housing project in East Baltimore about three weeks later. Police were able to link Booth with the abandoned car and arrested him on June 7, 1983. Booth had married Judy Edwards only five days earlier. They would never be together again.

The case against both Ace Booth and Sweetsie Reid was strong. The women, Veronda Mazyck and Judy Edwards, had also been charged as "accessories after the fact." Both testified for the prosecution in exchange for reduced charges. In Booth's case, the jury deliberated for only seven and a half hours before finding him guilty. Prosecutors had made it clear all along that they would be seeking the death penalty, given the brutality of the murders, but that still would take time. There would have to be a presentence investigation. Convicted in April of 1984, the sentencing hearing would not begin until October.

A "victims' rights" movement had been sweeping the country in the early eighties, and Maryland responded by amending its laws to require juries to consider the impact that murders have on the loved ones of the victims.[3] The impact on Barry Bronstein; his sister,

Phyllis; and their respective children would be devastating. The jury deciding Booth's fate would learn about it in excruciating detail.

Figure 10.5. Police examining the Bronsteins' abandoned Impala.

Since the Jewish religion dictates that birth and marriage are more important than death, the wedding of the Bronsteins' granddaughter had to proceed as planned on May 22. She had been eagerly looking forward to the wedding, but it turned out to be a morbid occasion of exceptional sorrow. Everyone was crying. The reception, which ordinarily would have been a celebration of several hours, was very brief. And the next day, instead of going on their honeymoon, she and her new husband attended her grandparents' funeral. She later described the events of these few days as a "completely devastating and life-altering experience."[4]

The victims' son, Barry Bronstein, said he was haunted by how he found his parents that afternoon, that he continues to feel their horror and fear. He said he was unable to drive through his parents' neighborhood or by his father's favorite restaurant or by the super-market where his parents shopped. His parents weren't just killed, he said. "They were butchered like animals."

Phyllis Bricker said she was unable to eat for days and that she cried every day for months following the murders. The jury heard how a part of Phyllis had also died along with her parents. The job of cleaning out her parents' home had fallen to her, and it took weeks. She saw the bloody carpet, knowing that her parents had been there, had died there, and she felt like getting down on the rug and holding them close to her.

The defense objected to this recitation but was overruled, given that such statements are not only allowed but even required under Maryland law. The Bronsteins' victim impact statement had been used in the trial of Willie "Sweetsie" Reid as well as that of John "Ace" Booth. And it appears to have been effective. Although the Maryland statute expressly prohibits those left behind from recommending the punishment, the jury got the message. Both defendants were sentenced to die in Maryland's seldom-used gas chamber.[5]

In Maryland, as in most states since the U.S. Supreme Court's decision in *Gregg v. Georgia*, death sentences are automatically reviewed by the state's highest court, which in Maryland is the Court of Appeals. Booth's court-appointed lawyers had raised nineteen different issues on which they claimed the conviction, death sentence, or both should be overturned, ranging from jury selection to jury instructions, from the sufficiency of the evidence to the allegedly inflammatory closing arguments by the prosecutor. The court rejected all nineteen claims in a thirty-page opinion, dismissing the defense's challenge to the victim impact statement in a few simple paragraphs.

The admissibility of the victim impact statement, however, would be the one and only question that would get the attention of the U.S. Supreme Court five months later on October 16, 1986, when it agreed to review the *Booth* case. The debate would focus less on arcane nuances of constitutional law than on simple issues of accountability and blame that could divide brother and sister around the breakfast table just as it would the Supreme Court.

Booth's attorneys had argued in the Maryland Court of Appeals that victim-impact evidence injects an arbitrary factor into the death-penalty decision and that it has no bearing on the defendant's culpability. His new team of lawyers tried to press that same point in the U.S. Supreme Court.[6]

Booth was represented by attorney George E. Burns, who specialized in appellate practice in the Baltimore Public Defender's Office: "The state argues that this [the impact of a murder on loved ones] is still part of the circumstances of the crime. The argument really comes down to no more than saying, 'If I cast a pebble into the ocean, the ripples just go on forever.' . . . The problem with that, I think, is not only has it never been used as a basis for criminal sentencing, it's probably not even a good basis for tort law. . . . The implications are simply staggering, because I think it's fair to say that each and every one of us is offended by violent crime. That being the case, there's no reason every citizen who is offended by this shouldn't come in and express that view. Indeed, we might have an 800-number linked up to the courtroom. People can call in."

Justice Sandra Day O'Connor appeared skeptical.

O'Connor: Mr. Burns, do you suppose that it's possible for a State to make it an aggravating circumstance to murder someone who is a policeman?
Burns: I think it is, Justice O'Connor, if I may add one thing. I think it would have to be that you would have to have reason to *know* it is a policeman as opposed to not.
O'Connor: Maybe, maybe not.

Most states do allow the judge or jury—whoever is doing the sentencing—to consider the impact of the crime on victims in non-capital cases. Burns's argument was that in cases where the punishment is death, the risk that the decision may be based on passion or sympathy for the victims may be too great. Burns emphasized that the punishment should be based on the defendant's "evil heart," that which he knew he was doing, and not based on some unforeseeable consequence, such as the impact on loved ones unknown to the perpetrator.

Justice Scalia wasn't buying, pointing out that unintended consequences are routinely a factor in sentencing.

> *Scalia:* Let's assume I'm pulling a bank robbery and I aim at a guard intending to kill him. If I happen to kill him, I'm liable for much graver punishment than if my aim is bad and he's only wounded, correct?
>
> *Burns:* I'm not sure, Your Honor, because in one case you have murder, and in one, attempted murder. . . . You have, in Maryland, at least life in each case.
>
> *Scalia:* Well, I think you certainly would not deny that a State can have different punishments, and considerably different, for a murder that goes awry, and one that is actually committed.
>
> *Burns:* I agree, Your Honor.
>
> *Scalia:* Although the evil of the person who pulls the trigger, the blackness of his soul, is exactly the same, right? He's just as bad a person.
>
> *Burns:* I agree, Your Honor.

The distinguished Supreme Court jurist, Oliver Wendell Holmes, has been famously quoted as saying that "the life of the law has not been logic; it has been experience."[7] Maybe Holmes had it wrong. This victim-impact issue does not turn on experience or any abstract nuances of constitutional law. Here, logical thinking may be more helpful than any deep understanding of what the framers said, or meant to say, when they drafted the Bill of Rights. This case, like many, is all about logic and illustrates—perhaps more than most—that sound logic can often lie on both sides of an issue.

The case split the Court 5–4,[8] with Justice Lewis Powell writing for the majority and departing from his conservative allies to throw out Booth's death sentence. Powell had already announced his retirement; he would be gone from the Court in two weeks. He was having growing doubts about capital punishment and deep concerns about what he considered irrelevant factors that seep into death-penalty sentencing. One of those factors was the role that race played and his own decision in *McCleskey v. Kemp* that he eventually would repudiate (see chap. 4). Another was the role of victim impact statements. Powell was joined by Justices Thurgood Marshall and William Brennan (whose votes were predictable given their opposition to capital punishment in all cases) as well as Justices John Paul Stevens and Harry Blackmun. Powell wrote that the impact on loved ones of the murder victim simply isn't relevant in determining whether the perpetrator should get a death sentence:

> While the full range of foreseeable consequences of a defendant's actions may be relevant in other criminal and civil contexts, we cannot agree that it is relevant in the unique circumstance of a capital [death penalty] sentencing hearing. When carrying out this task the jury is required to focus on the defendant as a "uniquely individual human being." The focus of a VIS [victim impact statement], however, is not on the defendant, but on the character and reputation of the victim and the effect on his family. These factors may be wholly unrelated to the blameworthiness of a particular defendant. As our cases have shown, the defendant often will not know the victim, and therefore will have no knowledge about the existence or characteristics of the victim's family. Moreover, defendants rarely select their victims based on whether the murder will have an effect on anyone other than the person murdered. Allowing the jury to rely on a VIS therefore could result in imposing the death sentence because of factors about which the defendant was unaware, and that were irrelevant to the decision to kill. This evidence thus could divert the jury's attention away from the defendant's background and record, and the circumstances of the crime.

Powell also expressed concerns that the sentencing hearing could degenerate into a mini-trial on the victim's character, the prospect of which "is more than simply unappealing; it could well distract the sentencing jury from its constitutionally required task—determining whether the death penalty is appropriate in light of the background and record of the accused and the particular circumstances of the crime."

Powell also observed that the Bronstein family was "articulate and persuasive in expressing their grief and the extent of their loss. But in some cases the victim will not leave behind a family, or the family members may be less articulate in describing their feelings even though their sense of loss is equally severe. The fact that the imposition of the death sentence may turn on such distinctions illustrates the danger of allowing juries to consider this information. Certainly the degree to which a family is willing and able to express its grief is irrelevant to the decision whether a defendant, who may merit the death penalty, should live or die."

Chief Justice William Rehnquist, Justice Byron White, Justice Sandra Day O'Connor, and Justice Antonin Scalia dissented. After reviving his bank-robbery hypothetical from the oral argument three months earlier, Scalia wrote:

> It seems to me, however—and I think to most of mankind—that the amount of harm one causes does bear upon the extent of his personal responsibility. We may take away the license of a driver who goes 60 miles an hour on a residential street; but we will put him in jail for manslaughter if though his moral guilt is no greater, he is unlucky enough to kill someone during the escapade.

And, added Scalia, it should make no difference in capital cases, drawing on the Tison brothers' case regarding non-triggermen (Chapter 8):

> Less than two months ago, we held that two brothers who planned and assisted in their father's escape from prison could be sentenced to death because in the course of the escape, their father and an accomplice murdered a married couple and two children. Had their father allowed the victims to live, the brothers could not

be put to death; but because he decided to kill, the brothers may. The difference between life and death for these two defendants was thus a matter "wholly unrelated to their blameworthiness." But it was related to their personal responsibility, i.e., to the degree of harm that they had caused. In sum, the principle upon which the Court's opinion rests—that the imposition of capital punishment is to be determined solely on the basis of moral guilt—does not exist, neither in the text of the Constitution, nor in the historic practices of our society, nor even in the opinions of this Court."

 For a video report on the *Booth* Supreme Court case, go to: http://murderatthesupremecourt.com/booth

The Court's decision was announced on June 15, 1987. Eleven days later, Powell's tenure on the Court was over. Might the conservative, law-and-order minded president Ronald Reagan appoint someone more sensitive to the rights of victims (and, by extension, *less* sensitive to the rights of criminal defendants)? Robert Bork, an academic who, only five years earlier, had been named to the U.S. Court of Appeals for the District of Columbia, was just such a candidate. The stage was set for a nasty confirmation fight, less perhaps because of the characteristics of the nominee than of the justice he would replace. For years, the Court had had a delicate ideological balance. Replacing a moderate like Lewis Powell with a conservative heavyweight like Robert Bork could shift the direction of the Court on victim impact statements and a whole lot more. The opposition was formidable, and successful. Bork's nomination was rejected by the full U.S. Senate by a vote of 58–42.

Powell's seat eventually went to Anthony Kennedy, a judge on the U.S. Court of Appeals for the Ninth Circuit, who was not as well-known as Bork but was still widely considered a reliable conservative, particularly on matters of criminal justice. Kennedy took his seat on the Court on February 18, 1988. The decision in *Booth* was only nine months old, and some felt, given the departure of its author, it was already ripe for the graveyard.

The first test would come soon enough. The following October, in Anthony Kennedy's first full term, the Court agreed to consider the case of *South Carolina v. Gathers*.[9] Demetrius Gathers was convicted of murder and sentenced to death for the killing of Richard Haynes, an unemployed thirty-one-year-old with a history of mental disorder.

The principle issue in *Booth v. Maryland* involved the impact of a murder on loved ones of the victim and only peripherally involved the characteristics of the victims themselves. In the *Gathers* case, the focus was exclusively on the victims and whether juries should be permitted to consider the personal characteristics of the victim in deciding the fate of his or her murderer. The Court's reasoning in the *Booth* case would come into play, giving the reconstituted Court an opportunity for an about-face. All eyes would be on Justice Kennedy (as they would be for the next twenty-five years, during which Kennedy has demonstrated a remarkable ability to almost always be on the winning side in cases decided 5–4, and often he would author the majority opinion).

The facts of the case were every bit as brutal as they were in the *Booth* case. Gathers and three companions were convicted of assaulting Haynes, beating and kicking him severely, and smashing a bottle over his head. They went through all his belongings, looking for something worth taking, apparently in vain. Before leaving the scene, Gathers beat Haynes with an umbrella, which he then stuffed into the victim's rectum. Sometime later, he apparently returned to the scene and stabbed Haynes with a knife, making sure he was dead.

Although he had no formal religious training, Haynes considered himself a preacher and referred to himself as "Reverend Minister"; his mother testified that he would "talk to people all the time about the Lord." He generally carried with him several bags containing articles of religious significance, including two Bibles, rosary beads, plastic statues, olive oil, and religious tracts. Among these items, on the evening of his murder, was a tract titled "The Game Guy's Prayer." Relying on football and boxing metaphors, it extolled the virtues of the good sport. He also carried a voter registration card.

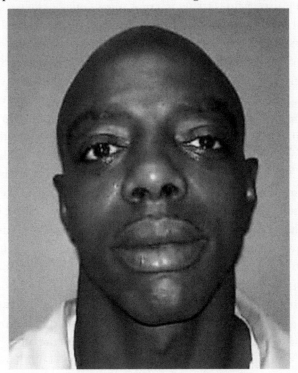

Figure 10.6. Demetrius Gathers.

Prosecutors offered no new evidence at the sentencing phase of Gathers's trial, but in their closing arguments, seeking the death penalty, they did comment on the victim's belongings recovered from the crime scene.

We know from the proof that Reverend Minister Haynes was a religious person. He had his religious items out there. This defendant strewn [*sic*] them across the bike path, thinking nothing of that.

Among the many cards that Reverend Haynes had among his belongings was this card. It's in evidence. Think about it when you go back there. He had this [*sic*] religious items, his beads. He had a plastic angel. Of course, he is with the angels now, but this defendant Demetrius Gathers could care little about the fact that he is a religious person. Cared little of the pain and agony he inflicted upon a person who is trying to enjoy one of our public parks.

But look at Reverend Minister Haynes' prayer. It's called the Game Guy's Prayer. "Dear God, help me to be a sport in this little game of life. I don't ask for any easy place in this lineup. Play me anywhere you need me. I only ask you for the stuff to give you one hundred percent of what I have got. If all the hard drives seem to come my way, I thank you for the compliment. Help me to remember that you won't ever let anything come my way that you and I together can't handle. And help me to take the bad break as part of the game. Help me to understand that the game is full of knots and knocks and trouble, and make me thankful for them. Help me to be brave so that the harder they come the better I like it. And, oh God, help me to always play on the square. No matter what the other players do, help me to come clean. Help me to study the book so that I'll know the rules, to study and think a lot about the greatest player that ever lived and other players that are portrayed in the book. If they ever found out the best part of the game was helping other guys who are out of luck, help me to find it out, too. Help me to be regular, and also an inspiration with the other players. Finally, oh God, if fate seems to uppercut me with both hands, and I am laid on the shelf in sickness or old age or something, help me to take that as part of the game, too. Help me not to whimper or squeal that the game was a frame-up or that I had a raw deal. When in the falling dusk I get the final bell, I ask for no lying, complimentary tombstones. I'd only like to know that you feel that I have been a good guy, a good game guy, a saint in the game of life." . . .

You will find some other exhibits in this case that tell you more about a just verdict. Again this is not easy. No one takes any pleasure from it, but the proof cries out from the grave in this case. Among the personal effects that this defendant could care little about when he went through it is something that we all treasure. Speaks a lot about Reverend Minister Haynes. Very simple yet very profound. Voting. A voter's registration card.

Reverend Haynes believed in this community. He took part. And he believed that in Charleston County, in the United States of America, that in this country you could go to a public park and sit on a public bench and not be attacked by the likes of Demetrius Gathers.

Was all this relevant in determining whether Gathers should get a death sentence? The Court said no, adhering to its decision in *Booth v. Maryland*. The Court again was divided 5–4, with Justice Brennan, the Court's premiere death-penalty opponent, writing the majority opinion. Justice Kennedy did as expected, voting to allow the jury to consider all the characteristics of the victim in deciding the fate of his killer. The surprise was Justice White, who had dissented in *Booth* and argued strongly that it was wrongly decided. White joined the majority opinion in the *Gathers* case, however, and explained why in a separate, two-sentence concurrence: "Unless *Booth v. Maryland*, 482 U.S. 496 (1987), is to be overruled, the judgment below must be affirmed. Hence, I join Justice Brennan's opinion for the Court." White's colleagues were not prepared to go so far as to overrule *Booth*, at least not in this case.

The Court has historically been loath to overrule itself, in part because doing so creates inconsistency in the law, which is generally thought undesirable. The principle is well known to students of the law as *stare decisis*, the policy of the Court to stand by precedent (the body of prior rulings that make up the core of the Court's history). The Latin term is actually short for *stare decisis et quieta non movere*—"to stand by and adhere to decisions and not disturb what is settled." Or, in the oft-quoted words of Justice Louis Brandeis, "In most matters, it is more important that the applicable rule of law be settled than that it be settled right."[10] The fact that a case has merely been determined to have been wrongly decided is seldom sufficient to overrule it. The justices may also ask whether the decision has turned out to be unworkable, whether it has won acceptance, whether overruling a decision would create more chaos than it resolves, and, as we have seen, whether the decision conflicts with "the evolving standards of

decency that mark the progress of a maturing society."[11] The fact that
a decision has endured for many years may also work in its favor, as
in *Roe v. Wade* (1973), the well-known ruling that legalized abortion.
The fact that *Booth* was of such recent vintage, only two years old,
made it more vulnerable.

Justice Antonin Scalia wrote separately in the *Gathers* case to say
he would overrule *Booth* in a heartbeat: "I would think it a violation
of my oath to adhere to what I consider a plainly unjustified intru-
sion upon the democratic process in order that the Court might save
face." But three other justices who had dissented in *Booth* felt that
Gathers was not the right case. Justice O'Connor, joined by Chief
Justice Rehnquist and Justice Kennedy, said she was "ready to overrule" but that it was not necessary in the *Gathers* case and that reaching
out to answer a question not presently before them might violate
time-honored principles of judicial restraint. It wouldn't take long,
however, for the "right" case to reach the Court's marbled doorstep.

The day after Justice Lewis Powell said good-bye to his colleagues
at the Supreme Court, events would unfold in the small town of
Millington, Tennessee, about fifteen miles north of Memphis, that
would test the opinion of the Court in *Booth v. Maryland*.[12] It was
Saturday, June 27, 1987. Pervis Payne was visiting his girlfriend,
Bobbie Thomas, with hopes of perhaps spending the weekend there.
But she was not at home. So he spent the time waiting around,
drinking malt liquor, using cocaine, and driving around town with
a friend, each taking turns reading a pornographic magazine. It was
now 3:00 p.m. and there was still no sign of his girlfriend. So Payne
entered the unlocked apartment across the hall where twenty-eight-
year-old Charisse Christopher lived with her two-year-old daughter,
Lacie, and her three-year-old son, Nicholas.

Payne began making sexual advances toward Charisse. When she resisted, Payne became violent. A neighbor who lived in the apartment directly beneath the Christophers heard Charisse screaming, "'Get out, get out,' as if she were telling the children to leave." The noise briefly subsided and then began again, "horribly loud." The neighbor called the police after she heard a "blood-curdling scream" from the Christophers' apartment.

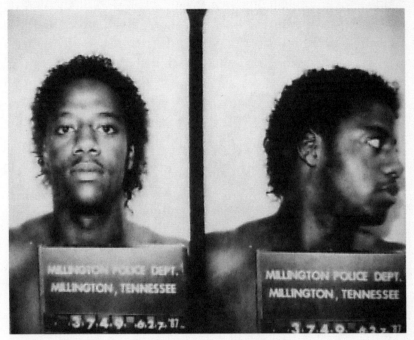

Figure 10.7. Pervis Payne.

When the first police officer arrived at the scene, he immediately encountered Payne, who was leaving the apartment building, so covered with blood that he appeared to be "sweating blood."[13] The officer confronted Payne, who responded, "I'm the complainant." When the officer asked, "What's going on up there?" Payne struck the officer with his overnight bag and fled.

Inside the apartment, the police encountered a horrifying scene. Blood covered the walls and floor throughout the unit. Charisse and her children were lying on the floor in the kitchen. Nicholas, despite

several wounds inflicted by a butcher knife that completely pene-
trated his body from front to back, was still breathing. Miraculously,
he survived, but only after undergoing seven hours of surgery and a
transfusion of 1,700 cc's of blood—400 to 500 cc's more than his estimated normal blood volume. Charisse and Lacie were dead.

Figure 10.8. Charisse Christopher.

Charisse's body was found on the kitchen floor; she was on her
back. She had sustained forty-two direct knife wounds and forty-two
defensive wounds on her arms and hands. The wounds were caused
by forty-one separate thrusts of a butcher knife. None of the eighty-
four wounds inflicted by Payne was individually fatal; rather, the
cause of death was most likely bleeding from all of the wounds.

Lacie's body was on the kitchen floor near her mother. She had
suffered stab wounds to the chest, abdomen, back, and head. The
murder weapon, the same butcher knife used on Charisse, was found
at her feet. Payne's baseball cap was snapped on her arm near her
elbow. Three cans of malt liquor bearing Payne's fingerprints were

found on a table near her body, and a fourth empty one was on the landing outside the apartment door.

Figure 10.9. A crime-scene photograph.

Payne was apprehended later that day, hiding in the attic of the home of a former girlfriend. As he descended the stairs of the attic, he stated to the arresting officers, "Man, I ain't killed no woman." He had blood on his body and clothes and several scratches across his chest. It was later determined that the blood stains matched the victims' blood types. A search of his pockets revealed a packet containing cocaine residue, a hypodermic syringe wrapper, and a cap from a hypodermic syringe. His overnight bag, containing a bloody white shirt, was found in a nearby dumpster. Payne was convicted of two counts of first-degree murder and one count of assault with intent to commit murder.[14]

Figure 10.10. A photograph from the crime scene of Charisse's hand.

Charisse's mother, Mary Zvolanek, was permitted to testify about how the murders had affected the surviving child, Nicholas, but she didn't say very much: "He cries for his mom. He doesn't seem to understand why she doesn't come home. And he cries for his sister, Lacie."

"He comes to me many times during the week and asks me, 'Grandmama, do you miss my Lacie?' And I tell him yes. He says, 'I'm worried about my Lacie.'"

In urging the jury to return a death sentence, the prosecutor amplified the grandmother's testimony:

We do know that Nicholas was alive. And Nicholas was in the same room. Nicholas was still conscious. His eyes were open. He responded to the paramedics. He was able to follow their directions. He was able to hold his intestines in as he was carried to the ambulance. So he knew what happened to his mother and baby sister. . . .

Somewhere down the road Nicholas is going to grow up, hopefully. He's going to want to know what happened. And he is going to know what happened to his baby sister and his mother. He is going to want to know what type of justice was done. He is going to want to know what happened. With your verdict, you will provide the answer.

You saw the videotape this morning. You saw what Nicholas Christopher will carry in his mind forever. When you talk about cruel, when you talk about atrocious, and when you talk about heinous, that picture will always come into your mind, probably throughout the rest of your lives. . . .

No one will ever know about Lacie Jo because she never had the chance to grow up. Her life was taken from her at the age of two years old. So, no there won't be a high school principal to talk about Lacie Jo Christopher, and there won't be anybody to take her to her high school prom. And there won't be anybody there—there won't be her mother there or Nicholas' mother there to kiss him at night. His mother will never kiss him good night or pat him as he goes off to bed, or hold him and sing him a lullaby.[15]

Figure 10.11. Three-year-old Nicholas survived the attack; his two-year-old sister, Lacie, did not.

Figure 10.12. Mary Zvolanek.

At one point during the closing argument, Assistant District Attorney Phyllis Gardner staged a grisly reenactment for the jury.

> Ladies and gentlemen of the jury, this is the last thing I am going to say to you. But I want you to think about this when you go back into your jury room. We have heard a lot about Charisse Christopher, Lacie Jo and Nicholas, and here they were as they appeared before Pervis Payne came into their lives. And this is what he did to them. Did they deserve it? Are you going to let it go unpunished?[16]

As Gardner uttered "And this is what he did to them," she approached one of the exhibits, a large diagram of Nicholas Christopher's body, and stabbed a hole through it with another exhibit, the butcher knife found between the bodies of Charisse and Lacie. Payne was sentenced to death for each of the murders and to thirty years in prison on the charge of assault with intent to murder.

The Tennessee Supreme Court was deeply offended by Gardner's stabbing demonstration during her closing argument, finding it "an improper argument, an improper, unprofessional act and an improper use of exhibits."[17] Given all the other evidence against Payne, however, the court felt it did not affect the outcome and thus was "harmless beyond a reasonable doubt."

The court also concluded that Mrs. Zvolanek's testimony about the impact of the murders on her grandson was not nearly as inflammatory as the testimony of the Bronsteins' family in *Booth v. Maryland* and, even if it were, allowing it would also have been harmless in light of the other evidence produced at the trial. The court concluded that given the "inhuman brutality" of the crime, once the identity of the perpetrator "was established by the jury's verdict, the death penalty was the only rational punishment available." The Tennessee court also took a parting shot at the U.S. Supreme Court's decisions in *Booth* and *Gathers*: "It is an affront to the civilized members of the human race to say that at sentencing in a capital case, a parade of witnesses may praise the background, character and good deeds of the defendant (as was done in this case), without limitation as to relevancy, but nothing may be said that bears upon the character of, or the harm imposed upon the victims."

Payne's attorneys took their appeal to the U.S. Supreme Court, but there was an unexpected new development that would seriously jeopardize their case. Four months after the Tennessee Supreme Court had ruled, Justice Brennan—who had joined the *Booth* majority and had written the decision of the Court in *Gathers*—appeared to have suffered a series of minor strokes. He was told by his doctors that he had to slow down, that continuing on the Court would entail enormous personal risk. On July 20, 1990, the word was out: Brennan was stepping down. President George H. W. Bush would choose as Brennan's successor David Souter, who only a few months earlier had been named to the First U.S. Circuit Court of Appeals in Boston after having served seven years on the New Hampshire Supreme Court.

Justice Kennedy had already played his hand on victim impact statements, agreeing with the *Booth* dissenters that such evidence should be allowed. Souter was perceived to be a likely ally for allowing the use of victim impact statements as well. The *Booth* and *Gathers* decisions appeared all but doomed. In their petition to the U.S. Supreme Court, Payne's lawyers argued only that the Tennessee Supreme Court had failed to apply the Court's precedents on victim impact statements, a failure that would require a new sentencing hearing. Some of the justices, however, were all but itching to have another look at the victim-impact issue; the time was right, given the new composition of the Court, and so was the case. As a result, the Court took the unusual step of ordering Payne's lawyers to also address whether the *Booth* and *Gathers* decisions should be overruled; and the justices took the unusual step of setting the case for "expedited consideration."[18] The hearing would be held in only two months. It was already mid-February and other cases accepted at this time would have their hearings scheduled in the succeeding term, which wouldn't begin until October. Both *Booth* and *Gathers* were 5–4 decisions, however, and two of the justices in the majority in each case—Powell and Brennan— were now gone. The three other justices who had prevailed in those cases—Marshall, Stevens, and Blackmun—all dissented from the Court's order expanding the issue and expediting review.

The U.S. Justice Department also had a stake in the outcome of the case because federal sentencing guidelines that had just been enacted could be affected. The department had filed a "friend of the Court" brief in support of Tennessee. Perhaps recognizing the significance of the issue, or perhaps foreseeing a slam dunk for the government, Attorney General Dick Thornburgh announced that he would personally argue for the government in the Supreme Court.

The Court's decision was announced on June 27, 1991, four years to the day after the brutal murders in Millington. To no great surprise, the Court overruled itself on both *Booth* and *Gathers* in its 6–3 decision. Given the extraordinary turn of events, Chief Justice Rehnquist assigned the opinion of the Court to himself. Justices Marshall, Stevens, and Blackmun again dissented.

Figure 10.13. Attorney General Richard "Dick" Thornburgh holds a news conference on the steps of the U.S. Supreme Court following arguments in *Payne v. Tennessee* (April 24, 1991).

Justice Marshall was particularly passionate in his dissent.

Power, not reason, is the new currency of this Court's decision-making. Four Terms ago, a five-Justice majority of this Court held that "victim impact" evidence of the type at issue in this case could not constitutionally be introduced during the penalty phase of a capital trial [*Booth v. Maryland*]. By another 5-4 vote, a majority of this Court rebuffed an attack upon this ruling just two Terms ago [*South Carolina v. Gathers*]. Nevertheless, having expressly invited respondent to renew the attack, today's majority overrules *Booth* and *Gathers* and credits the dissenting views expressed in those cases. Neither the law nor the facts supporting *Booth* and *Gathers* underwent any change in the last four years. Only the personnel of this Court did.

Figure 10.14. Justice Thurgood Marshall.

In dispatching *Booth* and *Gathers* to their graves, today's majority ominously suggests that an even more extensive upheaval of this Court's precedents may be in store. Renouncing this Court's historical commitment to a conception of "the judiciary as a source of impersonal and reasoned judgments," the majority declares itself free to discard any principle of constitutional liberty which was recognized or reaffirmed over the dissenting votes of four Justices and with which five or more Justices *now* disagree. The implications of this radical new exception to the doctrine of *stare decisis* are staggering. The majority today sends a clear signal that scores of established constitutional liberties are now ripe for reconsideration, thereby inviting the very type of open defiance of our precedents that the majority rewards in this case. Because I believe that this Court owes more to its constitutional precedents in general and to *Booth* and *Gathers* in particular, I dissent.[19]

The Payne decision was a triumph for Justice Scalia on an issue that he, too, felt passionately about, and in a concurring opinion, Scalia responded to Marshall's dissent.

The response to Justice Marshall's strenuous defense of the virtues of *stare decisis* can be found in the writings of Justice Marshall himself. That doctrine, he has reminded us, "is not 'an imprisonment of reason.'" If there was ever a case that defied reason, it was *Booth v. Maryland*, imposing a constitutional rule that had absolutely no basis in constitutional text, in historical practice, or in logic. Justice Marshall has also explained that "the jurist concerned with public confidence in, and acceptance of the judicial system might well consider that, however admirable its resolute adherence to the law as it was, a decision contrary to the public sense of justice as it is, operates, so far as it is known, to diminish respect for the courts and for law itself." . . .

Today, however, Justice Marshall demands of us some "special justification"—*beyond* the mere conviction that the rule of *Booth* significantly harms our criminal justice system and is egregiously wrong—before we can be absolved of exercising "power, not reason." I do not think that is fair. In fact, quite to the contrary, what would enshrine power as the governing principle of this Court is the notion that an important constitutional decision with plainly inadequate rational support *must* be left in place for the sole reason that it once attracted five votes.[20] (italics in the original)

Justice O'Connor, joined by Justices White and Kennedy, also wrote separately to point out that there is nothing in the decision to *compel* victim impact statements, and in some cases, they still may be inadmissible.

We do not hold today that victim impact evidence must be admitted, or even that it should be admitted. We hold merely that if a State decides to permit consideration of this evidence, "the *Eighth Amendment* erects no *per se* bar." If, in a particular case, a witness' testimony or a prosecutor's remark so infects the sentencing proceeding as to render it fundamentally unfair, the defendant may seek appropriate relief under the *Due Process Clause of the Fourteenth Amendment.*[21] (italics in the original)

 For a video report on the *Payne* Supreme Court case, go to: http://murderatthesupremecourt.com/payne

In 1953, Justice Robert Jackson described the authority of the Supreme Court this way: "We are not final because we are infallible, but we are infallible only because we are final."[22] As the *Booth-Gathers-Payne* trilogy of cases amply demonstrates, the decisions of the Supreme Court are not always final. And there are numerous other cases that also amply demonstrate that the Court is hardly infallible. The Court's *Dred Scott* decision all but ignited the Civil War by declaring slaves to be property[23]; *Plessy v. Ferguson*'s separate-but-equal ruling stood as a monument to racial segregation in public facilities for almost sixty years.[24] *Korematsu v. United* States,[25] upholding the internment of Japanese Americans during World War II solely because of their race, stands as a lasting monument to bigotry and how, in the words of Oliver Wendell Holmes, "hard cases make bad law."[26] *Korematsu* has never been overruled.

We tend to think of the U.S. Supreme Court as the last word on the Constitution and, as a result, may attribute power to the justices that they really do not enjoy. In some respects, Supreme Court justices have more restraints than any other judge. For one, they cannot

pass a difficult question on to a higher court. And if the Supreme
Court gets it wrong on an important question of constitutional law,
Congress is all but powerless and there is no other court around to
correct them. Accordingly, the justices have a unique responsibility
to get it right. And there are serious repercussions when they fail.
The damage can be enormous, the difference between life or death
in the context of the death-penalty debate. Supreme Court justices
must answer to their own conscience, future Supreme Courts that
can overrule them, and—as Chief Justice Roger Taney would understand were he around today—the long shadow of history. Taney was
widely regarded as a great chief justice and, in some quarters, still is.
But his standing in history is forever tarnished by his single opinion
in *Dred Scott*, igniting the Civil War.

So did the Supreme Court finally get it right on the victim-impact
question? Or did it merely take an ill-advised U-turn? The Court's
decision upheld the death sentence for Purvis Payne, but twenty-
five years after the double murder, he remains alive on death row
in Tennessee with appeals pending. Demetrius Gathers's death sentence was subsequently commuted to life without parole. As for John
Booth, whose case started it all, the decision in *Booth v. Maryland* led
to a new sentencing hearing without the victim impact statement.
He was resentenced to death again only to have the Maryland Court
of Appeals again reverse the sentence because of an improper jury
instruction. Booth was sentenced to death a third time, but that also
was reversed by the Maryland Court of Appeals because the jury was
not allowed to consider that Booth was high on heroin and alcohol on
the afternoon of the killings. He has been on death row in Maryland
for almost thirty years, longer than any other inmate in the state.
There is now a campaign in Maryland to do away with capital punishment, and the state's governor, Martin O'Malley, says there is not
enough sodium thiopental in the prison system to carry out executions. O'Malley, a death penalty foe, says the shortage "underscores
what a laborious and complicated and time-consuming resource-
wasting legal process goes into carrying out the death penalty."[27]

Phyllis and William Bricker have traveled to the state capitol in Annapolis and to court in Baltimore many times over the years in support of capital punishment. Booth attended one of the court hearings that seemed to go nowhere. At the end of the day, Phyllis remembers Booth turning from the defense table to look at her and whisper in her direction, "See you next year."[28]

11
THE MECHANICS OF DEATH

Commissioner Low: *It ran too smooth, Ralph, but don't screw it up next time.*
Warden Kemp: *OK . . . OK. We appreciate it. Just give us another one.*
—command post conversation after the execution of Ivon Ray Stanley in Jackson, Georgia, at 12:24 a.m. on July 14, 1984

D espite the careful oversight of legislators and the dutiful efforts of scientists and penal authorities, mishaps have dogged this country's executions from the scaffold to the gurney. Progress has been no guarantee of perfection. And a number of intriguing stories lie behind the veil of some of America's execution chambers.

The electric chair gained popularity fairly rapidly after its controversial debut with William Kemmler in 1890. Americans admire efficiency, and when the curtain was drawn on New York's execution chamber again, in July of 1891, prison officials electrocuted four prisoners without incident in the space of two hours. "Eminently satisfactory," proclaimed an eminent physician who witnessed the serial executions.[1]

The New York innovation attracted the attention of legislators across the country. The new method was initially less popular in the West, where hanging remained the political and cultural choice, but electricity became the dominant preference for execution chambers in the rest of the nation.

Some states, like Louisiana and Mississippi, used travelling electric chairs—powered by generators mounted on trucks—to bring executions to the towns and counties where the condemned had committed their crimes. The theory was that the local community affected by a crime would benefit from proximity to the law's satisfaction and that the specter of a nearby execution would bring home the message of deterrence.

Louisiana's chair, known as "Gruesome Gertie," suffered a spectacular failure in the rural town of St. Martinville on May 3, 1946. There, with wires strung from a generator truck to a room in the county courthouse, a seventeen-year-old black man, Willie Francis, was seated in the electric chair, rigged with electrodes, and fitted with a black hood. He had been condemned for the murder of the town druggist in a robbery that netted Francis twenty-three dollars.

Figure 11.1. Willie Francis. (AP Photo/Bill Allen)

Dr. Bernard de Mahy, a family practitioner in St. Martinville, was an official witness at the scheduled execution. He told the authors forty years later that he remembered it vividly: "It was a very embarrassing situation for the executioner. Because he said when he threw the switch, 'Goodbye, Willie'—and Willie didn't leave."[2] The words, and the result, were eerily similar to those at the Kemmler execution fifty-six years before. The chair didn't work.

Willie Francis was unstrapped, stood up, and walked away from the execution room unscathed. Asked what happened, he told bystanders, "The Lord fooled around with that chair." That phrase became the title of a popular song.

As Francis was led away from the execution site, one of the two technicians who had set up the chair called out to him, "I missed you this time, but I'll get you next week if I have to use a rock." Both technicians, according to witnesses, had been drinking.[3]

Bertrand de Blanc, a local attorney, took on Willie as a pro bono client after the aborted execution attempt. With the help of J. Skelly Wright, who would later become a distinguished federal appeals court judge, LeBlanc took the case to the U.S. Supreme Court, arguing that to put Willie Francis back in the electric chair would subject him to both double jeopardy and "cruel and unusual punishment." The Court didn't see it that way. The Court was split 5–4, with Justice Stanley Reed writing for the majority:

> We find nothing in what took place here which amounts to cruel and unusual punishment in the constitutional sense. . . . Petitioner's suggestion is that, because he once underwent the psychological strain of preparation for electrocution, now to require him to undergo this preparation again subjects him to a lingering or cruel and unusual punishment. . . . The cruelty against which the Constitution protects a convicted man is cruelty inherent in the method of punishment, not the necessary suffering involved in any method employed to extinguish life humanely. The fact that an unforeseeable accident prevented the prompt consummation of the sentence cannot, it seems to us, add an element of cruelty to a subsequent execution.[4]

Reed's opinion is what is called a *plurality opinion* because it drew the support of only three other justices—Chief Justice Fred Vinson, along with Justices Hugo Black and Robert Jackson. Justice Felix Frankfurter provided the fifth crucial vote but wrote separately about his misgivings. He was uncomfortable about giving Louisiana a second chance at putting Francis to death but did not view it as unconstitutional. Consequently, he wrote, "this Court must refrain from interference no matter how strong one's personal feeling of revulsion against a State's insistence on its pound of flesh."[5]

Behind the scenes, Frankfurter's revulsion was even stronger. In Conference, he told his colleagues: "This is not an easy case . . . cruel and unusual punishment is a progressive notion, shocking the feelings of the time. Here, though it is hardly a defensible thing for a state to do, it is not so offensive as to make me puke—it does not shock my conscience."[6] But Frankfurter would soon admit that the case "told on my conscience a great deal." He felt that a second execution might not violate the constitution, but, he said, "I was very much bothered by the problem; it offended my personal sense of decency to do this."[7] So in a highly unusual and extrajudicial move, Frankfurter secretly reached out from the privacy of his ornate Supreme Court chambers to a man he once described as "about the best lawyer South of the Mason Dixon Line," Monte E. Lemann.[8] Lemann had been Frankfurter's roommate at Harvard Law School and was a prominent and politically potent member of the Louisiana bar.

"This case has been so heavily on my conscience that I finally could not overcome the impulse to write to you," Frankfurter said in a letter to his old friend three weeks after the Court affirmed Francis's death sentence. He asked Lemann to use his political skills to prevent a second execution, saying, "I have little doubt that if Louisiana allows Francis to go to his death, it will needlessly cast a cloud upon Louisiana for many years to come."[9]

Frankfurter's furtive move on Francis's behalf—he sent a copy of his letter to only one fellow justice, Harold Burton—was highly unusual, and it provides an intriguing peek behind the mysteries and secrecy of the Supreme Court's inner workings concerning capital punishment. But Frankfurter's efforts failed. Lemann was not able to convince the state's pardons board to make a clemency recommendation; without one, the governor could not act.

So on May 9, 1947, the state's portable electric chair, which would eventually become permanently installed at the Louisiana State Penitentiary at Angola, was trucked back to St. Martinville's courthouse. It was, in keeping with the custom of the times, displayed on the courthouse steps for several hours that morning. James Theriot, later the clerk of the parish, told us he remembered coming with his grammar-school classmates to take in the sight. It was, he said, an amazing spectacle: "We were approximately thirteen years old at the time. We left the school during the noon hour so we could come by and visit the chair, which was set right in the middle of the courthouse porch."[10]

Early in the afternoon, the chair was moved inside the courthouse and connected to its generator—a new generator, ordered by the governor to prevent an embarrassing repeat of the botched execution attempt. The generator worked. Willie Francis, then eighteen years old, was dispatched successfully. His father had a coffin and hearse on hand, the same coffin and hearse he had brought to the St. Martinville courthouse almost exactly a year before.

The "humaneness" of electrocution was under continuing attack by death-penalty opponents whose cause was fueled by occasionally botched executions. In several states, in fact, condemned men would be "executed" twice, or would die amid flames, smoke, and stench. The authors vividly remember reporting on the case of John Evans in Alabama in 1983. Evans was a hardened criminal convicted of murdering a pawn shop owner after a seven-state crime spree that, by his own admission, involved nine kidnappings and thirty armed robberies. At his murder trial, Evans threatened that if the jury did not sentence him to death, he would escape and murder each of them. They apparently took him seriously: deliberations to convict and execute him took less than fifteen minutes.

Evans, while hardly contrite, accepted his fate. He told us from his cell on death row, "I'm glad it's almost over. And then when I sit in that chair, just before time, I'll be glad it's over."[11]

Figure 11.2. John Evans on death row.

He sat in the chair on April 22, 1983. It was Alabama's first execution in eighteen years, and it did not go well. Russell Canan, Evans's attorney, was a witness. "We had been told that one thirty-second administration of 1,900 volts of electricity would kill and execute John Evans," Russell told us, "but it took fourteen minutes."[12]

"At 8:30 p.m. you could hear the electricity go on," Canan said. "At that time the electrode that was fastened to his leg burst into flames and sparks. It looked like he was literally being burned alive.

He was in fact being tortured and burned alive right before our eyes." The medical examiner who conducted Evans's autopsy noted considerable burn patterns on the head and left leg. Dr. Gary Cumberland told us, "From the injuries I saw, there would have been an incredible amount of heat generated at these points." Cumberland said, though, that he thought it was a painless death because of the speed with which electricity brings about unconsciousness.[13]

The state's chief prison administrator was even more emphatic. Commissioner Fred Smith told us, "He was dead on the first jolt. I am convinced that it was painless and it's the way to go."[14] Skeptics point to the fact that according to prison doctors, John Evans's heart continued to beat, and his lungs to breathe, until the third jolt of electricity was administered in the execution chamber at Holman Prison. He was pronounced dead after that third jolt, at 8:44 p.m.

In the search for "more humane" methods, eleven states adopted the use of lethal gas for varying periods of time. Nevada was in the forefront of this new movement, building a gas chamber in Carson City and executing a Chinese Tong War murderer, Gee Jon, in 1924. "Gee Jon nodded and went to sleep," reported the *Nevada State Journal*, "it was as simple and painless as that."[15]

But, as with electrocution, this new method experienced some early problems. When in 1936 North Carolina sealed Allen Foster into its execution chamber and released the lethal gas, he gasped and retched convulsively for more than three minutes before losing consciousness, according to the research of legal scholar and author Stuart Banner. He described the warden as "sickened."[16]

"Never again for me," the coroner told a local newspaper. "It's slow torture, and I cannot see anything humane about it." Another witness said it was "just hell."[17]

In California, the gasping and choking suffered by the first two men to be executed in the state's gas chamber were enough to nauseate prison employees who had witnessed hundreds of hangings.[18] Banner said the early executions by gas proved to be just as variable as those by electrocution: "Like the electric chair, the gas chamber sometimes inflicted pain, and when it did, the results were just as troubling to watch."[19]

As executioners gained experience with lethal gas, the process became more reliably swift and less visibly agonizing. But the unspoken element in the search for "more humane" methods of execution was the effect on executioners, prison staff, and witnesses, not simply the pain of the condemned. San Quentin's Clinton Duffy, the warden who presided over the gas chamber ninety times, said the executioner liked gas better "because he didn't feel so directly responsible for the death of the condemned. . . . Death by lethal gas was more mechanical," he said, "which made it less personal."[20]

The gas chamber was still regularly attacked as "cruel and unusual" punishment, though such appeals did not gain much traction at the Supreme Court. Public support was growing for an alternative chemical method, lethal injection.

Although he concurred in a 1992 Court decision allowing California to send murderer Robert Alton Harris (Chapter 3) to the gas chamber, Justice John Paul Stevens was troubled. He wrote, "Execution by cyanide gas is in essence 'asphyxiation by suffocation or strangulation.' [It] is extremely and unnecessarily painful." He essentially urged California to join the growing number of states utilizing lethal injection.[21]

Lethal injection, while hailed by its advocates as the most humane method of carrying out executions, was also not without its problems. The killing chemicals had to be delivered intravenously, and finding suitable veins was an often-difficult process that required basic medical training. But doctors and other medical professionals felt constrained from participating in these tasks by the codes of their professions. Officials often depended upon less-skilled personnel, such as paramedics, and some executions were delayed or complicated by difficulties in locating, and connecting to, an appropriate vein.

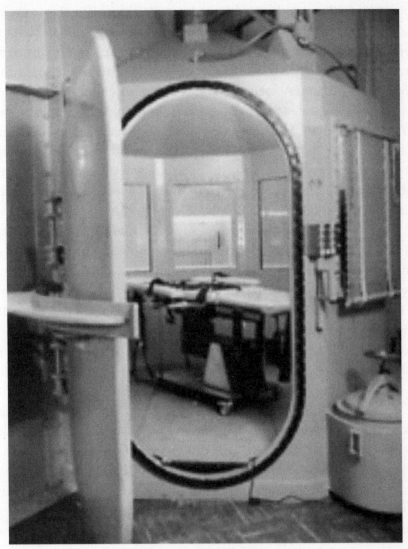

Figure 11.3. A gas chamber.

There was controversy, too, over the chemicals used. The Chapman-Deutsch formula, concocted in Oklahoma, called for a three-step process: first, a barbiturate (sodium thiopental) to induce a coma; then a paralytic agent (pancuronium bromide) to paralyze the body's muscles and interrupt breathing; and, finally, a dose of potassium chloride, which stops the heart.[22] Critics argue that we don't know for certain if the barbiturates produce a deep enough coma to prevent pain or sensation and that the use of pancuronium bromide as a paralytic is barbaric—its use is considered cruel by the American Veterinary Medical Association and is illegal for euthanizing animals in many of the states that use the same chemical for executions. But Dr. Jay Chapman, who developed the Chapman-Deutsch formula (still the most common formula in use), told us he is convinced the three-drug process is painless: "If the protocol is carried out properly, as it was set up, then there cannot be any possible issues of cruelty or unusual punishment or pain or suffering."[23]

Lethal injection faced a major Supreme Court test in 2008. Two Kentucky inmates, Ralph Baze and Thomas Bowling, claimed that the mixture of chemicals designed by Chapman posed a risk of excruciating pain—cruel and unusual punishment—if improperly administered. Their pleas to die painlessly point out a principal irony, paradoxically also a strength, of our system: brutal murderers are allowed to litigate for mercies they didn't grant their victims. Baze killed two police officers who were attempting to serve a warrant; Bowling shot and wounded a two-year-old, then orphaned the child by killing his parents.

The case for Baze and Bowling was argued (pro bono) by Donald B. Verrilli Jr., a high-profile Washington lawyer later to become U.S. Solicitor General. In 2012, he would successfully argue the watershed "Obamacare" case before the Supreme Court.[24]

During Verrilli's oral argument against Kentucky's lethal drug mixture, the subjects of pain and constitutionality prompted a courtroom dialogue that found the justices reaching back for comparisons:

Justice Alito: Isn't your position that every form of execution that has ever been used in the United States, if it were to be used today, would violate the Eighth Amendment?
Verrilli: No.
Alito: Well, which form that's been used at some time in an execution would not violate?

Verrilli: We would have to suggest it to the test that we are advocating, which it would . . . whether there is a risk of torturous pain.

Justice Scalia: Hanging certainly would, right?

Verrilli: Well, it would have to be subjected to the test.

Scalia: Is that a hard question? Is that a hard question, whether hanging would, whether you had experts who understood the dropweight, you know, that was enough that it would break the neck?

Verrilli: If there is a risk of torturous pain and if there are readily available alternatives that could obviate the risk, then any significant risk—

Scalia: Hanging's no good. What about electrocution?

Verrilli: Well, it would depend. The argument about electrocution, Justice Scalia, is whether or not it is painless, and that was its point when it was enacted, that it would be a painless form of death.

Scalia: It has to be, it has to be painless?

Verrilli: It does not, but that was its point, and I think one would have to subject it to the test to see whether it inflicts severe pain that is readily avoidable by an alternative.

Alito: You have no doubt that the three drug protocol that Kentucky is using violates the Eighth Amendment, but you really cannot express a judgment about any of the other methods that has ever been used?

Verrilli: Well, electrocution may well. But it would depend again, Your Honor. If it could be established that it was painless, that there wasn't a risk that it could go wrong in a way that inflicts excruciating pain then it would be upheld . . . but that would be the test, the mode of analysis here, and I—

Scalia: I would think you'd have to show it's unusual, not painless. I mean, cruel and unusual is what we're talking about—there's no painless requirement in there.[25]

In the end, the Court upheld Kentucky's chemical protocol by a vote of 7–2. (This is the same case, as noted in Chapter 8, that saw Justice Stevens reverse course on capital punishment.) Said Chief Justice Roberts in the controlling opinion: "Because some risk of pain is inherent in even the most humane execution method, if only from the prospect of error in following the required procedure, the Constitution does not demand the avoidance of all risk of pain."[26]

At this writing, Baze and Bowling still reside on Kentucky's death row. They have continued their fight against the three-drug system of lethal injection at the state level and could soon win the battle and lose their lives: Kentucky is considering following the lead of Ohio and Arizona in carrying out executions using one powerful sedative instead of the Chapman formula.

The search for the most efficient and "humane" method of execution, fine-tuning the process of death, continues.

12

"ACTUAL INNOCENCE"

I am innocent, innocent, innocent. . . . I am an innocent man, and something very wrong is taking place tonight.
—the last words of Leonel Torres Herrera,
spoken at the Texas State Penitentiary at
Huntsville at 4:35 a.m. on May 12, 1993

The last hour of Tuesday, September 29, 1981, was the last hour of Trooper David Rucker's life. The Texas Highway Patrol officer died shortly after 11:00 p.m.; his body was found on a stretch of rural highway east of Port Isabel and a few miles north of Brownsville. In the heart of the Rio Grande Valley, it was a dangerous neighborhood where drug trafficking was known to run rampant. Rucker, the father of three, was shot to death twenty-two days shy of his thirty-ninth birthday.

Only four minutes after Rucker's body was discovered, two police officers from the nearby town of Los Fresnos gave chase to a speeding car headed away from the place where the officer had been found. They pulled the car over and Officer Enrique Carrisalez approached the driver's side with a flashlight in hand. His partner, Enrique Hernandez, watched from the relative safety of their patrol car.

Hernandez saw the driver open the door and briefly exchange words with Carrisalez, and then he watched helplessly as the driver produced a gun and fired point-black at his partner. The car sped off; Carrisalez, hit in the chest, would die in the hospital nine days later.

A license-plate check revealed that the car belonged to the live-in girlfriend of Leonel Herrera, a thirty-four-year-old roofer. Hernandez identified Herrera as the shooter and, before he died, Carrisalez was shown a photograph of Herrera and nodded his head to confirm the identification. Herrera's Social Security card was found near Trooper Rucker's body, and blood of Rucker's type was later found on Herrera's jeans.

Figure 12.1. Trooper David Rucker.

When Herrera was arrested a week after the shootings, he still had the keys to the murder car in his pocket, as well as a rambling, handwritten letter in which he implied that he had known Officer Rucker and had killed him in connection with a perceived grudge, presumably a drug deal gone bad.

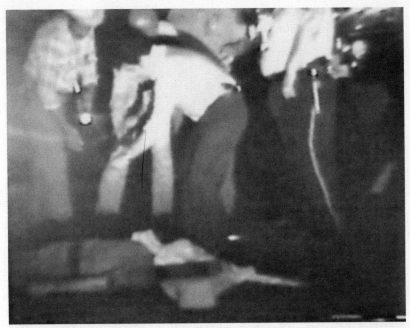

Figure 12.2. Texas state trooper Enrique Carrisalez died after
being shot by a motorist on September 29, 1981.

The cold-blooded killing of two local police officers ignited the community. Herrera would be charged separately with each murder and face trial within four months for the death of Officer Carrisalez. Every day of the trial, Texas law-enforcement officers showed up in force in full dress uniform. Even one of the jurors was a Brownsville police detective, his firearm in full display for the remaining jurors to see. Three other jurors were seated who had told the court that friends or close relatives were police officers.[1]

The case against Herrera was strong. In addition to the letter tying Herrera to both murders, investigators found small quantities of blood on Herrera's wallet and in his girlfriend's vehicle that matched Rucker's type-A blood. Herrera acknowledged that he had access to the car that was used in both murders but said that his brother was using it that night. As for the Social Security card found near Rucker's body, Herrera said he always kept the card in the glove compartment of the car.[2]

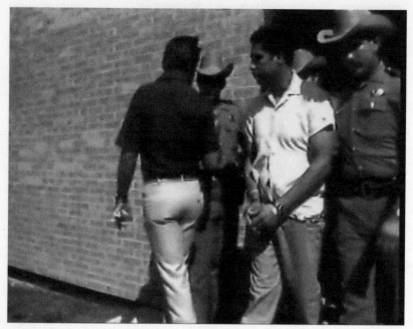

Figure 12.3. Leonel Hererra in custody.

While Herrera was in police custody and after he had invoked his right to counsel, an assistant district attorney walked into the interrogation room and asked Herrera why he had killed Officer Rucker. It was an improper inquiry for the DA to make. The law is clear that once a defendant requests an attorney, all questioning must cease. Herrera responded by jumping up and decking the attorney; he continued to beat the lawyer until forcibly restrained by police. The next morning, in a hospital room recovering from the incident, Herrera threatened to kill the police officers involved in his arrest upon his release. This did not help his case. He was convicted, and his attack on the assistant DA and threats to the police were introduced as evidence of Herrera's "future dangerousness" at the sentencing phase of his trial. Herrera was sentenced to death by lethal injection. Six months later, he pled guilty to Rucker's murder as well.

The case appeared to be open and shut—but Leonel Herrera would attempt to reopen it several times. He had an automatic right to review in the Texas Court of Criminal Appeals, the state's highest court for criminal matters. There, lawyers challenged the way in which the two officers had identified him—in Carrisalez's case, from his deathbed and with just a single photograph. Despite the challenge, the conviction and death sentence were affirmed. Herrera then appealed to the U.S. Supreme Court, which simply denied review, leaving the conviction and sentence intact.

In addition to direct appeals to the state's highest court and then the U.S. Supreme Court, a prison inmate can also challenge his conviction in both state and federal court if he can show that an aspect of his arrest or trial somehow violated the U.S. Constitution. The inmate submits what is called a petition for a writ of habeas corpus, the Latin words meaning essentially to "produce the body." Access to post-conviction habeas corpus review has long been controversial in capital cases. Critics say it allows for interminable delay, but others say it is essential to prevent death sentences from being meted out through an unfair—and unconstitutional—arrest or trial. Herrera had filed a number of such petitions, all of which failed. A new execution date was set for December 17, 1990. Herrera then filed yet another petition in the state courts, which again failed but allowed Herrera to put off his execution for more than a year. The next execution date was set for February 19, 1992.

The Texas Resource Center, a federally funded organization that represents most of the state's death row inmates, was severely strapped and turned to an experienced death-penalty litigator in Florida for help. Mark Olive had more than a decade of experience in the field and had previously served as director of the Texas Resource Center's sister facility in Georgia. Olive had followed closely the efforts of the Reagan administration to sharply reduce the opportunities for death-row inmates to delay execution through what many regarded as frivolous and unnecessary habeas petitions.[3]

Three days before Herrera was to be executed, Olive came up with yet another habeas petition raising a new claim that took all the judges and prosecutors familiar with the case quite by surprise—that Herrera was actually innocent, that he did not commit the murders but that his younger brother, Raul, did.

Figure 12.4. Attorney Hector Villareal.

Raul Herrera had died seven years earlier, shot to death by a former business partner who also may have been involved in the local drug trade.

But Leonel now produced affidavits from Raul's onetime lawyer, a former state-court judge, asserting that Raul Herrera had told him that he, not Leonel, had shot and killed both Rucker and Carrisalez. The lawyer, Hector Villareal, told Olive (and subsequently the authors) that the Herrera brothers were both involved in a drug-trafficking operation with Officer Rucker.[4]

Two other men, one of them a former cellmate, also claimed that Raul Herrera had confessed to them how he had shot the officers. Raul's son also provided an affidavit swearing that he, although only nine years old at the time, had witnessed his father commit both murders. According to the son, he had been hiding in the car his father was driving. (This contradicted the trial testimony of Enrique Hernandez that the killer was alone in the vehicle.)

Figure 12.5. Raul Herrera.

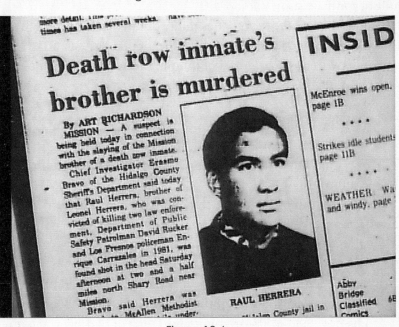

Figure 12.6.

The state district court again denied the application, finding that "no evidence at trial remotely suggested that anyone other than [Leonel Herrera] had committed the offense."[5] Having exhausted the state-court system, Olive had one last shot—that is, to file again in federal district court. Federal district judge Ricardo Hinojosa was skeptical but also troubled by the prospect, however slim, of executing an innocent person. Citing "a sense of fairness and due process," Hinojosa granted a stay so that Herrera's claim of actual innocence could be further considered. It would not be so simple.

Our criminal justice system leaves the determination of guilt to trial judges and juries. Whether the evidence was sufficient to support a conviction can be reviewed by a state's intermediate and supreme courts, and sometimes even by the U.S. Supreme Court. The standard for second-guessing a jury's verdict, however, is quite high. An appellate court does not sit as a thirteenth juror. It can only throw out a conviction on the grounds of insufficient evidence, should it conclude that "no rational trier of fact" could have found guilt beyond a reasonable doubt.[6]

Habeas review, however, does not ordinarily get into whether the defendant is guilty or innocent, only whether the arrest and trial were consistent with the guarantees of the Bill of Rights. Typical questions might include, for example, the following:

- Was the Fourth Amendment guarantee against unreasonable search and seizure violated?
- Was the Fifth Amendment guarantee against self-incrimination compromised?
- Did the defendant have the "effective assistance of counsel" guaranteed by the Sixth Amendment?

Herrera's lawyers argued that for the state to execute an individual who is innocent of the crime for which he was convicted and sentenced is *itself* a violation of the U.S. Constitution.[7]

It was now 8:30 in the evening and Herrera had been scheduled to be executed at dawn the following morning. The Texas Attorney General's Office immediately appealed Hinojosa's order to the Fifth U.S. Circuit Court of Appeals, which, within a few hours, lifted the stay. Herrera's execution was back on. The three-judge panel stated its decision in stark, unambiguous terms: "The rule is well-established that claims of newly discovered evidence, casting doubt on the petitioner's guilt, are not cognizable in federal habeas corpus."[8] Herrera's guilt had already been settled by the trial Court and could not be reconsidered by the federal court no matter how compelling the new evidence of innocence might be. That, said the judges, was the law.

At 11:00 p.m., attorney Mark Olive took his appeal for a stay to the U.S. Supreme Court. At 1:30 a.m., the media reported that the stay had been denied. Olive called the clerk's office, which was still staffed to handle this case, to learn the vote and was told it was 5–4 with Justices Sandra Day O'Connor, David Souter, John Paul Stevens and Harry Blackmun indicating they would have granted the stay.

Here, Olive's understanding of the internal workings of the Supreme Court took on special value. He was aware that it took five justices—a majority—to grant the stay and that he didn't have five. But he was also aware that it took only four justices to grant review of a case—that is, to accept it and schedule it for oral argument. And he did appear to have four justices who felt his argument was sound enough to grant a stay. He told the clerk that he wanted to convert his application for a stay into what is called a petition for certiorari, essentially, a request that the Court exercise its discretion to take the case. Olive handwrote his changes and faxed the new petition to the Court. It worked, sort of.

Reflecting the sharp divide within the Court on the use of successive habeas petitions in death-penalty cases, the Court accepted the case for later review but still refused to grant a stay. It was the legal equivalent of half a loaf, peculiar to the Supreme Court and a practice the Court has considered abolishing. Without a stay, Herrera would be executed in a matter of hours and his case would become moot. Olive, however, was ready for this. He and his team of lawyers were already scouring the Texas judiciary to find a state-court judge who, when told that the Supreme Court had accepted the case, would grant the stay to keep the case, not to mention Olive's client, alive.

In Texas, the vast majority of judges run for election—which didn't make the task any easier. Eventually they found two judges who would grant the stay (neither of whom would agree to do so separately), and Herrera's execution would be put on hold at least until the U.S. Supreme Court decided his case. It would be one of the first cases the justices would take up when the Court opened its new term the following October.

Figure 12.7. Delia Carrisalez.

The widow of Trooper Carrisalez spoke with the authors while the case was pending and she wept. "It just goes on and on and on. It just never ends."[9]

The risk of executing an innocent person has long been an important argument advanced by those who oppose capital punishment, and the leading anti-death-penalty groups pounced on the

Herrera case. Given the split vote denying the stay, Olive was well aware that his high Court argument would be a challenge, and he wanted an attorney of exceptional stature to present it to the justices. He didn't have to look far.

Talbot "Sandy" D'Alemberte, halfway through his term as president of the American Bar Association, maintained an office two blocks away from Olive's and would be just such a choice. Olive knew D'Alemberte from the latter's days as dean of the law school at Florida State University, where they had worked together on death-penalty appeals almost twenty years earlier. D'Alemberte, who went on to become president of FSU, was also highly regarded in the legal community for both his intellect and his integrity.

D'Alemberte spent much of the summer of 1992 scrupulously preparing for his high Court argument, including making a visit to the Rio Grande Valley and his new client, Leonel Herrera. He believed in Herrera's innocence and in the valley's reputation for drug violence. More than ten years had passed since Officers Carrisalez and Rucker had been shot to death, but D'Alemberte said he could still feel the tension in the community. "It was a violent, violent place. I detected a widespread perception of corruption within the sheriff's office. I felt uncomfortable and out of place. It was just spooky."[10]

After carefully studying the trial record, D'Alemberte felt that he might be able to pair Herrera's "colorable claim" of actual innocence with a constitutional violation. He initially believed that allowing a police officer to serve on the jury along with three other jurors who had close connections to law enforcement was so prejudicial that it might amount to ineffective assistance of counsel in violation of Sixth Amendment guarantees. After his visit, however, he concluded that having jurors who understood local law enforcement and its reputation for corruption might not have been such a bad strategy after all.

His argument in the Supreme Court got off to an inauspicious start.[11] Justice O'Connor seemed to view the question presented—whether the state could execute an individual who is innocent—as an oxymoron. She asked D'Alemberte, "Now you don't really think that's the way the case comes to us, do you? He comes to us as a guilty defendant. He has been found guilty." Herrera had been tried and convicted and sentenced. The conviction and sentence had been reviewed by the state's highest court. At least for this justice, that seemed to be the end of it. In the eyes of the law, Herrera was guilty.

D'Alemberte had anticipated the question and viewed getting the answer right as crucial. He had gone through a number of mock arguments with panels of distinguished lawyers in Florida, Georgia, and Washington, DC, in preparation for his argument in the Supreme Court. O'Connor's question was anticipated in each rehearsal. The answer D'Alemberte wanted to give was that Joan of Arc was also found guilty and burned at the stake at age nineteen for witchcraft and heresy. She's been considered one of the world's great martyrs ever since and was beatified by the Roman Catholic Church as a saint five hundred years later.

The panels D'Alemberte appeared before—which included some of the leading figures in the anti-death-penalty movement—didn't care for the reference. Leonel Herrera bore a striking *non*-resemblance to Joan of Arc, and some of D'Alemberte's mock inquisitors felt the analogy could rub some justices the wrong way. So D'Alemberte took their advice. "I recognized that many people had a great deal invested in this case and didn't want me screwing it up."

Twenty years after the fact, he lamented not using the Joan of Arc comparison. The point was not at all that Herrera was like Saint Joan. The point was that if even a courageous heroine could be wrongly convicted, a saint, so can anybody; and federal courts should have the power to undo the damage.

D'Alemberte's advice to lawyers arguing big cases in the Supreme Court is that you do have to listen to those around you, "but in the end you have to decide for yourself what is right, what will work."

Most states have strict time limits on the use of newly discovered evidence in petitions for a new trial. In Texas and a majority of states, a request for a new trial on the basis of newly discovered evidence must be submitted within thirty days of the conviction. The rationale is that there has to be some finality in court judgments, even death sentences, or the legal system would degenerate into chaos with each losing party seeking to reopen old cases.

Figure 12.8. Talbot "Sandy" D'Alemberte and coauthor Tim O'Brien leaving the Supreme Court following arguments in *Herrera v. Collins*, October 7, 1992.

But it wasn't just the thirty-day time limit that troubled D'Alemberte. Justice Byron White asked, "Would you be making this argument if Texas had a . . . say a 5-year time limit?" D'Alemberte responded, "Yes, sir. Your Honor, I believe that innocence is a value which trumps all other time limits."

Justice O'Connor pressed D'Alemberte to state precisely the rule he would have the Court adopt. D'Alemberte answered: "The rule that we would suggest is the rule that says that an inmate with a colorable claim of innocence may not be executed without provision for a hearing, due process to determine the merits of that claim—"

Justice Anthony Kennedy interrupted, "And if they commuted his sentence to life, then that would be the end of the case?" D'Alemberte: "That would be the end of this case, Your Honor. . . . I don't—"

Justice Antonin Scalia, who clearly was not persuaded, saw an opening. "That's not cruel and unusual? That's not cruel and unusual to leave him in prison for life although he has a colorable [claim of innocence]."

D'Alemberte replied that he didn't know how far the Eighth Amendment would go to protect a convicted person who had a "colorable claim" of innocence but that it at least must go far enough to prevent his execution. The prospect of countless new hearings to reconsider guilt and D'Alemberte's inability to articulate any limiting principle to the rule he sought weighed heavily on Scalia. "I think one has to consider how much damage we do to the system of criminal justice if we apply it across the board to all prisoners, no matter how much after the fact they choose to bring in new evidence raising a colorable claim of innocence. The witnesses from the prior trial are dead or gone. The burden this would put upon a system of justice is enormous."

Scalia was moving in for the kill. He got D'Alemberte to acknowledge that no state required the kind of new hearing to determine guilt that he, D'Alemberte, claimed the Constitution required and that such post-conviction hearings were unheard of in Anglo-Saxon common law. "What basis do you have for it other than your intuition?" D'Alemberte responded: "Your Honor, when I read the phrases used by this Court referring to miscarriages of justice and I began to put in my mind what is the greatest possible miscarriage of justice, it occurs to me that the greatest one that I could formulate would be the execution of an innocent person or the execution of a person who had a colorable claim of innocence. You would not want that person to be executed without hearing that case."

Justice Kennedy was similarly skeptical: "So, in other words, you have two shots at the judicial system? You can elect a strategy that fails and then because you're really innocent, you can start all over again? You can double deal the judicial system in that way just because death is at issue?" D'Alemberte again: "And because innocence is a paramount value, yes, Your Honor."

In one respect, the Court may have been between the proverbial rock and hard place. What if an individual convicted of a murder in the course of a robbery and sentenced to death could actually demonstrate that he was an astronaut on the moon at the time of the crime? Would Texas still be allowed to go through with the execution? It is a highly unrealistic hypothetical, but what if? The thought had occurred to Justice Kennedy, who asked Margaret Griffey, the assistant attorney general representing Texas, "Suppose you have a video tape which conclusively shows the person is innocent, and you have a state which as a matter of policy or law, or both, simply does not hear new evidence claims in its clemency proceeding. Is there a federal constitutional violation in your view?"

Griffey: "No, Your Honor, there is not." It turned out some justices agreed with Griffey, but not all.

 For a video report on the *Herrera* Supreme Court case, go to: http://murderatthesupremecourt.com/herrera

The Court announced its decision on January 25,[12] a relatively short turnaround for such an important case. It rejected Herrera's arguments. Chief Justice William Rehnquist, writing for a six-justice majority, said that absent some claim of a federal constitutional violation, the federal courts simply did not have the authority to even consider Herrera's "free-standing claim" of actual innocence. The court noted that the trial is the "paramount event for determining the defendant's guilt or innocence" and that Herrera's claims had to be evaluated "in light of the previous ten years of proceedings in this case. . . . Where, as here, a defendant has been afforded a fair trial and convicted of the offense for which he was charged, the constitutional presumption of innocence disappears."

Justice Blackmun wrote a passionate dissent that was joined by Justices Stevens and Souter. Blackmun concluded, "Just as an execution without adequate safeguards is unacceptable, so too is an execution when the condemned prisoner can prove that he is innocent. The execution of a person who can show that he is innocent comes perilously close to simple murder."[13]

The decision did leave Herrera an out. He could petition then governor Ann Richards for clemency; however, clemency was generally considered an empty remedy in Texas, which, since the Supreme Court reinstated capital punishment in 1976, had been putting more inmates to death than any other state. During the oral argument in the case, counsel for Texas acknowledged there had not been a death-penalty commutation in the state in the past fifteen to eighteen years. In Texas, executive clemency requires a recommendation from the Board of Pardons and Appeals and then action by the governor. Leonel Herrera received no clemency; he was executed by lethal injection on May 12, 1993.

 To see a preview of the Supreme Court's arguments in the *Herrera* case, go to: http://abcnews.go.com/Politics/video/tim-obrien-herrera-collins-17067566

The case produced six different opinions, and while the result for Herrera was clear—the state of Texas could proceed with his execution—the collection of opinions did not clearly answer the question Justice Kennedy had posed during oral argument regarding the plainly innocent inmate.

Justice White, in a separate concurring opinion, suggested a federal habeas court could stop an execution if it found that "no reasonable trier of fact" would have found the defendant guilty beyond a reasonable doubt. But no other justice joined White's opinion. Chief Justice Rehnquist, in his opinion for the Court, wrote that if the Court were to assume for the sake of argument that a posttrial demonstration of actual innocence would render an execution unconstitutional, Herrera's innocence claims fell far short. Rehnquist concluded that the threshold of proof "would necessarily be extraordinarily high because of the very disruptive effect that entertaining such claims would have on the need for finality in capital cases, and the enormous burden that having to retry cases based on often stale evidence would place on the states."[14]

Justice Scalia wrote separately to ridicule the dissenting justices. "If the system that has been in place for 200 years 'shocks' the dissenters' consciences, perhaps they should doubt the calibration of their consciences, or, better still, the usefulness of 'conscience shocking' as a legal test." Scalia concluded, "With any luck, we shall avoid ever having to face this embarrassing question again, since it is improbable that evidence of innocence as convincing as today's opinion requires would fail to produce an executive pardon."[15]

The decision, however, did little to dilute the long-standing concerns about the risk of error that some see as inherent in capital punishment. It continues to be one of the leading arguments advanced by opponents. Nor did the *Herrera* decision spare the Court from "ever having to face this embarrassing question again," as Justice Scalia had hoped. In fact, one of the side effects of the *Herrera* case may have been to demonstrate the effectiveness, if not the necessity, of adding an actual innocence claim in any federal death-penalty appeal. For one, Congress amended the federal habeas statute to prohibit federal courts from considering a second, or successive, petition from death-row inmates absent a plausible claim of innocence.[16] A plausible claim of innocence, and even one not so plausible, can also draw a faithful following in support of a lesser sentence.

The case of *O'Dell v. Netherland*,[17] which reached the Supreme Court in the fall of 1996, is illustrative.[18] Forty-four-year-old Helen Schartner left the County Line Lounge in Virginia Beach at about 11:30 p.m. on

February 5, 1985. Joseph O'Dell left the same club a few minutes later. The following day, Schartner's body was discovered in a muddy area across the highway from the nightclub. Tire tracks that matched the tires on O'Dell's car were discovered near Schartner's body.

Schartner had been strangled. She also had been pistol whipped, sustaining eight blows to the head, which had produced extensive bleeding. A handgun had been seen in O'Dell's car about ten days prior to the murder.

A few hours after leaving the County Line Lounge, O'Dell showed up at a convenience store with blood on his face and hands, in his hair, and down the front of his clothes. Later in the morning, he turned up at the home of a former girlfriend, Connie Craig, explaining that he had vomited blood all over his clothes and wanted her help in cleaning them up. Craig, however, had read about the murder at the County Line Lounge in the newspapers, knew that the lounge was a favorite watering hole of O'Dell, and called the police a few days later.

O'Dell explained to police that the blood on his clothing was the result of being struck in the nose while trying to stop a fight at another club the previous evening.

Forensic evidence established that the dried blood on O'Dell's shirt and jacket was the same type as Schartner's. (O'Dell's blood type was not the same as Schartner's, thus proving that it could not have been his own.) O'Dell's car was later seized, and dried blood found on objects in the car also had several enzyme markers consistent with Schartner's blood, but not O'Dell's. Vaginal and anal swabs disclosed the presence of seminal fluid in the victim's vagina and anus containing enzymes consistent with those in O'Dell's seminal fluid. A fellow jailhouse inmate, Steven Watson, testified that O'Dell admitted strangling Schartner after she refused to have sex with him.

At the time of Helen Schartner's death, O'Dell was on parole for kidnapping a convenience-store clerk at gunpoint. He had threatened to rape and kill her. He had spent much of his adult life in prison, where he had killed another inmate.[19] At the sentencing phase of O'Dell's trial for Schartner's murder, the jury learned of his troubled past and cited O'Dell's "future dangerousness" as an aggravating circumstance that would justify his death sentence.

At the time of his trial in 1986, DNA testing was still in its infancy and the blood-matching methods in use at the time were not nearly as reliable as what would soon become available. Given his consistent claims of innocence, DNA testing was permitted on O'Dell's clothing four years after the conviction, in 1990. It turned out that the blood on O'Dells shirt—contrary to what the jury was told at the trial— did not match either the victim or O'Dell. Although the DNA tests showed that numerous bloodstains on O'Dell's jacket did match that of the victim, O'Dell and his lawyers claimed the misidentified blood on his shirt exonerated him. The state of Virginia, they claimed, was about to execute an innocent man.

There was another, more persuasive issue surrounding O'Dell's death sentence. Eight years after O'Dell's trial, the U.S. Supreme Court ruled in *Simmons v. South Carolina*[20] that whenever "future dangerousness" is offered as an aggravating circumstance in support of a death sentence, the jury must be told if the defendant would be forever ineligible for parole if given a life sentence. Lawyers for O'Dell had asked for just such an instruction from the judge in his case, but the request had been denied. The jury was never told that if it returned a verdict of less than death, O'Dell would never be released from prison. The somewhat technical—but nonetheless crucial—question for the U.S. Supreme Court was whether its decision in the *Simmons* case should be applied retroactively to hundreds of other inmates sentenced to death by juries that had never received the instruction the Supreme Court now ruled was required by the U.S. Constitution.[21]

It was, however, the more inflammatory question of whether the United States could execute a man who had a plausible claim that he was wrongly convicted that caught fire. That was the way O'Dell supporters framed the issue, even though the trial judge and thirteen Virginia appeals-court judges concluded that O'Dell was guilty beyond a reasonable doubt, notwithstanding the misidentified blood sample from his shirt.

It may have started when O'Dell created his own Internet website to promote his case. Amnesty International, which opposes the death penalty in all cases, also took on a leading role in publicizing the innocence issue. It became a cause célèbre in Italy. The Vatican got involved, with Pope John Paul II sending personal letters to Virginia governor George Allen and President Bill Clinton urging clemency. Top Italian politicians followed, with President Oscar Luigi Scalfano and Prime Minister Romano Prodi speaking out on behalf of O'Dell. So did Mother Teresa, winner of the Nobel Peace Prize. Sister Helen Prejean wrote critically about the *O'Dell* case in her books *Death of Innocents*[22] and *Dead Man Walking*,[23] the latter of which formed the basis for the highly acclaimed motion picture of the same name.

Did any of this help? Probably not; although the Court did agree to hear O'Dell's appeal. When justices deny review to a case, it is not unusual for a justice to issue a dissent explaining why he or she thought the case should have been accepted. In the *O'Dell* case, Justice Scalia took the most unusual—to the authors, unheard-of—step of issuing a statement criticizing, and clarifying, the *grant* of review.[24] Scalia pointed out that the Court agreed to review only the question about the retroactivity of *Simmons v. South Carolina* and that the Court specifically did not intend to consider O'Dell's claim of actual innocence. Scalia is a devout Roman Catholic, and some Court insiders viewed his unusual opinion as, at least in effect if not in intent, a personal letter to the pope. Scalia would subsequently give a talk arguing that the question of capital punishment is not one on which the pope's word is decisive for Catholics.[25]

For a video report on the *O'Dell* Supreme Court case, go to:
http://murderatthesupremecourt.com/odell

Six months later, the Court issued its decision finding that the *Simmons* decision should not be applied retroactively, setting the stage for O'Dell's execution.[26] His last day alive was July 23, 1997. It was a day of vivid contrasts at the Greensville Correctional Center, just outside Jarratt, Virginia.

Shortly after noon, O'Dell was married to a Boston law student, Lori Urs, whom he had met through Sister Prejean's ministry. The ceremony was conducted through the bars of O'Dell's cell in the prison's L Unit, just steps from the execution chamber. The bride had been strip-searched on entering the unit; she and O'Dell were not allowed to touch during the ceremony. The rings were exchanged by proxy: Sister Prejean for the bride, a chaplain for the groom.[27]

Joseph O'Dell was put to death by lethal injection at 9:16 p.m., after the Supreme Court rejected a last-minute appeal. Lori Urs O'Dell, married for less than ten hours, was now a widow. The Court simply did not find O'Dell's claim of actual innocence convincing, just as it was not persuaded by Leonel Herrara's claim. In the *Herrera* case, however, as we'll see shortly, the Court did seem to leave the door open for reconsideration in a truly compelling case. In fact, actual innocence is an issue that is all but certain to dog the Court in years to come.

The U.S. criminal-justice system has entered an age where proof equivalent to being on the moon at the time of the crime is not completely unrealistic. While Herrera's claims were based on affidavits, legal instruments that for all of their weaknesses have an acknowledged place in the legal system, future cases will involve new forensic findings and technologies that are reshaping—and in some cases, redefining—criminal prosecution.

The "gold standard" of scientific evidence in the courtroom—as well as on *Law & Order, CSI*, and its television forebears—used to be fingerprint identification. No more. The courts have held that fingerprint comparison has components of art as well as science. Stephan Cowans spent seven years in a Massachusetts prison for the shooting of a Boston police officer, convicted primarily on the testimony of a fingerprint examiner who "matched" his print to one at a crime scene. The later testing of DNA strands, the genetic blueprints unique to individuals, proved the examiner wrong and proved Cowans's innocence.[28]

Hair and fiber comparisons are also subjective. In July of 2012, the Justice Department began a review of thousands of cases, going back to at least 1985, where convictions were obtained because of possibly flawed forensic examinations conducted by the prestigious FBI Laboratory.[29]

Arson evidence also relies heavily on interpretation. Cameron Willingham was executed in Texas in 2004 for the arson murders of his three young daughters. Months after his execution, five independent experts issued a report questioning the validity of the arson evidence and forensic testimony used to convict Willingham. Texas authorities have begun a reexamination of the state's forensic procedures.[30]

The reviews of the *Cowans* and *Willingham* cases were prompted by the Innocence Project, which has overturned almost three hundred felony convictions by uncovering new evidence and discrediting old evidence, primarily through DNA testing—the new "platinum standard" of forensic evidence.

The Innocence Project was born at Yeshiva University's Cardozo School of Law in 1992, the brainchild of faculty members Barry Scheck and Peter Neufeld. Now an independent nonprofit, although closely affiliated with Cardozo, it seeks to overturn wrongful convictions and to reform the criminal justice system.[31]

Since 1993, with the advent of DNA testing, and primarily through the work of the Innocence Project, seventeen condemned prisoners have been exonerated. *Exonerated*—as in, their convictions were not overturned because of a procedural error or legal technicality; instead, scientific evidence demonstrated conclusively that the accused had not committed the crimes for which they had been convicted. Although innocent of those crimes, they had been condemned to death.

Those seventeen condemned inmates had been convicted in eleven states and served a total of 187 years on death row. For one of them, exoneration came too late: Frank Lee Smith died in a Florida prison of cancer in January 2000 after serving fourteen years on

Florida's death row. DNA evidence subsequently showed he could not have committed the crime.[32]

 To view a PBS *Frontline* documentary on the Frank Smith case, go to: http://murderatthesupremecourt.com/smith

Frank Smith escaped the executioner because of a terminal disease; but for DNA testing, some or all of the sixteen other exonerated prisoners could well have been put to death.

Some proponents of capital punishment say, "So what?" They argue that, while mistakes were made in a limited number of cases, the system generally works. They challenge the opposition to identify a single case where a clearly innocent person has ever been executed.

That is difficult to do, but new evidence indicates that the Texas execution of Carlos DeLuna in 1989 may well be that case.[33]

DeLuna was convicted of the stabbing murder of Wanda Lopez, a twenty-four-year-old single mother who was tending the cash register at a gas station and convenience store. A chilling 9-1-1 recording begins with Lopez reporting a man with a knife threatening her, and it ends with Lopez pleading for her life. "Please!" she screams . . . and the phone goes silent.

A customer pumping gas outside, Kevan Baker, saw a scuffle and ran toward the door, briefly establishing what he called "eye-to-eye contact" with the fleeing attacker. Lopez slipped into unconsciousness as Baker reached her.

Forty minutes later, police arrested Carlos DeLuna, then twenty years old, after dragging him, drunk and disoriented, from under a pickup truck found several blocks away from the gas station. He matched several elements of descriptions provided by Baker and two other witnesses who saw a Hispanic man near the gas station. DeLuna had been arrested many times previously for public drunkenness; he had also served prison time for attempted rape and car theft. Police hustled him to a squad car and drove back to the gas station.

Figure 12.9. Scene of the crime: the Sigmor Shamrock gas station.

Researchers from Columbia University's law school have put together an exhaustive study of events following Wanda Lopez's death on the night of February 4, 1983. Under the direction of Professor James S. Liebman, they reconstructed the sequence of events by combing all the law-enforcement files in the case and directly reinterviewing the participants. The book-length report, titled *Los Tocayos Carlos*, was published in the *Columbia Human Rights Law Review* in the spring of 2012. Details of the case discussed here can be found in full in that report.

Kevan Baker recalled the night vividly when he talked with a private investigator connected with the Columbia project. He was at the gas station when officers arrived with a suspect in the backseat of their car. "Is this the guy you seen?" a police lieutenant had asked him. "Yeah, that's the guy," Baker had said. Later, at the station house, two other witnesses identified DeLuna's picture from a photo array. DeLuna was booked for capital murder.

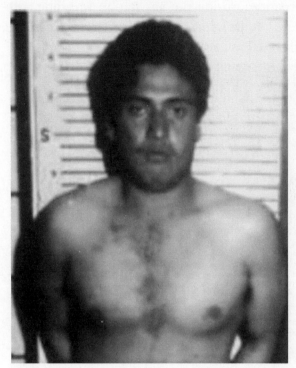

Figure 12.10. Carlos DeLuna at the police station.

"It was really tough," Baker told the Columbia investigator, but "it seemed like the right guy." It was also tough identifying DeLuna in court, Baker said, looking back, "But it just seemed right." His voice trailed off as he added, "Whether I was right or wrong . . ."

George Aguirre, another gas-station customer, also identified DeLuna as he sat in the squad car. But when he testified at DeLuna's trial, he balked: "I'm not too sure."

There was no forensic evidence introduced at the trial that linked DeLuna to the victim or the crime scene. No blood traces were found, either on his body or on the clothing police recovered near the location of his arrest. This, despite widespread patterns of pooled and spattered blood near Lopez's body.

At his trial, DeLuna testified that he had been on the street near Lopez's gas station, and that he had seen another man he knew, Carlos Hernandez, inside the gas station wrestling with a woman. Asked why he left, DeLuna said, "I know I got a record . . . I just kept running because I was scared, you know?"

Figure 12.11. Police crime-scene photographs.

Members of the jury may have reacted the same way Wanda's cousin, Becky Nesbitt, did as she heard DeLuna testify: "When Carlos DeLuna said that he did not do it, that it was another Carlos, when I heard that at the trial I thought, that's just a lie."

The jury deliberated for four hours, and during their deliberations the prosecutor offered to take the death penalty off the table in exchange for a guilty plea. DeLuna refused, proclaiming his innocence. When the jury returned to the courtroom, the verdict was read aloud: "The defendant, Carlos DeLuna, is guilty of capital murder as alleged in the indictment." And after a sentencing hearing, the same jury condemned him to death.

Judge Wallace Moore would later set the jury's verdict into motion with this formal, stark order:

> CARLOS DE LUNA . . . shall before the hour of sunrise on Wednesday, the 15th day of October A.D., 1986 at the state penitentiary at Huntsville, Texas, be caused to die by intravenous injection of a substance or substances in a lethal quantity sufficient to cause death into the body of the said Carlos De Luna.

The date was delayed several times by appeals, but the order of the court was finally carried out at 12:14 a.m. on December 7, 1989. The apparent truth of Carlos DeLuna's innocence surfaced only later.

The man DeLuna had accused of the crime, Carlos Hernandez, confessed to several relatives and friends that he murdered Wanda Lopez. The investigators from the Columbia Law School research project documented and cross-checked those confessions meticulously; the details of each account held up. The wooden-handled, seven-inch buck knife that was recovered at the crime scene was identified by a score of Hernandez's associates, friends, and relatives, as well as by police officers who had previously arrested him, as the type of knife he habitually carried. Despite dozens of arrests, DeLuna was never known to carry or use a knife or a weapon of any kind. A careful review of the witnesses' descriptions of the sloppily dressed, mustachioed man they saw reveals that their descriptions do not match

DeLuna, who was clean-shaven and in dress clothes when he was arrested nearby. His clothes didn't have a speck of blood on them, despite the blood-drenched crime scene. The witnesses' descriptions matched Hernandez's characteristic dress and grooming to a T.

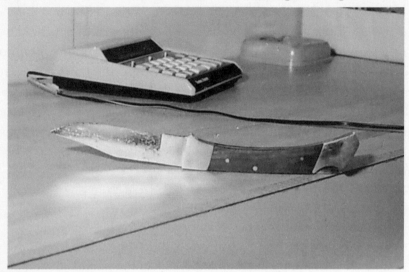

Figure 12.12. Photograph of the murder weapon.

The law school investigators used a photograph of the murder weapon; the original weapon was lost or misplaced after the trial, along with all of the physical evidence in the case, by the District Attorney's Office. But even Hernandez's own lawyer, Jon Kelly, had no doubt about the knife in the photograph: "Yes. He (Hernandez) had that on him all the time," he said. There was no way to conduct scientific tests on the knife, of course—the evidence had vanished.

Carlos DeLuna was convicted largely on the basis of the testimony of a single eyewitness to the crime. But any confusion by witnesses was understandable: relatives of both men described them as "tocayos"—twins. They were the same weight and height and looked very much alike. When investigators showed a picture of DeLuna to Hernandez's brother-in-law, Fernando Schilling, he first identified it as Hernandez. Told of his mistake, he said, "Man, he's a ringer [for] Carlos Hernandez. That gives me the goose bumps."

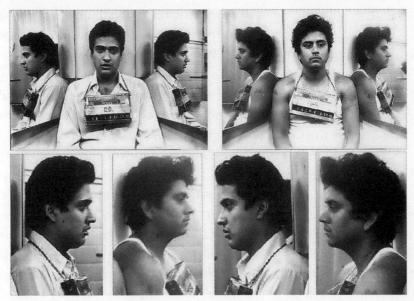

Figure 12.13. Carlos DeLuna *(left)*; Carlos Hernandez *(right)*.

Hernandez was both amoral and brutal. Throughout his life, he had raped and abused children, including his nine-year-old niece and younger brother. He had an extensive felony record, including prison terms for gas-station armed robberies and assault with a deadly weapon (a knife). He was found guilty of negligent homicide in an automobile death, and he narrowly escaped a murder conviction in the knifing death of a girlfriend. He was, his friends said, "a really mean guy" and "a badass." A police officer was even more direct, calling him a "mean motherfucker."

Hernandez would eventually die in prison of cirrhosis of the liver. He was serving a sentence for assault—his thirteenth arrest while carrying a knife. His mother refused to claim the body, allowing her son to be buried in a pauper's grave. "Dirt is dirt," she said.

The mistakes made in the prosecution of Carlos DeLuna are beyond remedy. The flaws in the evidence and the sloppiness by police and prosecutors, combined with lackluster defense, worked to send him to the death chamber. The eyewitness testimony against him turned out to be incorrect. The careful documentation of the Columbia investigation lead to the inescapable conclusion that the wrong man was put to death for Wanda Lopez's murder.

The claim of Carlos DeLuna's innocence was not asserted before his death and, accordingly, never reached the Supreme Court. But the case of Leonel Herrara will almost certainly not be the last to be considered by the Court on the grounds of "absolute innocence."

The Supreme Court will inevitably deal with that claim again, in the context of new and emerging technologies. However, the Court will not rush to either consideration or judgment; the institution is traditionally deliberate. It is no architectural accident that stone turtles are found in numerous locations around the iconic Supreme Court building, supporting lampposts at the entrances and exit at the ground level, and on one of the corners on the Second Street side. Justice Scalia once remarked in an interview, "Yes, we're slow, just like the turtle. But when was the last time you saw a turtle trip?"[34]

Both sides in the landmark *Herrera* case left the door open for future consideration. Justice Blackmun, voicing disappointment as he dissented, wrote, "I believe it contrary to any standard of decency to execute someone who is actually innocent. . . . I also believe that [a] petitioner may raise an Eighth Amendment challenge to his punishment on the ground that he is actually innocent."[35]

Supporting the majority, Justice O'Connor was nevertheless clear about the limitations of the *Herrera* ruling and about its implications: "The Court has no reason to pass on, and appropriately reserves, the question whether federal courts may entertain convincing claims of actual innocence. That difficult question remains open."[36]

13

INEFFECTIVE ASSISTANCE OF COUNSEL

WORST CRIMES?...OR JUST WORST LAWYERS?

> *So long as juries and judges are deprived of crucial infor-*
> *mation and the Bill of Rights is ignored . . . the death*
> *penalty will continue to be imposed, not upon those who*
> *commit the worst crimes, but upon those who have the*
> *misfortune to be assigned the worst lawyers.*
> —Stephen Bright, president and senior counsel
> for the Southern Center for Human Rights,
> in the *Yale Law Journal* 103 (1994)

Assume the following: You don't have a lot of money. You've led an exemplary life. But for one reason or another, you're wrongfully charged with a heinous crime. You're on trial for your life, and your lawyer shows up drunk or falls asleep, snoring loudly as the prosecution makes out its case against you. Assume for a moment you're a poor black man in Georgia and your lawyer turns out to be the former imperial wizard of the state Ku Klux Klan, who refers to you as a "nigger" in open court. Far fetched? Not at all. All of the above have occurred and, in each case, resulted in a death sentence. It is scandalous and it continues today.[1]

The Sixth Amendment to the U.S. Constitution guarantees all criminal defendants the effective assistance of counsel. Most of the defendants whose crimes have been recounted in this book have had good lawyers representing them at trial, some have even had outstanding lawyers arguing their appeals. Many capital defendants do get the kind of representation the Constitution requires. Alas, far too many do not. This chapter borrows heavily from the groundbreaking work of Stephen Bright and the Southern Center for Human Rights, which has taken a leading national role in promoting fairness and due process of law to those least able to afford adequate legal representation. The authors acknowledge their deep debt.

As discussed below, some of the nation's most prominent jurists and lawyers have recognized the problem of inadequate representation to poor people generally, and especially to those who are on trial for their lives, but little has been accomplished to remedy the problem. The Supreme Court has reviewed a number of cases involving standards for gauging the level of competency required of counsel in capital cases. The justices have had a wide range of opportunities to clarify the issue. The line between what is acceptable and what is not when a defendant's life is on the line, however, remains murky.

The case of George McFarland would seem to have presented an easy test.[2] McFarland was charged with capital murder arising out of the armed robbery of a grocery store in Houston, Texas. Kenneth Kwan had run the C&Y Food Center in Houston's low-income Trinity Gardens neighborhood for seventeen years. He knew that on Fridays, many customers would cash their payroll checks at his store. His routine was to go to the bank on Friday mornings accompanied by a security guard, James Powell, and withdraw enough cash to cover all the checks. Powell would carry a shotgun. On this particular Friday, November 15, 1991, they arrived back at the store to find two armed, young black men waiting for them.

As Kwan and Powell got out of their van, one of the men approached the security guard, pulled out a handgun, held it to the guard's head, and threatened, "Drop the gun. Drop the gun. If you don't, I'll blow your goddamned brains out." Powell said he complied but then heard a series of shots—"*pop, pop*"—fired at Kwan, who had rushed toward the store door. The two men ran off with $27,000 in cash, leaving Kwan bleeding to death on the sidewalk.

McFarland was arrested after his twenty-year-old nephew, Craig Burks, called Crime Stoppers to report that McFarland had boasted of holding up a grocery store and had displayed large quantities of cash. Crime Stoppers had paid Burks $900 for the tip; it turns out that Burks was also offered a reduced sentence on a separate aggravated robbery charge in return for his testimony.

The only other evidence against McFarland was from an eyewitness, Carolyn Bartie, who was sitting in her car outside the store about to buy some stamps when the shooting unfolded. She told detectives at the time that everything had happened so fast, she did not think she could identify either of the assailants. A month later, however, Bartie, who worked for the Houston Police Department in a secretarial capacity, tentatively identified McFarland as the shooter from a display of photos of six individuals. She subsequently picked him out at a lineup and identified him at trial. The security guard, James Powell, also testified at McFarland's trial. Asked if he saw the man who shot Kwan seated in the courtroom, Powell responded "No, I do not." Enough to create a reasonable doubt?

There was no forensic evidence connecting McFarland with the murder. No fingerprints. No murder weapon. Bartie initially told police that the man who shot Kwan was about five feet eight inches tall and weighed about 150 pounds. McFarland is six feet one and weighs over 200 pounds. He has consistently maintained his innocence.

Texas has no public-defender system for capital cases, and the court-appointed lawyers in Harris County had a reputation for moving capital cases through the system swiftly. Some of the lawyers favored by judges (but heavily criticized by the local bar) would be handling a dozen capital cases at the same time. Aware of this, McFarland scraped up all his money to hire his own attorney.

The idea was sound, but the selection of seventy-two-year-old John Benn turned out to be a fatally bad choice. Benn had forty-two years of trial experience but hadn't tried a capital case in the last twenty. He'd been around the block a few times, perhaps a few times too many. The trial judge, Doug Shaver, said later, "I knew John Benn. I knew he wasn't competent." Shaver said Benn had the appearance of a heavy drinker. "His clothes looked like he slept in them. He was very red-faced; he had protruding veins in his nose and watery red eyes. . . . I can't imagine anyone hiring him for a serious case."[3]

Benn spent only about four hours preparing for the trial. He failed to interview any of the witnesses. He prepared no motions and sought no subpoenas. Instead, he relied exclusively on what was in the prosecutor's file. He never went to the crime scene. He visited McFarland only twice prior to the trial.[4]

If the pretrial work was lacking (and it clearly was), the performance at the actual trial was even worse.

Benn slept through critical portions, including jury selection, at the very start of the trial, and at the end during the penalty phase. It was not just an occasional doze. The sleep was often accompanied by loud snoring. Benn did not deny it. At a posttrial hearing, Benn explained, "I customarily take a short nap in the afternoon." In an interview with the authors, Benn said he found the penalty phase of the trial "boring." We reminded Benn that this was the part of the trial when the jury would decide whether McFarland would live or die, that it wouldn't be boring for his client. Benn conceded, "No, it would not." McFarland's life was on the line. "Yes, it was."[5]

Speaking from death row at the Polunsky Correctional Center in West Livingston, Texas, McFarland told us that he was furious with his lawyer but didn't know how to show it, fearing the impact any visible display of anger might have on the jury. "He slept so hard," said McFarland, "I stuck my foot up on his chair and nudged him, and he jumped."[6]

The local papers carried stories about how Benn, on one of the last days of the trial, fell asleep in his chair, "head rolled back on his shoulders, his mouth agape."[7] Aware that Benn was not quite up to the task, Judge Shaver appointed another lawyer, Sandy Melamed, to assist Benn. Melamed, however, had never handled a death-penalty case. He says he had little communication with Benn before or during the trial other than to establish that Benn would be the lead attorney and would be making the critical decisions on trial strategy. Melamed later told the *Houston Chronicle*, "I think the poor old guy was tired at the end of the day. Being at trial for 10 or 12 days in a row, I think it wore him out."[8] Judge Shaver later allowed in his interview with us, "It's not the kind of defense I would want if I were on trial for my life."[9]

Figure 13.1. George McFarland on death row in Texas.

Could this, by any standard, have been a fair trial? The Texas Court of Criminal Appeals, dividing 7–2, concluded that it was. The Court noted that McFarland did have two attorneys, the one who was asleep (Benn) and the one who had no death-penalty experience (Melamed). The court's majority opinion pointed out that Melamed himself had said Benn's dozing off could have had the effect of winning the sympathy of the jury, a strategy the court found plausible.[10]

Judge Charlie Baird wrote a sharp dissent:

316 MURDER AT THE SUPREME COURT

I find the majority's suggestion that it was somehow reasonable trial strategy for appellant's lead counsel to take a "short nap" during trial utterly ridiculous. The possibility of jury sympathy can never be a reasonable alternative to effective representation. A sleeping counsel is unprepared to present evidence, to cross-examine witnesses, and to present any coordinated effort to evaluate evidence and present a defense. In my view, a sleeping attorney is no attorney at all.[11]

The Texas Court of Criminal Appeals is the state's highest court for criminal cases, and its decisions can be appealed directly to the U.S. Supreme Court. McFarland's new attorneys did appeal to the Supreme Court, but on November 29, 1993, the justices announced that they would not hear the case.[12]

Denial of review means the lower-court decision stands, but with neither approval nor disapproval from the nation's highest Court. The denial of review sets no binding precedent on other courts.

Curiously, the identical sleeping-lawyer issue came back to the U.S. Supreme Court almost ten years later, except that in this case, the lower court had ordered a new trial, finding the defendant's right to the effective assistance of counsel had been violated. The justices again, without comment, denied review, allowing that contrary decision to stand.[13]

The justices do try to resolve conflicts among the courts, especially when they arise out of different federal circuits on questions of federal law. But it takes the consent of at least four of the nine justices for a case to win review, and there can be some strong and little-understood reasons for voting not to review a case. The Supreme Court regularly takes up the most divisive questions facing our society, and it should come as no surprise that the Court itself is often sharply divided on some of these issues. The justices get along remarkably well, having recognized that serious disagreement goes with the job and that the weight of opposing viewpoints needs be taken into consideration when granting review to a case. A case may be denied review not because the justices believe it was correctly decided at the lower court level, but rather because they believe it was wrongly decided and it could only become worse—thereby setting a national precedent—should a majority of the Court vote to affirm. We do not know why, however, the Court declined to review these two sleeping-lawyer cases and pass up the opportunity to provide much-needed guidance to the states on the level of competence required of attorneys in capital cases. The justices rarely explain why they deny review, and they didn't in these cases.

At last report, McFarland was still on death row more than twenty years after the offense. He still has motions challenging the fairness of his trial pending before a federal judge in Houston. He is still angry about the representation he received. His attorney falling asleep, however, isn't what bothers him most. What he says bothers him most is that he spent the last twenty years of his life incarcerated for a crime he insists he did not commit.[14] No other suspect has been arrested.

McFarland had spent much of his life in trouble. He had a long arrest record. And as prosecutors had argued in the penalty phase of his trial, he may well have posed a continuing threat to society. He may be guilty as charged. Those to whom we entrust the power to enforce the rules, however, must also play by the rules. No matter how guilty the accused may appear to be—or may in fact be—the trial must be fair and appear to be fair. In all too many cases, it is neither. It has become readily apparent to those who have studied the issue that the abysmal representation of court-appointed counsel in death-penalty cases is the single most spectacular failure in the administration of criminal justice in America.[15] The McFarland case is but a small slice of a very large pie.

The *National Law Journal,* after an extensive study of capital cases in six Southern states, found that capital trials are "more like a random flip of the coin than a delicate balancing of the scales" because the defense lawyer is too often "ill trained, unprepared . . . [and] grossly underpaid."[16]

Figure 13.2. Eddie Lee Ross.

Like George McFarland, Eddie Lee Ross—charged with a gruesome murder in DeKalb County, Georgia, in 1983—didn't want to take a chance on a court-appointed lawyer. Or at least his family didn't. They were black and had little cash, but they scraped together whatever they could to hire seventy-seven-year-old James Venable to represent their son. What they didn't know was that Venable was also a former imperial wizard of the Ku Klux Klan in Georgia. For fifty consecutive years, he had hosted Klan rallies on Labor Day at Stone Mountain, Georgia, replete with cross-burning ceremonies.

Venable also slept through portions of the trial and sometimes didn't even show up. Recognizing a problem, presiding judge Clarence Peeler appointed back-up counsel. But unlike in the McFarland case, here the two lawyers could never agree on who was in charge and what strategy would be best for their client.

Venable wanted Ross to testify. The court-appointed lawyer adamantly resisted, believing it might undermine his own trial strategy of portraying Ross as merely a deeply troubled and disadvantaged youth. At the close of the state's case and without any preparation, Venable called Ross to the witness stand, where Ross proceeded to self-destruct.

Whether to testify or to assert one's Fifth Amendment right against self-incrimination can often be a difficult choice. Here, Venable's strategy made a conviction and death sentence all but inevitable. Did he have his client's best interest at heart? Was it merely a strategic error? During the course of the trial, Venable from time to time did show some hostility toward his client, referring to Ross in open court as a "nigger."[17]

Figure 13.5. DeKalb County Superior Court judge Clarence Peeler.

We went to DeKalb County, Georgia, to interview the presiding superior court judge Clarence Peeler about this. We found a warm, friendly, soft-spoken Southern gentleman who confirmed that Venable had repeatedly resorted to racial slurs during the course of the defense of his African American client.

Figure 13.3. James Venable.

Figure 13.4. Venable in Ku Klux Klan attire.

Did that not trouble you?" we asked. "No, not at all," said Peeler, "because I knew him to be a good lawyer who would do a good job."[18] Ross was convicted and sentenced to death in Georgia's electric chair.

The Georgia Supreme Court did not have quite as lofty an assessment of Venable's performance. It threw out Ross's death sentence on the ground of incompetent counsel. Venable later agreed to stop practicing law after the state bar association threatened to disbar him for senility.[19]

In the end, the experience may have been a lucky break for Ross. The crime he was convicted of was particularly brutal and the case against him was strong. According to his own statement to police, it was shortly after 5:30 in the morning when Ross, using a screwdriver, pried open the back window of the home of eighty-seven-year-old grandmother Ellen Funderburg. After rummaging around for money, Ross entered Mrs. Funderburg's bedroom and for some reason started bashing her with a vase.[20]

The Georgia Supreme Court, in its statement of the facts, picks up the story from there, quoting from Ross's statement to police.

> She woke up and screamed, to which he responded by stabbing her with a pair of scissors. She quit screaming. Then he "started to have sex with her." However, he only "juked about one or two times," and quit, because he "realized that wasn't me, you know." Ross got $11 in cash and some credit cards out of the victim's purse, took a wedding ring off the victim's finger, and took some other jewelry and some checks that he found in the house. He pawned one of the rings for $15 and then filled out one of the checks and tried unsuccessfully to cash it at a bank across the street from South DeKalb Mall. Next, he went to the mall and bought [a] radio, using the victim's credit card. That purchase, Ross recognized with regret, led to his arrest.[21]

It was about ten in the morning when Mrs. Funderburg's daughter stopped by just to say hello, as she frequently did. Immediately upon entering, Vivian Turner discovered that the house had been ransacked. She found the partially nude body of her mother lying on the bedroom floor, the handle end of a large pair of scissors protruding from her chest.

If Georgia is to have capital punishment, Eddie Lee Ross would seem to qualify absent some mental disease or defect not reflected in the police or court record. The Ross case stands for the proposition that it is not just the defendant who is harmed when the state fails to insure that a defendant on trial for his life is adequately represented. The state suffers, too. The failure to provide truly effective assistance of counsel raises the prospect that an innocent person is convicted, allowing the real murderer to go free.

But it can also mean that one who is clearly guilty of a horrible crime is not adequately punished or is not punished at all. In this case, Ross pleaded guilty rather than face a new trial. In exchange for his plea, he was sentenced to life in prison. He remains today in the custody of the Georgia Department of Corrections.

The murder rate in the United States has been declining over the last decade, but there are still around fifteen thousand homicides a year. The number of death sentences returned in recent years is also on the decline, now just over a hundred annually. Statistically, less than one percent of the homicides result in a death sentence. Most of the homicides do not satisfy the statutory requirements of a death sentence. Of those that do, whether a defendant lives or dies often depends on the competence and the tenacity of the defense lawyer.

The case of Rebecca Machetti and John Eldon Smith, coconspirators in a murder in Bibb County, Georgia, is illustrative. The crime is one of the most notorious in Bibb County history, and it resulted in Machetti becoming the only female on death row and Smith becoming the first person to actually be executed in Georgia following the reinstatement of capital punishment by the U.S. Supreme Court in 1976.

Figure 13.6. Rebecca Machetti and John Eldon Smith.

Machetti and Smith had schemed to murder Machetti's ex-husband, who had recently remarried. The plan was not the product of a spurned heart; rather it was simple greed. Machetti and Smith wanted to cash in her ex's $20,000 life-insurance policy. Machetti was the "brains" behind the operation, the "mastermind." Initially, she wanted to poison her ex-husband. But then she got to thinking in grander terms. The Mafia, she felt, could use a few good hit men, and her new husband might make a favorable impression by knocking off her old one. He would have to change his name, of course. Something with a little more Mafioso panache. Smith started going by the name of "Anthony Isalldo Machetti."[22]

If the name fit, the face and body didn't. Short, bald, chubby, with a walrus-like moustache, he looked every bit the TV repairman he pretended to be when he showed up at the home of Ronald Akins and his wife of twenty days, Juanita Akins. But he did the job, shooting them both dead at point-blank range with a 12-gauge shotgun. Juanita was killed solely because she was there, at the wrong place and the wrong time.[23]

Both Machetti and Smith were charged with capital murder, convicted in separate trials, and sentenced to death. Both had their death sentences affirmed by the Georgia Supreme Court. They had one other thing in common, too. In each case, women had been systematically, and unconstitutionally, excluded from jury service. Neither defendant was judged by an impartial jury of one's peers as the Sixth Amendment requires. The Supreme Court had struck down gender discrimination in jury selection only a few weeks earlier. The attorney for Machetti knew of the decision and knew enough to object promptly in state court. The attorney for Smith was unaware and failed to object. The Eleventh U.S. Circuit Court of Appeals ordered a new trial for Machetti. The court, however, refused to consider the identical issue in Smith's case because his lawyers had failed to preserve it with a timely objection.[24]

On December 15, 1983, the state of Georgia put John Eldon Smith to death at the Georgia Diagnostic and Treatment Center, fifty miles south of Atlanta. "Hey there ain't no point in pulling the straps so tight," protested Smith mildly, as prison guards strapped him into the state's brand-spanking-new electric chair. The execution made national news as evidence that the death penalty was back. United Press International sent out the news under the headline (adopted in many newspapers around the country): "Apprentice Hit Man Is Second Person Executed in Two Days."[25]

Machetti, however, was spared. In her new trial, with a more representative and more constitutional jury, she was given two life terms. Unlike today, "life in prison" in 1983 seldom really meant life in prison. Machetti was released on parole in June 2010 after having served thirty-six years in prison.[26]

Had Machetti been represented by Smith's lawyers in state court and Smith by Machetti's lawyers, Machetti would have been executed and Smith would have obtained federal habeas corpus relief.

So was the imposition of the death penalty because the crime was so bad or because the perpetrator was so incorrigible? Or might it be more a reflection of Smith's inadequate representation in court?

Figure 13.7. Stephen Bright of the Southern Center for Human Rights.

Stephen Bright, president of the Southern Center for Human Rights, is an outspoken opponent of capital punishment in all cases. He says that "a large part of the death row population is made up of people who are distinguished by neither their records nor the circumstances of their crimes, but by their abject poverty, debilitating mental impairments, minimal intelligence and the poor legal representation they received."[27]

Writing in the *Yale Law Journal*, Bright quotes a member of the Georgia Board of Pardons and Paroles, saying that if the files of one hundred cases punished by death and one hundred punished by life were shuffled, it would be impossible to sort them out by sentence based upon information in the files about the crime and the offender.[28]

George McFarland and Eddie Lee Ross had hired their own lawyers in the belief that court-appointed lawyers might not defend them as zealously as hired ones. While the strategy might not have worked for them, there is some validity to the underlying premise. Statistically, there is research showing that roughly 75 percent of capital defendants represented by court-appointed lawyers end up getting a death sentence. But only about a third of those represented by hired counsel go to death row.[29] A more recent study of the federal death penalty indicates that the greater the financial resources made available to the defense in a case, the less likely a death sentence will be handed down.[30]

According to the Death Penalty Information Center, which keeps tabs on such matters, the costs of defending a capital case are out of reach for most Americans. The center's executive director, Richard Dieter, says, "The reality today is that virtually no defendant can afford to hire fully adequate death penalty representation." Asked about research, he wryly replied, "The people with that kind of cash on hand probably are not going to face the death penalty very often, so it would be hard to do a reliable study of comparison."[31]

The vast majority of defendants in capital cases don't have the resources to hire a private attorney and have to take whatever the court will provide.[32] So it was for Gary Nelson, convicted and sentenced to death, though it turned out the state never had much of a case against him.

The case against Nelson was premised largely on a hair found on the victim's body that a prosecution witness testified could have come from Nelson. Nelson's attorney, Howard McGlasson, hired no investigators and offered no rebuttal witnesses. McGlasson (who was later disbarred on unrelated matters) was defensive when we caught up with him years later: "Out of what money, sir? I mean, you know, you've got to realize I was barely paying my rent, barely paying my mortgage, barely putting food on my table."[33] McGlasson was paid only between fifteen and twenty dollars an hour; his request for cocounsel was denied. He didn't even ask for an investigator, believing he did not stand a chance of getting one.

In subsequent appeals, Nelson was represented by attorneys who were willing to put up some of their own money to challenge the state's testimony on the hair evidence. It turned out the Federal Bureau of Investigation had previously determined the hair was in no condition to be linked to anyone, including Nelson. The Eleventh U.S. Circuit Court of Appeals eventually threw out Nelson's conviction for insufficient evidence, but only after he had spent eleven years on death row.[34]

Nelson later told us, "I had little or no representation. I knew he was a court-appointed attorney and I really didn't expect nothing from him. And he didn't give me anything."[35]

Figure 13.8. Gary Nelson.

These horror stories are not uncommon. Defendants on trial for their lives are typically represented by the "bottom of the bar"[36] and often have no representation at all in appeal and post-conviction proceedings.

It should come as no surprise that the level of representation accorded many capital defendants in these cases violates the Sixth Amendment guarantee of the effective assistance of counsel. What is remarkable, however, is the large number of cases where the courts have held the fundamental right to counsel had *not* been violated, notwithstanding what would appear to be egregious representation.

In 1984, the U.S. Supreme Court set out a two-part test for competency in the case of *Strickland v. Washington.*[37] To establish that one has been denied the effective assistance of counsel, the defendant must show that "counsel's representation fell below an objective standard of reasonableness" and that "there is a reasonable probability that, but for counsel's unprofessional errors, the result of the proceeding would have been different." Writing for the majority, Justice Sandra Day O'Connor warned that the "scrutiny of counsel's performance must be highly deferential," noting that it "is all too tempting to second-guess a lawyer's performance after the fact, and that courts should try to 'eliminate the distorting effects of hindsight.'"[38]

The language of the opinion in *Strickland v. Washington* made it easier for the Texas Court of Criminal Appeals to find attorney John Benn's dozing off to be part of a strategy that should not be second-guessed through "the distorting effect of hindsight." In *Strickland* itself, the Court upheld a death sentence even though the defendant's lawyer chose not to offer any mitigating evidence at all at the sentencing phase of the trial, although there was plenty of information that would have helped Washington and could well have saved his life.[39] Justice Thurgood Marshall dissented.

Among other things, Marshall took issue with the Court's pronouncement that trial lawyers must have wide latitude and that reviewing courts must be "deferential." Much of the work, he felt, is subject to uniform standards such as applying for bail, conferring with one's clients, making timely objections to questionable rulings by the trial judge, meeting deadlines for motions and appeal notices. Marshall suggested failure to meet those standards should not be subject to any deference at all.

Marshall also took issue with the majority's view that the determination of whether a defendant's right to counsel was effective should hang on the fairness of the outcome. The fairness of the procedure, said Marshall, matters just as much. "The majority contends that the Sixth Amendment is not violated when a manifestly guilty defendant is convicted after a trial in which he was represented by a manifestly ineffective attorney. I cannot agree."[40]

Marshall also argued that attorneys in capital cases should be held to a higher standard than those in noncapital cases given the severity and irrevocability of a death sentence. The Supreme Court itself has been through a gauntlet of test cases, much of it documented in this book, that has left death-penalty litigation more complex than ever.

The Court's majority, and the legislatures of states desiring capital punishment, would have done well to heed Justice Marshall's advice. The quality of representation in the years since the *Strickland* decision was announced does not appear to have gotten any better. Death-penalty critics make a strong case that it has only degenerated further, quite often attributing the decline to the high Court's decision in *Washington v. Strickland*.[41]

Most court-appointed lawyers simply do not have the training necessary to represent someone on trial for his life. The playing field is anything but level. As Stephen Bright put it in his *Yale Law Journal* article,

> Many death penalty states have two state-funded offices that specialize in handling serious criminal cases. Both employ attorneys who generally spend years—some even their entire careers—handling criminal cases. Both pay decent annual salaries and provide health care and retirement benefits. Both send their employees to conferences and continuing legal education programs each year to keep them up to date on the latest developments in the law. Both have at their disposal a stable of investigative agencies, a wide range of experts and mental health professionals anxious to help develop and interpret facts favorable to their side. Unfortunately, however, in many states both of these offices are on the same side: the prosecution.[42]

In general, court-appointed lawyers, and many private attorneys, are simply no match for the professionals working for the district attorney and in the offices of the state attorney general. In fact, according to one study, in the states with the largest number of death sentences, a third of the lawyers practiced mostly civil law and most had never handled a capital case before. And having tried it once, more than half said they'd never do it again.[43]

In addition to extensive training, capital cases also take a great deal of time. And yet, states pay next to nothing for the work. The rates vary not only from state to state but also from county to county and city to city. In Philadelphia, court-appointed attorneys in capital cases have recently been getting only about forty dollars an hour for preparation time.[44] No wonder there might be little pretrial preparation. For years, Alabama had set a flat rate of $2,000 for trial preparation, even though a good capital defense could easily run up a thousand hours of work. That has since changed but, as of this writing, they are paid around only seventy dollars an hour, and Alabama law does not require any death-penalty litigation experience when representing clients on trial for their lives.[45] Often judges end up having to choose from the least able or least experienced lawyers, those who cannot get clients any other way.[46]

The *Houston Chronicle* reports that Texas lawyers have repeatedly missed filing deadlines between 2009 and 2011, resulting in the dismissal of their clients' appeals. At least six of those clients have since been executed. Taxpayers appear loathe to pay the price for adequate representation of those charged with murder.[47] The defendants are generally poor, disproportionately of color, often afflicted with mental disabilities, and always accused of a horrible crime. And when the community talks about "justice," it is more in the nature of revenge than of a just legal system and the guarantee of a fair trial.

And even if they wanted to, providing true justice may be beyond the means of some jurisdictions. Consider the case of Robert Haggart, accused of shooting seven people to death—three of them children— in one of the worst crimes in Michigan history.[48] The crime occurred in 1982 in Clare County, which, with a 19 percent unemployment rate and $3,700 per capita income, ranked among the poorest counties in the state. Yet getting the case to trial meant staggering expenses: Haggert fled to Tennessee and had to be brought back to Michigan along with many of the witnesses. That cost an estimated $24,000. Add in $40,000 for police overtime, $4,500 for autopsies and other lab work, plus the cost of attorneys, and the total bill came to over $200,000, or 7 percent of the county's annual budget. Trash collection was reduced to once a week; school budgets were frozen.

The victims were lifelong residents of the area, widely known and well liked. The murders traumatized the community, as did the bill. Charged with both prosecuting and defending an accused mass murderer, the county was left in the worst financial straits in its history, with no one to turn to for help. Haggart ended up being sentenced to life in prison without parole. He died in prison in 2003. Clare County did what it had to do. After all, the right to a fair trial is fundamental. Courts may be standing in line to guarantee it, but as the citizens of Clare County sadly learned, no one is standing in line to pay for it.

Add to all of the above that many clients tend to be undesirable from a variety of standpoints. Many have actually committed the horrible crimes of which they are accused. While they are still entitled to a fair trial, there can be social pressure against taking on such clients, particularly in small, rural communities where many capital crimes arise. In sum, the work is hard, a defendant's life is on the line, the hours are long, and the pay is low. And when all else fails, the capital defendant's final resort is to challenge the competency of his lawyer. It is all but guaranteed, even in many cases where counsel performed exemplary service.

The climate has improved somewhat in recent years. In 1994, the Court extended the right to counsel beyond the trial and direct appeals to federal habeas corpus petitions. Even after all direct appeals have been exhausted, a defendant in state court has the right to challenge the fairness of his trial in federal court, and counsel must be provided in death-penalty cases.[49]

The Court has also somewhat refined its decision in *Strickland*. Lower courts may not have carte blanche to second-guess a defense lawyer's strategy of not providing any mitigating evidence at the punishment phase of a capital trial, but the attorney still must undertake a meaningful inquiry to determine what mitigating evidence might exist. The Supreme Court ruled in 2003 that the failure to even research and consider factors that might result in mercy is per se ineffective assistance of counsel.[50]

More still needs to be done. The American Law Institute (ALI),[51] made up of about four thousand judges, lawyers, and law professors, was instrumental in drafting the framework for capital punishment legislation that the Supreme Court upheld in *Gregg v. Georgia* (setting the stage for a revival of capital punishment in thirty-eight states). But in October 2009, the ALI pronounced the project a failure, citing among other things the apparent and historic inability of states to fund competent defense counsel. In backing off from what had at one time been considered a monumental achievement, the ALI cited "the current intractable institutional and structural obstacles to ensuring a minimally adequate system for administering capital punishment."[52]

Since 1997, the American Bar Association has called for a moratorium on executions in large part because of the failure to provide adequate counsel to defendants on trial for their lives. Citing the "quality of legal representation that capital defendants receive and the fairness of capital proceedings," ABA president Laurel Bellows says the association "encourages jurisdictions not to carry out executions until critical reforms are implemented." Although the association opposes the death penalty for juvenile offenders and mentally impaired defendants, it has not taken a position on the death penalty itself.[53]

The right to counsel in death-penalty cases since the Supreme Court reinstated capital punishment in 1976 has been, at best, illusory, raising the question of whether it can ever be "done right." Whatever one's position on capital punishment, and particularly for those who might embrace it, this condition is intolerable and needs to be remedied. The chronic failure to provide effective assistance of counsel, compounded by the slim prospect of improvement, has emerged as one of the leading arguments for doing away with capital punishment once and for all.

 For a video report on ineffective assistance of counsel, go to: http://murderatthesupremecourt.com/counsel

14

CLOSING ARGUMENTS

THE VIEW OF THE AUTHORS

You want a fair death penalty? You kill; you die. That's fair.
> —Antonin Scalia, speaking at the Pew Forum
> on Religion and Public Life,
> University of Chicago, January 2002

If a state wishes that its citizens respect human life, then the state should stop killing.
> —Clarence Darrow, remarks from a debate on
> capital punishment with Judge Alfred J. Talley,
> New York City, October 27, 1924

The murderers you've met in this book are no run-of-the-mill felons. Most of them are stone-cold killers; all of them have committed horrific crimes. Their victims were often chosen at random, innocent but merely at the wrong place at the wrong time. They could have been your spouse, your parents, your children—or you. In many cases, the murder victim suffers less than the survivors, the loved ones who are victims in their own right and who may suffer loss and feel pain for the rest of their lives. The perpetrators were callously indifferent, both to their victims and to the value of human life.

The offenses chronicled in the preceding chapters are not at all comparable to the vast majority of homicides, which are the result of sudden passion or simple negligence and which rarely bring a death sentence. In every state that allows it, capital punishment is reserved for the vicious and premeditated taking of another's life.

The leading cases before the Supreme Court illustrate some of the thorny and, in our view as authors, fascinating questions that surround the death-penalty debate. Who may be executed? Who is immune from being executed? What crimes do and do not justify death? What procedural protections must be applied for the ultimate punishment? None of the cases we have set our sights on, however, raised the ultimate question of whether the United States should have a death penalty at all.

We pointed out in the beginning of this book that the gruesome facts of these crimes and the lasting impact on loved ones are often lost in the capital-punishment debate, an omission we hope to correct. As we also noted, those who oppose capital punishment tend to focus on the flaws in the system that make its application appear arbitrary and capricious, as the Court found in *Furman*. Our primary focus on the crimes and the criminals who committed them may have seemed to give these pages a pro-death-penalty tilt. But we do have misgivings about how capital punishment is practiced in the United States; this book would be incomplete if we didn't share them.

DETERRENCE

The most widely heard argument for the death penalty has been that it deters would-be murderers. The claim is asserted as authoritatively in neighborhood bars as it is in presidential debates. "I think the reason to support the death penalty is because it saves other people's lives," said candidate George W. Bush in a 2000 debate. He got no argument from candidate Al Gore, who said, "I support the death penalty in the most heinous cases."[1]

To watch the exchange between Bush and Gore, go to:
http://murderatthesupremecourt/debate

The concept of deterrence is almost intuitive; it is logical to assume that the threat of death would discourage someone considering murder. It may be logical, but it is not necessarily true. There always have been, and continue to be, grave doubts about the deterrent effect of capital punishment.

According to a 2009 FBI crime report, states that allow the death penalty have a homicide rate almost twice that of those states that prohibit it: 4.9 murders per 100,000 people, as opposed to 2.8 per 100,000.[2] And actual executions do not appear to have had any impact at all. Since the death penalty was reinstated in 1976, there have been more than a thousand executions in the South and only four in the Northeast, yet the homicide rates are markedly higher in the South than in the Northeast.[3]

In fact, some contend those numbers suggest that the threat of being executed is making criminals even more likely to pull the trigger: dead witnesses cannot testify. Proof, perhaps, that statistics can be manipulated to support *any* theory. The argument for deterrence was forcefully made to the Supreme Court in *Gregg v. Georgia*, where the death penalty was reinstated. An amicus brief filed by U.S. Solicitor General Robert Bork on behalf of the Department of Justice cited a university study purporting to show a direct link between the death penalty and lower crime rates, that for every execution, eight would-be murder victims are spared.

The study, conducted by respected economist Isaac Ehrlich at the State University of New York at Buffalo, is often cited as the first scientific study on the deterrent effect of the death penalty and one of the most persuasive. It failed to persuade a majority of the Court. Some of the justices felt that while the study demonstrated the death penalty might be a deterrent in some cases, it would have no deterrent effect in many other cases and, thus, the overall impact was inconclusive.[4]

We are convinced that the death penalty has never been proved a deterrent. We doubt it ever will be, for a number of reasons.

Criminologists agree that for any punishment to be a meaningful deterrent, it must be swift and certain. The death penalty is neither. Most of the current occupants of death row have been languishing there for more than a decade. The evidence is overwhelming that most will die like the rest of us, of old age and not by the executioner's hand. That may be due, in part, to a historic commitment to fundamental fairness, born of our common law and the old adage, "Better that ten guilty persons escape than one innocent suffer."[5]

Our judicial system allows a capital defendant greater protections at trial than any other criminal defendant and considerable opportunity for appeal if convicted, making the journey from crime to punishment a long and arduous one. Allegiance to our values— especially our commitment to due process—makes delay inevitable and may well exact a price in terms of a meaningful death-penalty system. The death penalty in modern America not only lacks both the speed and the certainty to be a meaningful deterrent, but there is also no credible evidence that it provides any more deterrence than the lesser punishment of life in prison with no parole.

RETRIBUTION

The vast majority of those Americans currently supporting capital punishment, as noted in Chapter 8, do so in the belief that it serves society's interest in what proponents call "justice" and opponents call "revenge." Whatever you call it, the desire for retribution is instinctive. We crave it.

Retribution has a strong emotional pull in the public arena, as demonstrated in the reaction to Michael Dukakis's answer to a presidential debate question in 1988. Reporter Bernard Shaw asked the Democratic nominee, "If Kitty Dukakis were raped and murdered, would you favor an irrevocable death penalty for the killer?" Dukakis calmly and dispassionately answered that he would not, that he had long opposed the death penalty and believed there were "better ways to deal with violent crime."[6]

 To watch the Dukakis/Shaw exchange, go to:
http://murderatthesupremecourt/dukakis

It was certainly a reasonable, defensible reply. But political pundits concluded that Dukakis's bland, emotionless consideration of the hypothetical rape and murder of his own wife cost him the debate and contributed to his defeat in the general election. Americans want passion in their politicians, and our thirst for blood needs quenching. Dukakis might have done better to answer Shaw with another question: "If you were the defendant in the case, would you want *me* on the jury?"

Dukakis, of course, could not serve on the jury of that fictional case any more than Detective Steven Baker would be allowed to consider the fate of Robert Alton Harris, who shot Baker's weeping fifteen-year-old son at point-blank range. But society, removed from the trauma and emotion of the specific crime, does need to take into account that a murder is more than merely a crime against the person who is killed and the loved ones of that person. It is a crime against society itself, and society has a right, some would say an obligation, to exact just punishment.

Murder is also a crime against our shared social fabric, so society itself needs to be avenged. And if society did not act to punish offenders, it would risk vigilante reprisals by those left behind. So retribution is a legitimate function of the law and has become the strongest argument in favor of capital punishment.[7]

We are persuaded, however, that the legitimate interest in retribution is—like deterrence—also insufficient to overcome flaws in the death-penalty system; the risks, which we outline in the following pages, outweigh the retributive benefits. Life without parole sufficiently serves the purposes of retribution, delivering incapacitating and continuing punishment without those risks.

THE RACE FACTOR

Race continues to be an astonishingly arbitrary and undeniably influential factor in determining who gets sentenced to death. When compared with the general population, racial minorities do comprise a disproportionately larger percentage of those who are sentenced to death. There are, however, more whites on death row than blacks and all other minorities combined. What is much more striking than the race of the defendant is the race of the victim. When the victim is white, the defendant is much more likely to get a death sentence than when the victim is African American. Arbitrary? Irrational? Racist? It is all three. We are reminded of the dissent in *McClesky v. Kemp* by Justice John Paul Stevens who, after leaving the Court, wrote, "that the murder of black victims is treated as less culpable than the murder of white victims provides a haunting reminder of once-prevalent Southern lynchings."[8]

The race of the defendant and the race of the victim should have no bearing on whether a defendant gets a death sentence. But the history of the past forty years shows it is not only a significant factor, it may be a controlling one. Although unacceptable, the role of race now also appears to be inherent and eradicable in our death-penalty system.

UNEQUAL APPLICATION

The features that most distinguish occupants of death row in the United States do not involve race but rather backgrounds marked by poverty, lack of education, and child abuse.[9] These features should be irrelevant to punishment, but they show up with undeniable and astonishing frequency among death-row inmates. It is not a coincidence.

Poverty is generally considered a contributing factor to crime. After all, bank presidents do not hold up gas stations. Yet it may not be so much poverty itself that is the culprit as it is the hopelessness that poverty can breed in some circumstances. Poverty, when combined with an abusive childhood and little or no education, provides fertile ground for the scourge of hopelessness. This is not a do-gooder observation; it is sociological fact.[10]

Proponents of capital punishment are quick to respond that if these are the people who are doing the crimes, they are the people who should be paying the price. However, are they the only ones responsible? We are troubled by the questions raised in Chapter 3 by the case of Robert Alton Harris—arguably among the more deserving candidates for execution. But the complications of his upbringing raise a spectral and unnerving question: Was he put to death, *at least to some limited extent,* because of the sins of his parents?

INEFFECTIVE REPRESENTATION

In a high-profile capital case, particularly with a defendant of means, the quality of legal representation is often superb. Very few get or even need the supercharged representation of O. J. Simpson's famous "dream team"; fewer still can pay for it. But in a large number of less-sensational murder cases, as documented in Chapter 13, the quality of legal representation has been deplorable.

Some states, such as Georgia, provide no funds at all for the appointment of counsel or investigative tools to indigent defendants, ceding that role to individual counties or municipalities. Many of those jurisdictions are already impoverished and incapable of providing the level of resources that death-penalty cases often require. They have learned to their dismay that while appeals courts freely write orders to require fair trials, no one is waiting to write the check to pay for them.

Providing capital defendants with quality representation would actually be cost-effective, helping to avoid costly appeals and retrials. In some cases, it would prevent conviction and possible execution of the innocent—which also allows the guilty to escape justice. But lawmakers (and the taxpayers they represent) have historically resisted putting up the money to finance fairly matched trials. It is now clearly established that many of the current occupants of death row are there not because they committed the worst crimes, but—in the words of Stephen Bright, because they had the worst lawyers.[11]

THE RISK OF ERROR

If an error has been made in sending a prisoner to his execution, it is irreversible once the lethal chemicals start to flow. New evidence or proof of a flawed prosecution cannot turn back the clock or restore a heartbeat. The prisoner is dead.

The risk of error is significant; recent history suggests it is much greater than anyone could have imagined back in 1972 when the Supreme Court put the death penalty on hold in *Furman v. Georgia.*

A forensic revolution got underway in 1993 when DNA testing began to be applied in capital cases. More precise than any scientific identification process ever known, the comparison of DNA samples provides certainty: the comparison is of genetic blueprints unique to each individual. DNA testing leaves such previously revered forensic tools as fingerprint analysis in the laboratory dust.

In the last twenty years, as we noted in Chapter 12, seventeen condemned prisoners have been completely exonerated by DNA evidence. The emergence of DNA as a forensic tool, while illustrating the risk of executing an innocent person, also diminishes the risk of such errors. But it does so only in those cases where there actually is DNA evidence; in many cases, there is none.

POLITICAL SOLUTIONS

In 1993, in the *Herrera* case we examined in Chapter 12, the U.S. Supreme Court noted that a state has an interest in the finality of its judgments and that "executive clemency has provided the 'fail safe' in our criminal justice system."[12] In most states, the governor has the authority to grant clemency and even a full pardon. It doesn't happen often and is hardly a fail-safe. Vigorously fighting crime produces votes, and few political candidates can afford to be viewed as in any way "soft on crime." In California, for example, no governor has commuted a death sentence since the administration of Governor Ronald Reagan, who granted clemency to a brain-damaged inmate in 1967.[13]

Even so, there does seem to be a trend in the state legislatures, albeit a slow one, against capital punishment. In 2012, Connecticut repealed its death-penalty law notwithstanding an estimated 62 percent of the state's voters claiming to favor it.[14] When Governor Dan Malloy quietly and without fanfare signed the bill that would end Connecticut's death penalty, he acknowledged that "many people whom I deeply respect, including friends and family, believe the death penalty is just."[15] It may not have been as politically risky as it seemed. The number of voters favoring the death penalty in the state dropped from 62 percent to 47 percent when those polled were given the option of life in prison with no parole.[16]

In 1994, the Supreme Court ruled that juries must be told if a capital defendant may be sentenced to life without parole in any case where "future dangerousness" is given as an aggravating circumstance.[17] The decision is often cited as one reason for a national decline in the number of death sentences that juries return.

In 2011, Illinois repealed its death penalty statute after a ten-year moratorium. In 2003, Governor George Ryan had commuted the death sentences of 164 inmates to life in prison after the *Chicago*

Tribune, working with Northwestern University law students, exposed more than a dozen faulty convictions based on forced confessions, unreliable witnesses, and incompetent legal representation. Said Ryan, "There is a flaw in the system, without question."[18] And while a handful of states have moved away from capital punishment, no state in recent decades has moved from not having the death penalty to adopting it. This trend is important. As we have seen in the case of offenders who are underage or who suffer mental impairment, today's trend may ultimately reflect the "evolving standards of decency that mark the progress of a maturing society."[19]

Scott Turow, attorney and novelist, was a member of a special commission Ryan created to study the death penalty. A former prosecutor who had also represented two condemned prisoners, Turow considered himself "a death penalty agnostic" at the beginning of the commission's two-year inquiry. By the end of its work, he was a reluctant convert to abolition: "There will always be cases that cry out to me for ultimate punishment. That is not the true issue. The pivotal question instead is whether a system of justice can be constructed that reaches only the rare, right cases, without also occasionally condemning the innocent or the undeserving."[20]

JUDICIAL SOLUTIONS

Given the determination of at least some Southern states to retain capital punishment, any nationwide ban would likely have to come in a decision from the U.S. Supreme Court.[21] As of this writing, there does not appear to be a single justice on the Court so disposed.

Curiously, five justices sitting on the Supreme Court presided over by Chief Justice Warren Burger (1969–1986) came out against capital punishment but not at the same time and certainly not in the same case (which would have ended capital punishment once and for all).

Justices William Brennan and Thurgood Marshall opposed it in all cases. In 1991, four years after his retirement, Justice Lewis

Powell—who had voted to uphold the death penalty throughout his fifteen-year tenure on the Court—later repudiated those votes, telling his biographer that they were among the few regrets he had come to have after his service on the Court.[22] "I would vote the other way in any capital case," he said; "I have come to think that capital punishment should be abolished." Powell's doubts about capital punishment had been growing for some time.

One year after his retirement, Chief Justice William Rehnquist named Powell to head a commission to examine why it was typically taking almost a decade to carry out a death sentence. The Powell Committee, as it became known, concluded there were too many opportunities for collateral appeals on procedural issues and that capital defendants rarely got the legal representation required when one's life is on the line. Powell believed the opponents of capital punishment, the defense bar in particular, were part of the problem. Streamlining the system and making it more efficient would hardly be in their clients' best interest, hastening their own demise.

In all other criminal cases, the defense has a vested interest in moving the case along in the hope that finality may bring freedom or at least an earlier release from prison. When it comes to the death penalty, however, it has been among the proponents who have been most forceful in pushing for reform. Among them is Charles Lane, the author and articulate *Washington Post* columnist, who argues that the death penalty should be "more specifically targeted." "If capital punishment in general were more clearly aimed at 'the worst of the worst,'" Lane writes, "and if it were more centrally and consistently applied within states, individual sentences would probably be that much less vulnerable to challenges in federal court."[23]

Justice Powell, however, had lost hope. His long-awaited report was released at a rare news conference at the Supreme Court[24] in which he allowed that as a judge he had no problems upholding death penalty laws; were he sitting in the state legislature, however, he would vote against it: "Capital punishment has so far not deterred murder," said Powell, adding that it "creates too many collateral problems." But Powell was now gone, replaced by Justice Anthony Kennedy, who harbored no such doubts.

As reported in Chapter 8, Justice John Paul Stevens, toward the end of his almost-thirty-five-year tenure on the Court, also shared his misgiving about the death penalty, finding that it represents "the pointless and needless extinction of life with only marginal contributions to any discernible social or public purposes."[25]

Figure 14.1. Justice John Paul Stevens.

Shortly after his retirement, Stevens explained further, writing in the *New York Review of Books*.[26] Stevens defended his vote in *Gregg v. Georgia* to reinstate the death penalty, writing that he still believed the decision established a framework for the fair and impartial implementation of capital punishment. But that framework, he wrote, had been undermined by an activist Court with little regard for precedent, a Court that—among other things—failed to adequately consider the role of race and politics in death sentences.

Stevens echoed the lament of Justice Marshall on the Court's about-face on victim-impact evidence in *Payne v. Tennessee*, complaining that the reversal was solely the result of changes in personnel on the Court rather than allegiance to what had been thought to be settled principles of constitutional law.

In 1994, Justice Harry Blackmun—who had also consistently voted to uphold death sentences throughout his thirty years on the federal bench—announced that he could no longer support it, that he would "no longer tinker with the machinery of death."[27] Blackmun had served with Brennan and Marshall for more than twenty years but never joined their death-penalty dissents. Now they were both gone. Brennan had retired in 1990, Marshall in 1991. And Blackmun stood alone on the Court in his opposition to capital punishment.

Blackmun had been planning his announcement for some time. The idea for a turnaround came from one of his law clerks, Andrew Shapiro, who had observed Blackmun's growing frustration with the Court's death-penalty decisions. Shapiro and another clerk, Michelle Alexander, collaborated on the opinion—a generic treatise about the intractable problems that have come to be associated with capital punishment. They and the justice agreed the opinion should be filed in some garden-variety death-penalty case—as if there ever could be such a thing—that would not raise other issues that might detract from Blackmun's central message.

They settled on an appeal brought by Bruce Callins, who was sentenced to die for the shooting death of a patron at a Texas bar in the course of a robbery.[28] It was a case that the Court would not accept for review, but it did provide Blackmun a choice opportunity to air his growing doubts about capital punishment as practiced in the United States.

Figure 14.2. Justice Harry A. Blackmun.

On February 23, 1994, at approximately 1:00 a.m., Bruce Edwin Callins will be executed by the State of Texas. Intravenous tubes attached to his arms will carry the instrument of death, a toxic fluid designed specifically for the purpose of killing human beings. The witnesses, standing a few feet away, will behold Callins, no longer a defendant, an appellant, or a petitioner, but a man, strapped to a gurney, and seconds away from extinction. . . .

Twenty years have passed since this Court declared that the death penalty must be imposed fairly, and with reasonable consistency, or not at all, see *Furman* v. *Georgia*, and, despite the effort of the States and courts to devise legal formulas and procedural rules to meet this daunting challenge, the death penalty remains fraught with arbitrariness, discrimination, caprice, and mistake. This is not to say that the problems with the death penalty today are identical to those that were present 20 years ago. Rather, the problems that were pursued down one hole with procedural rules and verbal formulas have come to the surface somewhere else, just as virulent and pernicious as they were in their original form. Experience has taught us that the constitutional goal of eliminating arbitrariness and discrimination from the administration of death, see *Furman* v. *Georgia, supra,* can never be achieved without compromising an equally essential component of fundamental fairness—individualized sentencing. See *Lockett* v. *Ohio.*

And Blackmun concluded his lengthy dissent as follows:

Perhaps one day this Court will develop procedural rules or verbal formulas that actually will provide consistency, fairness, and reliability in a capital sentencing scheme. I am not optimistic that such a day will come. I am more optimistic, though, that this Court eventually will conclude that the effort to eliminate arbitrariness while preserving fairness "in the infliction of [death] is so plainly doomed to failure that it—and the death penalty—must be abandoned altogether." *Godfrey* v. *Georgia,* 446 U.S. 420, 442 (1980) (Marshall, J., concurring in the judgment). I may not live to see that day, but I have faith that eventually it will arrive. The path the Court has chosen lessens us all. I dissent.[29]

It is not unusual for justices to dissent from the denial of review in a case. It is unusual, however, for a justice to respond to another justice's dissent in such a case—but that is precisely what Justice Antonin Scalia did. As you have seen, Justice Scalia has been one of the Court's most forceful proponents of the right of the states to allow capital punishment. In his "Letter to Harry," Scalia did not mince words.

> Justice Blackmun begins his statement by describing with poignancy the death of a convicted murderer by lethal injection. He chooses, as the case in which to make that statement, one of the less brutal of the murders that regularly come before us, the murder of a man ripped by a bullet suddenly and unexpectedly, with no opportunity to prepare himself and his affairs, and left to bleed to death on the floor of a tavern. The death-by-injection which Justice Blackmun describes looks pretty desirable next to that. It looks even better next to some of the other cases currently before us, which Justice Blackmun did not select as the vehicle for his announcement that the death penalty is always unconstitutional, for example, the case of the 11-year-old girl raped by four men and then killed by stuffing her panties down her throat. How enviable a quiet death by lethal injection compared with that!"

In their respective opinions, Blackmun and Scalia addressed a large chunk of the capital-punishment debate. The views expressed by Scalia are no doubt shared by millions of Americans and, accordingly, are entitled to consideration and respect. Scalia, however, did not directly contradict Blackmun. Where Scalia was addressing the desirability of the death penalty (which has long been debated), Blackmun was addressing the efficacy of society's ultimate sanction, questioning what it accomplishes in light of widely acknowledged failings.

We find the opinion of Justice Blackmun more persuasive.[30]

As a matter of strict constitutional law, it is hard to take issue with the death penalty. Given its deep roots in our history and the specific references to the practice in the Constitution, we agree with proponents that the death penalty is not unconstitutional per se. We also agree with the opponents, however, that the nation's experience with capital punishment over the last forty years strongly suggests that we, as a society committed to due process and the rule of law, have become incapable of implementing it in a meaningful, rational, nondiscriminatory manner.

Figure 14.3. Justice Antonin Scalia.

Our conclusion is that the system of capital punishment is broken and cannot be fixed. That functional judgment makes it unnecessary for us to offer conclusions about what for many is the larger and more vexing question, whether the death penalty is immoral. This aspect of morality is arguably more of an issue for philosophers, and perhaps state legislators, than for journalists and judges. Moreover, there is no consensus in this country about the morality of capital punishment. Nor is there in the Bible itself, which teaches "An eye for an eye" alongside "Vengeance is Mine, so sayeth the Lord."

Our political and legal system is ill-equipped to deal with moral issues—and we are in no position to make moral judgments. While we have our own views on capital punishment, our experiences in the field leave us uncomfortable telling others what to think. Each reader will arrive at a personal conclusion on this compelling matter of life and death; for us as the authors, a crucial measure of this book's success will be the extent to which it provokes and informs those decisions.

We fully understand why so many Americans find the death penalty desirable. Were we to agree that in addition to being desirable it was also appropriate, the concerns of Justices Blackmun, Stevens, and Powell—as well as many other critics—about how the death penalty has been implemented would still give us pause. We share their concerns and their doubts about whether the problems so engrained in the system can ever be remedied.

We acknowledge that there are forceful arguments on all sides of this debate, that it is an issue that admits of immeasurably more opinions than answers. Yet this is not like exploring outer space or finding a cure for cancer; it is not an investigation of the unknown. The evidence is right there before us, much of it is in this book. All that is required is careful consideration. The answer lies in our minds and hearts. We respect the views of those with whom we may disagree.

THE GEORGIA
DEATH-PENALTY STATUTE

T he U.S. Supreme Court's opinion in *Gregg v. Georgia* made the Georgia death-penalty statute a model for other states. It is reproduced below. The Court's comments about the statute have been retained, the italics are from the original document, and the original footnotes have been converted to endnotes.

II

Before considering the issues presented it is necessary to understand the Georgia statutory scheme for the imposition of the death penalty.[3] The Georgia statute, as amended after our decision in *Furman v. Georgia, 408 U.S. 238 (1972),* retains the death penalty for six categories of crime: murder,[4] kidnaping for ransom or where the victim is harmed, armed robbery,[5] rape, treason, and aircraft hijacking.[6] Ga. Code Ann. §§ 26-1101, 26-1311, 26-1902, 26-2001, 26-2201, 26-3301 (1972). The capital defendant's guilt or innocence is determined in the traditional manner, either by a trial judge or a jury, in the first stage of a bifurcated trial.

If trial is by jury, the trial judge is required to charge lesser included offenses when they are supported by any view of the evidence. *Sims v. State, 203 Ga. 668, 47 S.E. 2d 862 (1948).* See *Linder v. State, 132 Ga. App. 624, 625, 208 S.E. 2d 630, 631 (1974).* After a verdict, finding, or plea of guilty to a capital crime, a presentence hearing is conducted before whoever made the determination of guilt. The sentencing procedures are essentially the same in both bench and jury trials. At the hearing:

"The judge [or jury] shall hear additional evidence in extenuation, mitigation, and aggravation of punishment, including the record of any prior criminal convictions and pleas of guilty or pleas of nolo contendere of the defendant, or the absence of any prior conviction and pleas: Provided, however, that only such evidence in aggravation as the State has made known to the defendant prior to his trial shall be admissible. The judge [or jury] shall also hear argument by the defendant or his counsel and the prosecuting attorney . . . regarding the punishment to be imposed." § 27-2503 (Supp. 1975).

The defendant is accorded substantial latitude as to the types of evidence that he may introduce. See *Brown v. State, 235 Ga. 644, 647-650, 220 S.E. 2d 922, 925-926 (1975).*[7] Evidence considered during the guilt stage may be considered during the sentencing stage without being resubmitted. *Eberheart v. State, 232 Ga. 247, 253, 206 S.E. 2d 12, 17 (1974).*[8]

In the assessment of the appropriate sentence to be imposed the judge is also required to consider or to include in his instructions to the jury "any mitigating circumstances or aggravating circumstances otherwise authorized by law and any of [10] statutory aggravating circumstances which may be supported by the evidence." § 27-2534.1(b) (Supp. 1975). The scope of the nonstatutory aggravating or mitigating circumstances is not delineated in the statute. Before a convicted defendant may be sentenced to death, however, except in cases of treason or aircraft hijacking, the jury, or the trial judge in cases tried without a jury, must find beyond a reasonable doubt one of the 10 aggravating circumstances specified in the statute.[9] The sentence of death may be imposed only if the jury (or judge) finds one of the statutory aggravating circumstances and then elects to impose that sentence. § 26-3102 (Supp. 1975). If the verdict is death, the jury or judge must specify the aggravating circumstance(s) found. §

27-2534.1(c) (Supp. 1975). In jury cases, the trial judge is bound by the jury's recommended sentence. §§ 26-3102, 27-2514 (Supp. 1975).

In addition to the conventional appellate process available in all criminal cases, provision is made for special expedited direct review by the Supreme Court of Georgia of the appropriateness of imposing the sentence of death in the particular case. The court is directed to consider "the punishment as well as any errors enumerated by way of appeal," and to determine:

(1) Whether the sentence of death was imposed under the influence of passion, prejudice, or any other arbitrary factor, and

(2) Whether, in cases other than treason or aircraft hijacking, the evidence supports the jury's or judge's finding of a statutory aggravating circumstance as enumerated in section 27.2534.1 (b), and

(3) Whether the sentence of death is excessive or disproportionate to the penalty imposed in similar cases, considering both the crime and the defendant." § 27-2537 (Supp. 1975).

If the court affirms a death sentence, it is required to include in its decision reference to similar cases that it has taken into consideration. § 27-2537 (e) (Supp. 1975).[10]

A transcript and complete record of the trial, as well as a separate report by the trial judge, are transmitted to the court for its use in reviewing the sentence. § 27-2537 (a) (Supp. 1975). The report is in the form of a 6 1/2-page questionnaire, designed to elicit information about the defendant, the crime, and the circumstances of the trial. It requires the trial judge to characterize the trial in several ways designed to test for arbitrariness and disproportionality of sentence. Included in the report are responses to detailed questions concerning the quality of the defendant's representation, whether race played a role in the trial, and, whether, in the trial court's judgment, there was any doubt about the defendant's guilt or the appropriateness of the sentence. A copy of the report is served upon defense counsel. Under its special review authority, the court may either affirm the death sentence or remand the case for resentencing. In cases in which the death sentence is affirmed there remains the possibility of executive clemency.[11]

[NOTES]

3. Subsequent to the trial in this case limited portions of the Georgia statute were amended. None of these amendments changed significantly the substance of the statutory scheme. All references to the statute in this opinion are to the current version.

4. Georgia Code Ann. § 26-1101 (1972) provides:

"(a) A person commits murder when he unlawfully and with malice afore-thought, either express or implied, causes the death of another human being. Express malice is that deliberate intention unlawfully to take away the life of a fellow creature, which is manifested by external circumstances capable of proof. Malice shall be implied where no considerable provocation appears, and where all the circumstances of the killing show an abandoned and malignant heart.

"(b) A person also commits the crime of murder when in the commission of a felony he causes the death of another human being, irrespective of malice.

"(c) A person convicted of murder shall be punished by death or by imprisonment for life."

5. Section 26-1902 (1972) provides:

"A person commits armed robbery when, with intent to commit theft, he takes property of another from the person or the immediate presence of another by use of an offensive weapon. The offense robbery by intimidation shall be a lesser included offense in the offense of armed robbery. A person convicted of armed robbery shall be punished by death or imprisonment for life, or by imprisonment for not less than one nor more than 20 years."

6. These capital felonies currently are defined as they were when *Furman* was decided. The 1973 amendments to the Georgia statute, however, narrowed the class of crimes potentially punishable by death by eliminating capital perjury. Compare § 26-2401 (Supp. 1975) with § 26-2401 (1972).

7. It is not clear whether the 1974 amendments to the Georgia statute were intended to broaden the types of evidence admissible at the presentence hearing. Compare § 27-2503(a) (Supp. 1975) with § 27-2534 (1972) (deletion of limitation "subject to the laws of evidence").

8. Essentially the same procedures are followed in the case of a guilty plea. The judge considers the factual basis of the plea, as well as evidence in aggravation and mitigation. See *Mitchell v. State, 234 Ga. 160, 214 S.E. 2d 900 (1975)*.

9. The statute provides in part:

    (a)   The death penalty may be imposed for the offenses of aircraft hijacking or treason, in any case.

    (b)   In all cases of other offenses for which the death penalty may be authorized, the judge shall consider, or he shall include in his instructions to the jury for it to consider, any mitigating circumstances or aggravating circumstances otherwise authorized by law and any of the following statutory aggravating circumstances which may be supported by the evidence:

        (1)   The offense of murder, rape, armed robbery, or kidnapping was committed by a person with a prior record of conviction for a capital felony, or the offense of murder was committed by a person who has a substantial history of serious assaultive criminal convictions.

        (2)   The offense of murder, rape, armed robbery, or kidnapping was committed while the offender was engaged in the commission of another capital felony, or aggravated battery, or the offense of murder was committed while the offender was engaged in the commission of burglary or arson in the first degree.

        (3)   The offender by his act of murder, armed robbery, or kidnapping knowingly created a great risk of death to more than one person in a public place by means of a weapon or device which would normally be hazardous to the lives of more than one person.

        (4)   The offender committed the offense of murder for himself or another, for the purpose of receiving money or any other thing of monetary value.

        (5)   The murder of a judicial officer, former judicial officer, district attorney or solicitor or former district attorney or solicitor during or because of the exercise of his official duty.

        (6)   The offender caused or directed another to commit murder or committed murder as an agent or employee of another person.

        (7)   The offense of murder, rape, armed robbery, or kidnapping was

outrageously or wantonly vile, horrible or inhuman in that it involved torture, depravity of mind, or an aggravated battery to the victim.

(8)   The offense of murder was committed against any peace officer, corrections employee or fireman while engaged in the performance of his official duties.

(9)   The offense of murder was committed by a person in, or who has escaped from, the lawful custody of a peace officer or place of lawful confinement.

(10) The murder was committed for the purpose of avoiding, interfering with, or preventing a lawful arrest or custody in a place of lawful confinement, of himself or another.

(c)   The statutory instructions as determined by the trial judge to be warranted by the evidence shall be given in charge and in writing to the jury for its deliberation. The jury, if its verdict be a recommendation of death, shall designate in writing, signed by the foreman of the jury, the aggravating circumstance or circumstances which it found beyond a reasonable doubt. In non-jury cases the judge shall make such designation. Except in cases of treason or aircraft hijacking, unless at least one of the statutory aggravating circumstances enumerated in section 27-2534.1(b) is so found, the death penalty shall not be imposed." § 27-2534.1 (Supp. 1975).

The Supreme Court of Georgia, in *Arnold v. State, 236 Ga. 534, 540, 224 S.E. 2d 386, 391 (1976)*, recently held unconstitutional the portion of the first circumstance encompassing persons who have a "substantial history of serious assaultive criminal convictions" because it did not set "sufficiently 'clear and objective standards.'"

10. The statute requires that the Supreme Court of Georgia obtain and preserve the records of all capital felony cases in which the death penalty was imposed after January 1, 1970, or such earlier date that the court considers appropriate. § 27-2537 (f) (Supp. 1975). To aid the court in its disposition of these cases the statute further provides for the appointment of a special assistant and authorizes the employment of additional staff members. §§ 27-2537 (f)-(h) (Supp. 1975).

11. See Ga. Const., Art. 5, § 1, [*] 12, Ga. Code Ann. § 2-3011 (1973); Ga. Code Ann. §§ 77-501, 77-511, 77-513 (1973 and Supp. 1975) (Board of Pardons and Paroles is authorized to commute sentence of death except in cases where Governor refuses to suspend that sentence).

APPENDIX B
BRONSTEIN VICTIM IMPACT STATEMENT

The victim impact statement in this case was prepared by the Maryland Division of Parole and Probation. The information presented here has been taken from page 14 of the Supreme Court's opinion in **Booth v. Maryland,** *482 U.S. 496, 510 (1987).*

"Mr. and Mrs. Bronstein's son, daughter, son-in-law, and granddaughter were interviewed for purposes of the Victim Impact Statement. There are also four other grandchildren in the family. The victims' son reports that his parents had been married for fifty-three years and enjoyed a very close relationship, spending each day together. He states that his father had worked hard all his life and had been retired for eight years. He describes his mother as a woman who was young at heart and never seemed like an old lady. She taught herself to play bridge when she was in her seventies. The victims' son relates that his parents were amazing people who attended the senior citizens' center and made many devout friends. He indicates that he was very close to his parents, and that he talked to them every day. The victims' daughter also spent lots of time with them.

"The victims' son saw his parents alive for the last time on May 18th. They were having their lawn manicured and were excited by the onset of spring. He called them on the phone that evening and received no answer. He had made arrangements to pick Mr. Bronstein up on May 20th. They were both to be ushers in a granddaughter's wedding and were going to pick up their tuxedos. When he arrived

359

at the house on May 20th he noticed that his parents' car wasn't there. A neighbor told him that he hadn't seen the car in several days and he knew something was wrong. He went to his parents' house and found them murdered. He called his sister crying and told her to come right over because something terrible had happened and their parents were both dead.

"The victims' daughter recalls that when she arrived at her parents' house, there were police officers and television crews everywhere. She felt numb and cold. She was not allowed to go into the house and so she went to a neighbor's home. There were people and reporters everywhere and all she could feel was cold. She called her older daughter and told her what had happened. She told her daughter to get her husband and then tell her younger daughter what had happened. The younger daughter was to be married two days later.

"The victims' granddaughter reports that just before she received the call from her mother she had telephoned her grandparents and received no answer. After her mother told her what happened she turned on the television and heard the news reports about it. The victims' son reports that his children first learned about their grandparents' death from the television reports.

"Since the Jewish religion dictates that birth and marriage are more important than death, the granddaughter's wedding had to proceed on May 22nd. She had been looking forward to it eagerly, but it was a sad occasion with people crying. The reception, which normally would have lasted for hours, was very brief. The next day, instead of going on her honeymoon, she attended her grandparents' funerals. The victims' son, who was an usher at the wedding, cannot remember being there or coming and going from his parents' funeral the next day. The victims' granddaughter, on the other hand, vividly remembers every detail of the days following her grandparents' death. Perhaps she described the impact of the tragedy most eloquently when she stated that it was a completely devastating and life altering experience.

"The victims' son states that he can only think of his parents in the context of how he found them that day, and he can feel their fear and horror. It was 4:00 p.m. when he discovered their bodies and this stands out in his mind. He is always aware of when 4:00 p.m. comes each day, even when he is not near a clock. He also wakes up at 4:00 a.m. each morning. The victims' son states that he suffers from lack of sleep. He is unable to drive on the streets that pass near his parents' home. He also avoids driving past his father's favorite restaurant, the supermarket where his parents shopped, etc. He is constantly reminded of his parents. He sees his father coming out of synagogues, sees his parents' car, and feels very sad whenever he sees old people. The victims' son feels that his parents were not killed, but were butchered like animals. He doesn't think anyone should be able to do something like that and get away with it. He is very angry and wishes he could sleep and not feel so depressed all the time. He is fearful for the first time in his life, putting all the lights on and checking the locks frequently. His children are scared for him and concerned for his health. They phone him several times a day. At the same time he takes a fearful approach to the whereabouts of his children. He also calls his sister every day. He states that he is frightened by his own reaction of what he would do if someone hurt him or a family member. He doesn't know if he'll ever be the same again.

"The victims' daughter and her husband didn't eat dinner for three days following the discovery of Mr. and Mrs. Bronstein's bodies. They cried together every day for four months and she still cries every day. She states that she doesn't sleep through a single night and thinks a part of her died too when her parents were killed. She reports that she doesn't find much joy in anything and her powers of concentration aren't good. She feels as if her brain is on overload. The victims' daughter relates that she had to clean out her parents' house and it took several weeks. She saw the bloody carpet, knowing that her parents had been there, and she felt like getting down on the rug and holding her mother. She wonders how this could have happened to her family because they're just ordinary people. The victims' daughter reports that she had become noticeably withdrawn and depressed at work and is now making an effort to be more outgoing. She notes that she is so emotionally tired because she doesn't sleep at night, that she has a tendency to fall asleep when she attends social events such as dinner parties or the symphony. The victims' daughter states that wherever she goes she sees and hears her parents. This happens every day. She cannot look at kitchen knives without being reminded of the murders and she is never away from it. She states that she can't watch movies with bodies or stabbings in it. She can't tolerate any reminder of violence. The victims' daughter relates that she used to be very trusting, but is not any longer. When the doorbell rings she tells her husband not to answer it. She is very suspicious of people and was never that way before.

"The victims' daughter attended the defendant's trial and that of the co-defendant because she felt someone should be there to represent her parents. She had never been told the exact details of her parents' death and had to listen to the medical examiner's report. After a certain point, her mind blocked out and she stopped hearing. She states that her parents were stabbed repeatedly with viciousness and she could never forgive anyone for killing them that way. She can't believe that anybody could do that to someone. The victims' daughter states that animals wouldn't do this. They didn't have to kill because there was no one to stop them from looting. Her father would have given them anything. The murders show the viciousness of the killers' anger. She doesn't feel that the people who did this could ever be rehabilitated and she doesn't want them to be able to do this again or put another family through this. She feels that the lives of her family members will never be the same again.

"The victims' granddaughter states that unless you experience something like this you can't understand how it feels. You are in a state of shock for several months and then a terrible depression sets in. You are so angry and feel such rage. She states that she only dwells on the image of their death when thinking of her grandparents. For a time she would become hysterical whenever she saw dead animals on the road. She is not able to drive near her grandparents' house and will never be able to go into their neighborhood again. The victims' granddaughter also has a tendency to turn on all the lights in her house. She goes into a panic if her husband is late coming home from work. She used to be an avid reader of murder mysteries, but will never be able to read them again. She has to turn off the radio or T.V. when reports of violence come on because they hit too close to home. When she gets a newspaper she reads the comics and throws the rest away. She states that it is the small everyday things that haunt her constantly and always will. She saw a counselor for several months but stopped because she felt that no one could help her.

"The victims' granddaughter states that the whole thing has been very hard on her sister too. Her wedding anniversary will always be bittersweet and tainted by the memory of what happened to her grandparents. This year on her anniversary she and her husband quietly went out of town. The victims' granddaughter finds that she is unable to look at her sister's wedding pictures. She also has a picture of her grandparents, but had to put it away because it was too painful to look at it.

"The victims' family members note that the trials of the suspects charged with these offenses have been delayed for over a year and the postponements have been very hard on the family emotionally. The victims' son notes that he keeps seeing news reports about his parents' murder which show their house and the police removing their bodies. This is a constant reminder to him. The family wants the whole thing to be over with and they would like to see swift and just punishment.

"As described by their family members, the Bronsteins were loving parents and grandparents whose family was most important to them. Their funeral was the largest in the history of the Levinson Funeral Home and the family received over one thousand sympathy cards, some from total strangers. They attempted to answer each card personally. The family states that Mr. and Mrs. Bronstein were extremely good people who wouldn't hurt a fly. Because of their loss, a ter-

rible void has been put into their lives and every day is still a strain
just to get through. It became increasingly apparent to the writer as
she talked to the family members that the murder of Mr. and Mrs.
Bronstein is still such a shocking, painful, and devastating memory to
them that it permeates every aspect of their daily lives. It is doubtful
that they will ever be able to fully recover from this tragedy and not
be haunted by the memory of the brutal manner in which their loved
ones were murdered and taken from them."

ACKNOWLEDGMENTS

MARTIN:

We started talking about this book more than twenty years ago, but until recently it was all talk, no work. The catalyst, for both of us, was the gentle prodding of Mary Dee Clancy. She never stopped asking, "Well, how's it going?" Eventually, we simply had to get going.

Tim and I have strong wills and often-divergent opinions, but our partnership has flourished, in television and now in print, because of mutual respect and a deep friendship. We both love chasing stories. Tim has spent years learning the law and the courts—and how to keep my writing legally kosher—but he was born a reporter. Reporting has always been my first love, too, and this book gave me an opportunity to focus on it without worrying about cameras, lights, or satellite feeds. I did miss the network expense account.

Journalism is a collaborative business, and the debts I owe to others would fill another book. I've been incredibly lucky to work with such icons as Fred Friendly, Shad Northshield, and Barbara Walters, and alongside many enormously gifted people with less recognizable names, all of whom have been generous in sharing their insights and their knowledge. My career is the sum of many talents—and many of them aren't mine.

At ABC, Roone Arledge, David Burke, and Av Westin helped me enormously. David Sloan, who has a gift for bringing out the best in his colleagues, has been a believer and a motivator from the day I met him. Bill Moyers and I met at PBS almost forty years ago; he has been a teacher, an inspiration, and a treasured friend ever since.

David Birenbaum and Tom O'Herron were kind enough to read drafts of this book, offering gentle corrections and sage advice; they are responsible for many improvements, but Tim and I are solely responsible for any errors that survive. Also absolved in the error department, but included in our enthusiastic applause, is the supportive creative team at Prometheus Books: Mariel Bard, Melissa Shofner, Cate Roberts-Abel, Brian McMahon, and the man with the prescience to make the purchase, Steven L. Mitchell.

I owe a special debt to Bill Peterson and to a group I think of as the Saturday Morning Irregulars—a tight group of friends who regularly provide encouragement and ruthlessly discourage self-importance. My son, Ty, is a powerful motivator; my guiding star is the aforesaid Mary Dee Clancy.

TIM:

Mary Dee Clancy never asked me, "How is it going?" But instead of saying "Hello," she would always greet me with a warm, loving smile and simply whisper, "Well?" I knew what she meant.

While Mary Dee was indeed the catalyst, our work at ABC News made this book possible. I was particularly blessed by the carte blanche the network gave me to hit the road whenever I wanted to cover virtually any Supreme Court case I perceived to be newsworthy. For more than twenty years, they never said no. Not once. Such luxury was unheard of in network news then, just as it is today. The resulting experience has enhanced my appreciation of the breadth and beauty of our country; it has deepened my respect for our Constitution and for the justices who dutifully seek to interpret it; it has enriched my life, personally and professionally. I am duly thankful.

Ben Sherwood, the president of ABC News, made it possible for us to include pictures and content from stories we have covered over the years and to link to many of those stories at abcnews.com. We are grateful to Sara Just and Sarah Burke for their generous help and uncommon diligence in digging out and organizing the material; their professionalism was matched only by their patience.

I am also grateful to the PBS broadcast *Religion and Ethics Newsweekly*, which has been my home (well, one of them) over the past decade. Working with executive producer Arnie Labaton and executive editor Bob Abernethy, I've had the professionally gratifying experience of putting together in-depth reports on a wide range of issues. Two of those issues—whether to allow the death penalty for juvenile offenders and whether to allow it for child molesters—are now topics of chapters in this book. Arnie and Bob have also agreed to allow us to use pictures taken from those reports, and we thank them for that. I particularly thank them for their support, guidance, and friendship over the years.

Special thanks to Kathy Arberg and her terrific staff in the press office at the Supreme Court. Kathy and I go back a long way at the Court, long before any of the current justices were even there. I thank her not only for her assistance on this project, but also for the many kindnesses she has shown me and the professionalism she has demonstrated to everyone over all those years.

Martin and I began our journalism careers together in local television news in Washington, DC, more decades ago than either of us care to admit. I am pleased to get back with him again on this book. His reputation as a skilled writer and producer is legendary within the network. His editorial experience is vast. My background has been exclusively in gathering and writing news stories. Doing so for television, perhaps more than any other medium, requires the reporter to be both precise and succinct. Efforts at precision and succinctness in *legal* reporting, however, run the risk of producing a work that reads more like a statute than a story. While I take great pride in my handle on both the facts and the law of the cases I cover, my coauthor's assistance was indispensable in translating legal abstractions into comprehensible stories. There is no "legalese" in this book. Martin has spared you, not I.

We are both grateful to our friend and agent Ron Goldfarb, who linked us up with Prometheus Books, a publisher that shares our approach to combining great stories with great issues. Ron made it happen, and we look forward to continuing the relationships with him and Prometheus Books long into the future.

I am, as all who know me attest, most indebted to my wife "Petie," to whom my efforts here are now dedicated. She has been a constant source of encouragement and support in this and all my endeavors. There wouldn't be a book without her. There wouldn't be anything. Forty-two years and counting, still loving every minute of it. Here's to you, Pete.

Finally, we are grateful to you, the reader, for purchasing this book. Please continue the conversation with us at: http://murderat thesupremecourt.com

Martin Clancy and Tim O'Brien
Washington, DC
January 2013.

NOTES

INTRODUCTION: A HOUSE OF SECRETS

1. Del Dickson, ed., *The Supreme Court in Conference, 1940–1985: The Private Discussions behind Nearly 300 Supreme Court Decisions* (New York: Oxford University Press, 2001), p. 610.

2. Ibid.

3. David O. Stewart, "A Life on the Court," *American Bar Association Journal* 77 (February 1991): 62.

4. *Reynolds v. Sims*, 377 U.S. 533, 589 (1964), Harlan J., dissenting.

5. Dickson, *Supreme Court in Conference*, p. 611.

6. William Brennan to William O. Douglas (personal note), April 1, 1969, William Brennan Papers, part II, box 1470, no. 13, Library of Congress.

7. *Witherspoon v. Illinois*, 391 U.S. 510 (1968). The Court said, "Whatever else might be said of capital punishment, it is at least clear that its imposition by a hanging jury cannot be squared with the Constitution. The State of Illinois has stacked the deck against the petitioner. To execute this death sentence would deprive him of life without due process of law." The Court did say, however, that jurors who indicate they could not return a death sentence under any circumstances could be dismissed for cause.

8. Earl Warren, *The Memoirs of Chief Justice Earl Warren* (Lanham, MD: Madison Books, 2001), p. 283.

9. Stuart Banner, *The Death Penalty: An American History* (Cambridge, MA: Harvard University Press, 2002), p. 256.

10. Jeffrey Toobin, *The Nine* (New York: Doubleday, 2007), p. 340.

CHAPTER 1. ROAD TO THE DEATH HOUSE

1. *Wilkerson v. Utah*, 99 U.S. 130 (1879).

2. William Bradford, *Of Plymouth Plantation: 1620–1647*, ed. Samuel Eliot Morison (New York: Knopf, 1991), p. 234.

3. "State by State Database," Death Penalty Information Center, http://www .deathpenaltyinfo.org/state_by_state (accessed November 6, 2012).

4. Ibid.

5. "State's Last Public Hanging in Ripley 53 Years Ago," *Jackson Herald* (Ripley, WV), March 9, 1951.

6. New York State, Commission on Capital Punishment, *Report of the Commission to Investigate and Report the Most Humane and Practical Method of Carrying into Effect the Sentence of Death in Capital Cases* (Troy, NY: Troy Press, 1888).

7. Mark Regan Essig, *Edison & The Electric Chair: A Story of Light and Death* (New York: Walker, 2003).

8. *People* (ex rel. Phelps) *v. Fancher*, 2 Hun, 226 (4 T. & C. 467).

9. "Far Worse than Hanging," *New York Times*, August 7, 1890.

10. "Westinghouse Is Satisfied; He Thinks There Will Be No More Electrical Executions," *New York Times*, August 7, 1890.

11. "A Crime in Itself," *20/20*, ABC News, October 17, 1985.

12. Ibid.

13. Stuart Banner, *The Death Penalty: American History* (Cambridge, MA: Harvard University Press, 2002), p. 204.

14. Letter from Stanley Deutsch, professor of anesthesiology, University of Oklahoma Health Sciences Center, to Oklahoma state senator Bill Dawson, February 28, 1977, cited in *Human Rights Watch* 18, no. 1 (April 2006).

15. "Technician Executes Murderer in Texas by Lethal Injection," *New York Times*, December 7, 1982.

16. "An Eye for an Eye," *20/20*, ABC News, May 4, 2001.

CHAPTER 2. THE DEATH PENALTY LIVES AGAIN

1. " Slayer Fails in Suicide Dies Today," *Salt Lake Tribune*, April 12, 1967.

2. Terje Langeland, "The Executioner's Song," *Colorado Springs Independent*, July 18, 2002, p. A1.

3. Leonard A. Stevens, *The Death Penalty* (New York: Coward, McCann & Geoghegan, 1978), pp. 15–20.

4. Ibid.

5. "B. Clarence Mayfield Obituary," *Savannah Morning News*, September 3, 1996.

6. Stevens, *Death Penalty*, p. 39.

7. Ibid.

8. *Furman v. the State*, 225 Ga. 253, 167 S.E.2.d 628 (1969).

9. Arthur Goldberg, "Memorandum to the Conference Re: Capital Punishment," *South Texas Law Review* 27 (1986): 493.

10. William J. Brennan, "Constitutional Adjudication and the Death Penalty: A View from the Court," *Harvard Law Review* 100 (December 1986): 313.

11. Cong. Globe, 39th Cong., 1st Sess. (1866), p. 2766.

12. Bob Woodward and Scott Armstrong, *The Brethren: Inside the Supreme Court* (New York: Simon & Schuster, 1979), p. 253.

13. Del Dickson, ed., *The Supreme Court in Conference, 1940–1985: The Private Discussions behind Nearly 300 Supreme Court Decisions* (New York: Oxford University Press, 2001), p. 617.

14. Ibid.

15. Ibid., p. 617

16. *Furman v. Georgia*, 408 U.S. 238 (1972).

17. Ibid.

18. Ibid.

19. *Furman v. Georgia*, 408 U.S. 238 (1972), Blackmun dissenting.

20. Robert Weisberg, "Deregulating Death," *Supreme Court Review* 305 (1983).

21. Edward Lazarus, *Closed Chambers: The Rise, Fall, and Future of the Modern Supreme Court* (New York: Penguin Books, 1969) p. 109.

22. Anti-hijacking Act of 1974, 49 U.S.C. § 1472(i) (1974).

23. Christopher Davis, *Waiting for It: Life on Death Row* (New York: Harper & Row, 1980), p. 45.

24. As recounted in the decision by the Georgia Supreme Court affirming Gregg's conviction and sentence, 210 S.E.2d 1059 at 1060.

25. *Gregg v. the State*, 233 Ga. 117; 210 S.E.2d 659; LEXIS 698 (1974).

26. Davis, *Waiting for It*, p. 120.

27. James B. Ginty, "Memorandum to the Conference," January 8, 1976, as found in the Powell Archives at the Washington and Lee School of Law, available online at http://law.wlu.edu/deptimages/powell%20archives/74-6257_GreggGeorgia1976Jan8-12.pdf.

28. The other four cases were *Woodson v. North Carolina*, 428 U.S. 280 (1976); *Proffitt v. Florida*, 428 U.S. 242 (1976); *Roberts v. Louisiana*, 428 U.S. 325 (1976); and *Jurek v. Texas*, 428 U.S. 262 (1976).

29. Supreme Court oral argument, *Jurek v. Texas*, 428 U.S. 262 (1976), March 31, 1976, available online at http://www.oyez.org/cases/1970-1979/1975/1975_75_5394/argument-2.

30. Ibid.

31. Ibid.

32. Stuart Banner, *The Death Penalty: An American History* (Cambridge: Harvard University Press, 2002), p. 271.

33. *Gregg v. Georgia*, 428 U.S. 153 (1976).

34. Figures derived from "U.S. Executions since 1976," Clark County Prosecuting Attorney's Office (website), http://www.clarkprosecutor.org/html/death/usexecute.htm (accessed November 21, 2012).

35. These quotes along with details of the escape and Isaac's Seminole County massacre are all chronicled in Thomas H. Cook, *Blood Echoes* (New York: Penguin Books, 1993).

36. "Four Death-Row Inmates Escape Reidsville Prison," *Rome News-Tribune* (Rome, GA), July 29, 1980.

37. Cook, *Blood Echoes*, p. 269.

CHAPTER 3. GOOD GUY/BAD GUY? SAME GUY?

1. *Furman v. Georgia*, 408 U.S. 238 (1972) (see chap. 2 for more information on this case).

2. *Gregg v. Georgia*, 428 U.S. 153 (1976).

3. *Woodson v. North Carolina*, 428 U.S. 280, 305 (1976).

4. *Lockett v. the State*, 49 Ohio St. 2d 48, 358 N.E.2d 1062 (1976).

5. Imposition of Sentence for Aggravated Murder, Ohio Rev. Code § 2929.03 (1975).

6. See Ohio Rev. Code Ann. §§ 2929.03, 2929.04 (1975).

7. *Lockett v. Ohio*, 438 U.S. 586 at 591.

8. *Lockett*, 438 U.S. at 593.

9. Ibid. at 593.

10. Ibid. at 591.

11. Ibid. at 595.

12. The Supreme Court arguments in this case can be heard at "*Lockett v. Ohio*," Oyez Project at Chicago-Kent College of Law, http://www.oyez.org/cases/1970-1979/1977/1977_76_6997 (accessed October 29, 2012).

13. Quotations relating to this case come from ibid. (see specifically the oral argument full transcript text).

14. Harry A. Blackmun Papers, Library of Congress; see http://www.loc.gov/rr/mss/blackmun/.

15. Ibid.

16. Ibid.

17. *Lockett*, 438 U.S. at 604.

18. Ibid. at 623.

19. *Callins v. Collins*, 510 U.S. 1141 (1994), Scalia, J., dissenting.

20. *Lockett*, 438 U.S. at 628.

21. The facts of the case presented here are taken from *People v. Harris*, 28 Cal.3d 935, 623 P.2d 240, 244 (1981).

22. Ibid.

23. Paul Litton, "The 'Abuse Excuse' in Capital Sentencing Trials: Is It Relevant to Responsibility, Punishment, or Neither?" *American Criminal Law Review* 42 (Summer 2005): 1027–72.

24. Trial transcript from Case No. CR44135, San Diego Cty. Super. Ct. (1978).

25. *Harris*, 28 Cal. at 945.

26. *World News Tonight*, November 7, 1983.

27. The Supreme Court arguments in this case can be heard at "*Pulley v. Harris*," Oyez Project at Chicago-Kent College of Law, http://www.oyez.org/cases/1980-1989/1983/1983_82_1095 (accessed October 29, 2012).

28. 1982 U.S. Briefs 1095, Respondent's Brief on the Merits.

29. *People v. John Zimmerman*, Los Angeles Cty. Supr. Ct. No. A077363.

30. *People v. Willie Thomas*, Los Angeles Cty. Super. Ct. No. A018108.

31. *People v. Paul Roberts*, San Bernardino Cty Super. Ct. No. SCR 35302.

32. *Harris*, 1983 U.S. Trans. LEXIS 35, at 19.

33. *Coker v. Georgia*, 433 U.S. 584 (1977).

34. Quoted from *Lockett*, 438 U.S. at 605.

35. "Death Row USA," NAACP Legal Defense Fund, http://www.naacpldf.org/death-row-usa (accessed October 29, 2012). According to these statistics, from 1992 to 2011, the number of inmates sentenced to death in California more than doubled to 707.

36. *Daniel Vasquez, Warden, v. Harris* 503 U.S. 1000 (April 21, 1992).

37. *James Gomez and Daniel Vasquez v. United States District Court for the Northern District of California et al.*, No. A-767, 503 U.S. 653 (April 21, 1992).

38. The supervisory power of the Supreme Court over lower federal courts has historical roots in the All Writs Act, which states, "The Supreme Court and all courts established by Act of Congress may issue all writs necessary or appropriate in aid of their respective jurisdictions and agreeable to the usages and principles of law." See the All Writs Act, 28 U.S.C. § 1651(a) (1988).

39. Had Harris not been executed on the day indicated on the death warrant, the warrant would have expired and his execution would have to have been rescheduled, a process that could have taken another thirty to sixty days. See Cal. Penal Code, § 1227 (1992).

40. As recorded by prison warden Daniel Vasquez and widely reported.

41. CNN, April 21, 1992; Transcript no. 36-1.

42. The order by U.S. District Court judge Marilyn Patel has not been pub-

lished; see "Video of Harris Execution Destroyed," *Los Angeles Times*, February 11, 1994.

43. *Fierro v. Gomez*, 865 F. Supp. 1387, at 1415 (N.D. Cal. 1994).

44. *Fierro v. Gomez*, 77 F.3d 301, 309 (9th Cir. 1996).

45. *Gomez v. Fierro*, 519 U.S. 918.

46. Gary Watson, "Responsibility and the Limits of Evil: Variations on a Strawsonian Theme," in *Responsibility, Character, and the Emotions*, ed. Ferdinand Schoeman (Cambridge, UK: Cambridge University Press, 1987), pp. 256–86.

47. Ibid., pp. 268–70.

48. Ibid.

49. Ibid.

50. Nearly all share another characteristic: they are nearly all male, 98.1 percent, according to Tracy L. Snell, "Capital Punishment, 2010—Statistical Tables," Bureau of Justice Statistics, Department of Justice, December 2010.

51. Ibid.

52. C. S. Widom, "The Cycle of Violence: Research in Brief," National Institute of Justice, Department of Justice, October 1992; Thornberry Smith, "The Relationship between Childhood Maltreatment and Adolescent Involvement in Delinquency," *Criminology* 31 (1993): 173–202.

53. "Criminal Investigative Analysis," National Center for the Analysis of Violent Crime, Federal Bureau of Investigation, 1990. The National Center for the Analysis of Violent Crime is part of the FBI's Critical Incident Response Group (CIRG). The center provides investigative support to law enforcement agencies around the world. See https://www.fbijobs.gov/232.asp

54. Watson, "Responsibility and the Limits of Evil," pp. 256–86; also see Robert Kane, ed., *Free Will*, Blackwell Readings in Philosophy (Malden, MA: Blackwell, 2002).

55. Retribution as justification for capital punishment is discussed in further detail in Chapter 8.

56. Governor Wilson was speaking live to a statewide television audience, as reported in "Wilson Rejects Plea of Mercy for Harris: Capital Punishment—Murderer's Lawyers Are Seeking a Court to Stay His Execution, Scheduled in Four Days," *Los Angeles Times*, April 17, 1992, http://articles.latimes.com/1992-04-17/news/mn-706_1_robert-harris (accessed November 26, 2012).

57. Ibid.

58. *Enmund v. Florida*, 458 U.S. 782 (1982).

59. *Tison v. Arizona*, 481 U.S. 137 (1987).

60. Lori Hearn, "Brother Ready for Harris to Die," *San Diego Times Union*, March 22, 1992.

61. *People v. Harris*, 2004 Cal. Appl Unpul. LEXIS 4420 (April 30, 2004).

62. Debra Dennis, "Woman Who Broke Ohio Death Penalty Faces Prison Again," *Cleveland Plain Dealer*, March 5, 1997, p. 1A.

63. Information found through the Ohio Department of Corrections, www.drc .ohio.gov/offendersearch/search.aspx (accessed October 29, 2012).

64. "Family of Victim Wants Defendants to Stay in Prison," *Akron Beacon Journal*, April 29, 2006.

CHAPTER 4. BLACK ON WHITE

1. "Policeman Shot Dead in Holdup," *Atlanta Journal-Constitution*, May 14, 1978.

2. *McCleskey v. the State*, 245 Ga. 108; 263 S.E.2d 146 (1980).

3. Ibid., see also "Robbery Victim: McCleskey Was 'Guilty as Sin,'" *Atlanta Journal-Constitution*, September 25, 1991.

4. "Policeman Shot Dead in Holdup."

5. "Schlatt a Careful Cop, Buddies Say," *Atlanta Journal-Constitution*, May 14, 1978.

6. John Turner, interview with authors, February 22, 2012.

7. Russell Parker, interview with authors, February 28, 2012.

8. The Honorable Thomas Thrash, interview with authors, March 2, 2012.

9. Edward Lazarus, *Closed Chambers: The Rise, Fall, and Future of the Modern Supreme Court* (New York: Penguin Books, 1969) p. 177.

10. Thrash, interview with authors.

11. Lazarus, *Closed Chambers*, p. 178.

12. Ibid., p. 176.

13. Ibid., pp. 179–80.

14. Thrash, interview with authors.

15. Lazarus, *Closed Chambers*, pp. 179–80.

16. Thrash, interview with authors.

17. Parker, interview with authors.

18. Linda Carter and Ellen Kreitzberg, *Understanding Capital Punishment Law* (Newark, NJ: LexisNexis, 2004), p. 292.

19. Lazarus, *Closed Chambers*, p. 189.

20. Kenneth Worthen, "Shirt-Tales: Clerking for Byron White," *Brigham Young University Law Review* 349 (1994): 353.

21. Lazarus, *Closed Chambers*, p. 199.

22. Ibid., p. 202.

23. Ibid.

24. The facts of the case presented here are taken from the oral argument of John Charles Boger, *McCleskey v. Kemp*, 481 U.S. 279 (1986).

25. *McCleskey*, 481 U.S. at 279.

26. Ibid.

27. Ibid.

28. John Calvin Jeffries, Jr., *Justice Lewis F. Powell, Jr.: A Biography* (New York: Charles Scribner's Sons, 1994), p. 451.

29. "McCleskey Put to Death after Hours of Delays, Final Apology," *Atlanta Journal-Constitution*, September 26, 1991. An audio record of the communications in the prison command post can be heard at: http://soundportraits.org/on-air/execution_tapes/complete_audio.php (accessed November 26, 2012).

30. "Execution Delayed for 8 Hours by 7 Stays," *Orlando Sentinel*, September 26, 1991.

31. Peter Applebome, "Georgia Inmate Is Executed after 'Chaotic' Legal Move," *New York Times*, September 26, 1991.

32. Ibid.

CHAPTER 5. MENTAL INCAPACITY AND "EVOLVING STANDARDS OF DECENCY"

1. The facts of the case presented here are taken from *Trop v. Dulles*, 356 U.S. 86 (1958).

2. Ibid. at 101.

3. Trial transcript from *Commonwealth v. Atkins*, Cir. Ct. for York Cty., Va., Case No. 99-R1-8229.

4. Ibid.

5. See *Atkins v. Virginia*, 536 U.S. 304 (2002).

6. *Atkins v. Commonwealth*, 257 Va. 160, 168 (1999).

7. Ibid. at 168.

8. The facts of the case presented here are taken from the trial transcript from *Commonwealth v. Atkins*, Case No. 99-R1-8229.

9. *Atkins*, 536 U.S. at 391.

10. Ibid. at 392.

11. *Penry v. Lynaugh*, 492 U.S. 302 (1989).

12. Ibid. at 338, 339.

13. *Atkins v. Commonwealth*, 260 Va. 375, 392, 394 (2000).

14. Jim Ellis, interview with the authors, March 10, 2012.

15. *Atkins v. Virginia*, 536 U.S. 304 (2002).

16. A transcript of the oral argument and an audio recording can be found at "*Atkins v. Virginia*," Oyez Project at IIT Chicago-Kent College of Law, http://www.oyez.org/cases/2000-2009/2001/2001_00_8452/ (accessed November 26, 2012).

17. *Atkins*, 536 U.S. at 304.

18. Justice John Paul Stevens, quoting from *Enmund v. Florida*, 458 U.S. 782, 798 (1982).

19. *Atkins*, 536 U.S. at 316.

20. Ibid. at 338.

21. *Thompson v. Oklahoma*, 487 U.S. 815 at 865 (1988), Scalia, J., dissenting.

22. *Atkins*, 536 U.S. at 348, Scalia, J., dissenting.

23. *Giles v. California*, Supreme Court Docket 07-6053; 554 U.S. 353 (2008).

24. *Melendez-Diaz v. Massachusetts*, Supreme Court Docket 07-591; 557 U.S. 305 (2009).

25. *Maryland v. Craig*, 497 U.S. 836 (1990).

26. *Brady v. Maryland*, 373 U.S. 83 (1963).

27. Troy Lyons, telephone interview with authors, March 5, 2012.

28. In re Commonwealth of Virginia, 677 S.E.2d 236 (2009); *Jones v. Commonwealth*, 278 Va. 1 (2009).

29. Mary Sloan, telephone interview with authors, March 1, 2012.

30. Virginia State Bar Docket No. 08-060-073840, entered by Pleasant S. Brodnax III of the Virginia State Disciplinary Board, August 23, 2011, also available online at http://www.vsb.org/docs/Addison-082511.pdf (accessed November 27, 2012).

CHAPTER 6. JUVENILE KILLERS

1. Cheryl Hayes, interview with authors, September 22, 2004, for *Religion and Ethics Newsweekly*, PBS, October 1, 2004.

2. In a post-conviction appeal, Simmons's new lawyers argued that the trial lawyers should have disclosed these problems as mitigating factors that would justify a sentence less than death and that their failure to do so denied Simmons the effective assistance of counsel that the Sixth Amendment guarantees. The argument was rejected. See *State v. Simmons*, 944 S.W.2d 165, 170 (Mo. banc 1997).

3. Ibid. at 165–71. Also see Simmons's videotaped confession at www.murder-atthesupremecourt.com/simmons.

4. Trial testimony of Brian Moomey, from *Simmons*, 944 S.W.2d.

5. The facts of the case presented here are taken from the decisions of the

Missouri Supreme Court (944 S.W.2d 165 and 112 S.W.3d 397) and the Supreme Court of the United States in *Roper v. Simmons*, 540 U.S. 1160 (2004).

6. "Hanged on the Gallows," *New York Times*, June 27, 1885.

7. Evidence later surfaced making it highly unlikely that Stinney could have committed the crime. See David Stout, *Carolina Skeletons* (New York: Mysterious Press, 1991).

8. *Thompson v. Oklahoma*, 487 U.S. 815 (1988).

9. Justice Kennedy did not participate. Justices rarely explain why they take themselves out of a case and, true to form, Justice Kennedy offered no explanation in this case.

10. *Stanford v. Kentucky*, 492 U.S. 361 (1989).

11. Portions of Appelbaum's closing argument to the jury can be viewed on our website, www.murderatthesupremecourt.com.

12. John Appelbaum, interview with authors, September 21, 2004, for *Religion and Ethics Newsweekly*, PBS, October 1, 2004.

13. Pertie Mitchell, interview with authors, September 20, 2004, for *Religion and Ethics Newsweekly*, PBS, October 1, 2004.

14. David Crosby, interview with authors, September 22, 2004, for *Religion and Ethics Newsweekly*, PBS, October 1, 2004.

15. *Simmons*, 944 S.W. 2d 165, 171 (1997).

16. *Penry v. Lynaugh*, 492 U.S. 302 (1989).

17. Kevin Murphy, "Researchers: Immature Brains Abet Youths on Death Row," *Bowling Green Daily News*, June 13, 2004, p. 15 A; available at http://news.google .com/newspapers?nid=1696&dat=20040613&id=9CgqAAAAIBAJ&sjid=OUgEAAAA IBAJ&pg=6819,1391211 (accessed December 4, 2012).

18. "Stay for Killer Angers Sister of Victim," *St. Louis Post-Dispatch*, May 30, 2002, p. B1.

19. *Chutzpah* refers to "supreme self-confidence; audaciousness," *Merriam-Webster*, s.v. "chutzpah."

20. State ex rel. *Simmons v. Roper*, 112 S.W.3d 397; LEXIS 123 (2003).

21. Ibid. at 420.

22. A rule surpassed in importance only by the "Rule of Five." Arguments will continue for decades over how a case should come out, but, right or wrong, whatever argument gets five votes carries the day.

23. Former U.S. diplomats Morton Abramowitz, Stephen W. Bosworth, Stuart E. Eisenstadt, John C. Kornblum, Phyllis E. Oakley, Thomas R. Pickering, Felix G. Rohatyn, J. Stapleton Roy, and Frank G. Wisner were all in support of Simmons.

24. The ACLU, the NAACP Legal Defense Fund, Amnesty International, Human Rights Watch, the National Association of Criminal Defense Lawyers, and many others filed briefs in support of Simmons.

25. *Roper v. Simmons*, No. 03-633, Brief of the States of Alabama, Delaware, Oklahoma, Texas, Utah, and Virginia as amici curiae in support of Petitioner.

26. Conversations with two justices on separate occasions on the condition of anonymity.

27. The emotional center of the brain is the limbic system. Within the limbic system is the amygdala, which is associated with aggressive and impulsive behavior. See also American Medical Association et al., *Brief of American Medical Association*, U.S. Briefs 633 (2003), in *Roper v. Simmons*, 543 U.S. 551 (2005).

28. *Simmons*, 543 U.S. at 617, Scalia, J., dissenting.

29. April Witt and Justin Blum, "John Allen Muhammad," *Washington Post*, October 25, 2002.

30. Paul Ebert, interview with authors for *Religion and Ethics Newsweekly*, PBS, October 1, 2004; in re *Stanford*, 537 U.S. 968 at 972 (2002).

31. In re *Stanford*, 537 U.S. at 972.

32. *Planned Parenthood v. Casey*, 505 U.S. 833 (1992).

33. *Johnson v. Texas*, 491 U.S. 397 (1989).

34. *Lawrence v. Texas*, 539 U.S. 558 (2003).

35. *Lee vs. Weisman*, 505 U.S. 577 (1992).

36. See Robert H. Bork, *Slouching toward Gomorrah* (New York: Harper-Collins, 2003).

37. The authors attended the event; there does not appear to be any published record of these informal remarks.

38. Federal Death Penalty Act of 1994, 18 U.S.C. § 3591 (1994).

39. *Simmons*, 543 U.S. at 572–97.

40. Adopted in 1789, the same year the U.S. Constitution was adopted and two years prior to the ratification of the Bill of Rights.

41. Most recently, and memorably, in his surprise opinion joining the Court's more liberal justices in upholding the Obama healthcare legislation, Chief Justice John Roberts famously wrote, "But the Court does not express any opinion on the wisdom of the Affordable Care Act. Under the Constitution, the judgment is reserved to the people." *National Federation of Independent Business et al. v. Sebelius, Secretary of Health and Human Services*, Case No. 11-393 at 59. See the October term 2011 syllabus at www.supremecourt.gov/opinions/11pdf/11-393c3a2.pdf (accessed November 27, 2012).

42. *Simmons*, 543 U.S. at 587.

43. Ibid. at 607.

44. Nico U. F. Dosenbach et al., "Prediction of Individual Brain Maturity Using fMRI," *Science* 329, no. 5997 (September 2010): 1358–61.

45. Chief Justice John Roberts voted with the majority, making the outcome

6–3. Roberts, however, did not join the opinion in that it applied to all juvenile offenders. In his view, each case should be decided on its own merits; in the case before the Court, the death penalty would have been excessive. See *Graham v. Florida*, 560 U.S. (2010), Supreme Court Case No. 08-7412.

46. *Miller v. Alabama*, Supreme Court Case No. 10-9646, decided June 25, 2012, forbidding automatic life sentences.

47. Hayes, interview with authors.

48. See Jennifer Brewer, Patrick J. Berrigan, and Caryn Platt Tatelli, "In the Matter of Christopher Lee Simmons, Petition for a Commutation of, or Reprieve of, a Sentence of Death, Submitted to Office of the Governor," http://www .americanbar.org/content/dam/aba/publishing/criminal_justice_section_newsletter/ crimjust_juvjus_simmonsclemency.authcheckdam.pdf (accessed November 27, 2012).

49. "Man's Defense Aided by Science," *Kansas City Star*, June 7, 2004.

50. J. Cardozo, holding that the Fifth Amendment guarantee against double jeopardy is so "implicit in the concept of ordered liberty" that it must apply to states as it does to the federal government even though the amendment itself applies only to the federal government. See *Palko v. Connecticut*, 301 U.S. 319 (1937).

51. Justice Antonin Scalia, interview with authors, November 20, 2012.

52. *Simmons*, 543 U.S. at 587, Stevens, J., concurring.

53. "Man's Defense Aided by Science."

CHAPTER 7. MEDICATE TO EXECUTE?

1. Doris Bacon, "When Fans Turn into Fanatics, Nervous Celebs Call for Help from Security Expert Gavin de Becker," *People*, February 12, 1990, http://www.people .com/people/archive/article/0,,20116769,00.html (accessed November 27, 2012).

2. Letter introduced into evidence at Perry trial.

3. Gavin de Becker, interview with author, September 6, 1990.

4. Deanne Lemain, interview with the authors, October 11, 2010.

5. Pookie Marceau, *Guilty but Insane* (Bloomington, IN: Author House, 2005), p. 8.

6. Ibid., pp. 4–18.

7. Melinda Shelton, "Witnesses Say Perry Confessed," *Baton Rouge Morning Advocate*, October 31, 1985.

8. Testimony of Herbert L. Durkes Jr., as reported in ruling of Louisiana Supreme Court in *Louisiana v. Perry*, 502 So. 2d 543; 1986 La. LEXIS 7831 (1986).

9. Chet Kaufman, "Two Jailers Say Perry Described Murder of 5," *Baton Rouge State Times*, October 30, 1985.

10. *Louisiana v. Perry*, 86 La. 0460 S. Ct. La. 502 So. 2d 543; 1986 LEXIS 7831 (1986).

11. Ibid.

12. "Testimony Reveals Confession," *Baton Rouge Morning Advocate*, August 23, 1985.

13. Melinda Shelton, "7 Jurors Selected as Multiple Murders Defendant Perry Fidgets," *Baton Rouge Morning Advocate*, October 22, 1985.

14. Melinda Shelton, "12 Picked for Jury in Perry Trial," *Baton Rouge Morning Advocate*, October 24, 1985.

15. "Pathologist Says Victim May Have Been Asleep When Killed by Shotgun," *Baton Rouge State Times*, October 26, 1985.

16. Melinda Shelton, "Murder Scene Photos Leave Jurors in Tears," *Baton Rouge Sunday Advocate*, October 27, 1985.

17. Chet Kaufman, "Jurors Find Perry Guilty on 5 Counts," *Baton Rouge State Times*, October 31, 1985.

18. *Perry*, 1986 La. LEXIS 7831.

19. Melinda Shelton, "Perry Convicted; Jury Recommends Death," *Baton Rouge Morning Advocate*, November 1, 1985.

20. Chet Kaufman, "The Chair Is Too Good for Him," *Baton Rouge State Times*, November 1, 1985.

21. Don Lewis, "Court Upholds Perry Death Sentence," *Baton Rouge State Times*, November 25, 1986.

22. *Perry*, 1986 La. LEXIS 7831.

23. Ibid.

24. Howard Hoffman, "Condemned Killer Cites Suicidal Thoughts," *Baton Rouge State Times*, April 21, 1988.

25. Aris Cox, interview with Tim O'Brien, *ABC World News Tonight with Peter Jennings*, October 12, 1990.

26. *Ford v. Wainwright*, 477 U.S. 399 (1986).

27. *Riggins v. Nevada*, 504 U.S. 127 (1992).

28. N. S. Gill, "Is 'First Do No Harm' from the Hippocratic Oath? Myth vs Fact," Ancient/Classical History, About.com, http://ancienthistory.about.com/od/greekmedicine/f/HippocraticOath.htm (accessed November 27, 2012).

29. "An Insane Remedy," *USA Today*, September 24, 1991, p. 10A.

30. "Help, Don't Kill Insane," *USA Today*, September 26, 1991.

31. "First Cure Him; Then Kill Him," *St. Louis Post-Dispatch*, November 19, 1990.

32. Linda Chavez, "Treating a Killer: To Execute Him Is Right," *USA Today*, October 9, 1990, p. A10.

33. Oral argument in *Perry v. Louisiana*, 498 U.S. 38 (1990).

34. Linda Greenhouse, "New Hearing on Forced Medication of Inmate," *New York Times*, November 14, 1990.

35. De Becker, interview with author.

36. Ibid.

37. Letter from Sandra Day O'Connor, as broadcast on *ABC World News Tonight*, October 12, 1990. See also "Video: Rewind: Sandra Day O'Connor," http://murder atthesupremecourt.com/oconnor.

38. Order of L. J. Hymel, East Baton Rouge District Court, April 24, 1991.

39. Tim Talley, "State Can Medicate Inmate, Judge Says," *Baton Rouge Morning Advocate*, April 26, 1991.

40. L. J. Hymel, interview with authors, October 19, 2010.

41. Fred Kalmbach, "Court Denies Request to Rehear Perry Case," *Baton Rouge State Times*, January 28, 1991.

42. *State v. Perry*, 610 So. 2d 746; 1992 La. LEXIS 3170 (1992).

43. *Perry*, 1992 La. LEXIS 3170.

CHAPTER 8. GETTING EVEN

1. Taken from videotapes of the news coverage surrounding the crime introduced at the trial and subsequently contained in the Supreme Court record in *Kennedy v. Louisiana*, Case No. 07-343.

2. "Jefferson Parish Sheriff Harry Lee Dies," *New Orleans Times-Picayune*, October 1, 2007.

3. The chain of events reported here is taken from the detailed statement of the facts in the Louisiana Supreme Court decision in this case. See *State v. Kennedy*, 957 So.2d 757 (La. 2007).

4. From the Supreme Court record, *Kennedy v. Louisiana*, Case No. 07-343.

5. Ibid.

6. "Jefferson Parish Sheriff Harry Lee Dies."

7. Dr. Lee's report was submitted into evidence in Kennedy's trial, Case No. 98-125, Parish of Jefferson, 24th Judicial District, Div. O.

8. *Kennedy*, 957 So.2d.

9. Ibid. at 761.

10. Luminol ($C_8H_7N_3O_2$) is a versatile chemical that exhibits chemiluminescence, with a striking blue glow, when mixed with an appropriate oxidizing agent. Luminol is used by forensic investigators to detect trace amounts of blood left at crime scenes as it reacts with iron found in hemoglobin.

11. "Notable Awards," Pete Schneider State Senator District 11, http://pete

schneider.com/cgi-bin/psc07/sbpg/rt_hdln_dsply2.cgi?Autoincrement=000108&
value_6=Home Page Main (accessed December 4, 2012).

12. Pete Schneider, interview with authors, May 25, 2008, portions of which
were broadcast on PBS on June 13, 2008. See "Retribution for Child Molesters,"
Religion and Ethics Newsweekly, PBS, June 13, 2008, http://www.pbs.org/wnet/
religionandethics/episodes/june-13-2008/retribution-for-child-molesters/53/
(accessed November 27, 2012).

13. "Sourcebook of Criminal Justice Statistics, Table 2.55," Department of
Justice, Bureau of Justice Statistics, 2003, http://www.albany.edu/sourcebook/pdf/
t255.pdf (accessed November 27, 2012).

14. *Furman v. Georgia*, 408 U.S. 238, 308 (1972).

15. Justice William Brennan, interview with authors, April 2, 1986, aired on
Perspective, ABC Radio News, April 22, 1986.

16. *Gregg v. Georgia*, 428 U.S. 153, 184 (1976), Marshall, J., dissenting, quoting
from *Furman*, 408 U.S. at 394, 395.

17. John Stuart Mill, "An Examination of Sir William Hamilton's Philosophy,"
in *Free Will*, ed. Sidney Morgenbesser and James Walsh (Upper Saddle River, NJ:
Prentice Hall, 1962), pp. 59, 63.

18. Ibid, p. 64.

19. Schneider, interview with authors.

20. *Coker v. Georgia*, 433 U.S. 584 (1977).

21. See *State v. Wilson*, 685 So.2d 1063 (1996).

22. Ibid. at 1070.

23. *Kennedy*, 957 So.2d.

24. *Coker*, 433 U.S. at 598.

25. Montana, Oklahoma, South Carolina, Texas, and Florida. All those state
statutes, however, unlike Louisiana's, require a prior sexual-assault conviction.
Florida's statute was invalidated by the state supreme court in 2003.

26. A transcript of the oral argument in *Kennedy v. Louisiana*, Case No. 07-343,
can be found at "*Kennedy v. Louisiana*," Oyez Project at Chicago-Kent College of Law,
http://www.oyez.org/cases/2000-2009/2007/2007_07_343 (accessed November
27, 2012).

27. *Baze v. Rees*, 533 U.S. 35, 86 (2008), quoting from *Furman*, 408 U.S. at 455.

28. See Antonin Scalia and Bryan A. Garner, *Reading Law: The Interpretation
of Legal Texts* (St. Paul, MN: Thompson/West, 2012). Acclaimed even by many of
Scalia's critics, this comprehensive work explains Scalia's approach to interpreting
the Constitution, statutes, and ordinary contracts.

29. *Kennedy v. Louisiana*, 554 U.S. 407, 431 (2008).

30. Ibid. at 435.

31. Joint Brief of the National Association of Social Workers, the Louisiana Foundation against Sexual Assault, the Texas Association against Sexual Assault, and the National Alliance to End Sexual Violence as amici curiae in support of Petitioner, *Kennedy v. Louisiana*, 2007 U.S. Briefs 343.

32. Brief of the National Association of Criminal Defense Lawyers as amicus curiae in support of Petitioner, *Kennedy v. Louisiana*, 2007 U.S. Briefs 343.

33. Angola Inmate Delinquency Report, Case No. 07-343, on file at the Supreme Court of the United States.

34. "Jefferson Parish Sheriff Harry Lee Dies."

35. Section 552(b) of the National Defense Authorization Act for Fiscal Year 2006, 119 Stat. 3136, 3264 (2006), provides that "until the President otherwise provides pursuant to" UCMJ article 56, "the punishment which a court-martial may direct for an offense under" the amended UCMJ article 120 "may not exceed the following limits: . . . For an offense under subsection (a) (rape) or subsection (b) (rape of a child), death or such other punishment as a court-martial may direct."

36. Dwight Sullivan, "The Supremes Dis the Military Justice System," *CAAFlog* (blog), June 28, 2008, http://www.caaflog.com/2008/06/28/the-supremes-dis-the -military-justice-system/ (accessed November 27, 2012).

37. Linda Geenhouse, "In Court Ruling on Executions, a Factual Flaw," *New York Times,* July 2, 2008.

38. 554 U.S. 942.

39. See Tony Mauro, "Government's 'Duty to Defend' Not a Given," *National Law Journal,* October 27, 2010. There are some notable exceptions, however, where an administration declines to defend federal statutes. The Obama administration, for example, declined to defend the Defense of Marriage Act, which authorizes the federal government to treat same-sex marriages differently than heterosexual marriages.

40. *Kennedy,* 554 U.S. at 945.

41. Ibid. at 948.

42. See "Cary Police Charge Jailed Suspect Who Tried to Solicit the Murder of Wife and Stepdaughter," news release, May 24, 2006, http://www.townofcary.org/ Departments/Administration/pio/News_Releases/news2006/cokercharges-pd.htm (accessed November 27, 2012).

CHAPTER 9. NON-TRIGGERMEN

1. Perry Knight, interview with authors, January 18, 2012.
2. Newton Murdock, interview with authors, February 1, 2012.

3. Mary Lee Albritton, interview with authors, January 17, 2012.

4. Knight, interview with authors.

5. Albritton, interview with authors.

6. Jeanette Armstrong, taped statement to Florida Dept. of Law Enforcement investigators, May 1, 1975. This recording was introduced into evidence at her trial, August 14, 1975.

7. Albritton, interview with authors; Murdock, interview with authors.

8. Murdock, interview with authors.

9. *Enmund v. Florida*, 458 U.S. 782 (1982).

10. James W. Clarke, *Last Rampage: The Escape of Gary Tison* (Phoenix: University of Arizona Press, 1999), pp. 42–43.

11. Ibid., p. 10.

12. Gary Tison, interview with William B. McGrath, October 5, 1961, cited in Clarke, *Last Rampage*, p. 38.

13. Clarke, *Last Rampage*, p. 6.

14. Ibid.

15. "Member of Infamous Tison Gang in Line for Execution in Arizona," *Lubbock Avalanche-Journal*, Associated Press, January 20, 1997, http://lubbockonline.com/news/012097/memberof.htm (accessed November 27, 2012).

16. Clarke, *Last Rampage*, p. 267.

17. Oral argument on November 3, 1986, in *Tison v. Arizona*, 481 U.S. 137 (1987).

18. *Tison*, 481 U.S.

19. Edward Lazarus, *Closed Chambers: The Rise, Fall, and Future of the Modern Supreme Court* (New York: Penguin Books, 1969), p. 209.

20. Clarke, *Last Rampage*, p. 292.

CHAPTER 10. THE VICTIMS LEFT BEHIND

1. *Booth v. Maryland*, 306 Md. 172, 190 (1984).

2. Trial testimony of Judy Edwards, Case No. 18318813, Cir. Ct. for Baltimore City, Criminal Division.

3. Md. Ann. Code, Art. 41 § 4-609(d) (1983); "In any case in which the death penalty is requested . . . a presentence investigation, including a victim impact statement, shall be completed by the Division of Parole and Probation, and shall be considered by the court or jury before whom the separate sentencing proceeding is conducted."

4. This characterization of the impact on the Bronstein family is taken directly,

in some cases verbatim, from the victim impact statement taken by Agent Michelle Swann of the State Division of Parole and Probation (DPP). The statement is reproduced in its entirety as Appendix B in this book.

5. Maryland did not change to using lethal injection until March 1994.

6. The colloquy that follows is taken from the transcript of the oral argument in the U.S. Supreme Court. Case No. 86-5020, *Booth v. Maryland,* 1987 U.S. Trans. LEXIS 177 (1987).

7. Oliver Wendell Holmes, *The Common Law* (Boston: Little, Brown, 1881), p. 1.

8. *Booth v. Maryland,* 482 U.S. 496, 504 (1987).

9. The facts of this case are taken directly from the Supreme Court's decision in *South Carolina vs. Gathers,* 490 U.S. 805 (1989).

10. *Burnet v. Coronado Oil and Gas Co.,* 285 U.S. 393, 405 (1932).

11. *Trop v. Dulles,* 356 U.S. 86, 101 (1958).

12. The facts of the case are taken directly from the opinion of Chief Justice William Rehnquist, some parts verbatim; see *Payne v. Tennessee,* 501 U.S. 808 (1991).

13. *Payne v. Tennessee,* Supr. Ct. Case No. 90-5721; Brief for the Respondent at p. 6.

14. Ibid. at 9.

15. From the trial transcript, Case No. 87-04408-10, Shelby County Criminal Court.

16. Ibid.

17. *State v. Payne,* 791 S.W.2d 10, 33 (Tenn. 1990).

18. *Payne v. Tennessee,* 498 U.S. 1076 (mem. granting cert. 1991).

19. *Payne,* 501 U.S. at 844, Marshall, J., dissenting.

20. Ibid. at 741, Scalia, J., concurring.

21. *Payne,* 501 U.S. 808 at 831.

22. *Brown v. Allen,* 344 U.S. 443, 540 (1953), Jackson, J., concurring.

23. *Dred Scott v. Sanford,* 60 U.S. 393 (1857).

24. *Plessy v. Ferguson,* 163 U.S. 537 (1896).

25. *Korematsu v. United States,* 323 U.S. 214 (1944).

26. *Northern Securities Co. v. United States,* 193 U.S. 197, 401 (1904); "Great cases, like hard cases, make bad law. For great cases are called great not by any reason of their real importance in shaping the law of the future, but because of some accident of overwhelming interest which appeals to the feelings and distorts the judgment. These immediate interests exercise a kind of hydraulic pressure which makes what previously was clear seem doubtful, and before which even well-settled principles of law will bend."

27. "A Slow Death; Capital Punishment in Maryland an Unofficial Moratorium on Executions Tests the Patience of Prosecutors and the Perseverance of Victims'

Families and Leaves the Condemned Awaiting an Uncertain Fate," *Baltimore Sun*, February 13, 2011, p. A1.

28. Ibid. See also a video of Phyllis Bricker's statement, "Phyllis Bricker Talks about Death Penalty," YouTube video, 3:19, discussing her efforts to have the man who killed her parents executed, posted by "wbalam," May 19, 2010, http://www .youtube.com/watch?v=mIox1QICAOY (accessed November 29, 2012).

CHAPTER 11. THE MECHANICS OF DEATH

1. "A Success, Say the Witnesses," *New York Times*, July 8, 1891.

2. Bernard de Mahy, interview with authors for "A Crime in Itself," *20/20*, ABC News, October 17, 1985.

3. Arthur S. Miller and Jeffrey H. Bowman, *Death by Installments* (New York: Greenwood Press, 1988), pp. 7, 11.

4. *Louisiana v. Resweber*, 329 U.S. 459 (1947).

5. Ibid.

6. Del Dickson, ed., *The Supreme Court in Conference, 1940–1985: The Private Discussions behind Nearly 300 Supreme Court Decisions* (New York: Oxford University Press, 2001), p. 605.

7. Miller and Bowman, *Death by Installments*, p. 124.

8. Felix Frankfurter, personal letter to Franklin Roosevelt, 1938, as cited by Miller and Bowman, *Death by Installments*, p. 125.

9. Felix Frankfurter, personal letter to Monte E. Lemann, February 3, 1947. A copy of this letter was found in Justice Harold Burton's files, box 171, Library of Congress, by Miller and Bowman, cited in *Death by Installments*, p. 126.

10. James Theriot, interviews with authors, September 8, 1985, and July 12, 2012.

11. John Evans, interview with authors for "A Crime in Itself," *20/20*, ABC News, October 17, 1985.

12. Russell Canan, interview with authors for "A Crime in Itself," *20/20*, ABC News, October 17, 1985.

13. Dr. Gary Cumberland, interview with authors for "A Crime in Itself," *20/20*, ABC News, October 17, 1985.

14. Commissioner Fred Smith, interview with authors for "A Crime in Itself," *20/20*, ABC News, October 17, 1985.

15. *Nevada State Journal*, February 9, 1924, as cited by Stuart Banner, *The Death Penalty: An American History* (Cambridge, MA: Harvard University Press, 2002), p. 198.

16. Banner, *Death Penalty*, p. 200.

17. *Raleigh News and Observer,* January 25, 1936; *Charlotte Observer,* January 25, 1936 (as cited by Banner in *Death Penalty*).

18. *Los Angeles Times,* December 3, 1938, and *San Francisco Chronicle,* December 3, 1938 (as cited by Banner in *Death Penalty*).

19. Banner, *Death Penalty,* p. 200.

20. Clinton T. Duffy with Al Hirshberg, *88 Men and 2 Women* (Garden City, NY: Doubleday, 1962), p. 101.

21. *Gomez et al. v. United States District Court for the Northern District Of California et al.,* 503 U.S. 653 (1992).

22. "So Long as They Die: Lethal Injections in the United States," part 1, "Development of Lethal Injection Protocols," *Human Rights Watch* 18, no. 1 (2006): 9–20.

23. Jay Chapman, interview with Tim O'Brien for *Religion & Ethics Newsweekly,* PBS, March 28, 2008.

24. *National Federation of Independent Business et al. v. Sebelius, Secretary of Health and Human Services, et al.* (Supreme Court Case No. 11-393).

25. Oral argument for *Baze v. Rees,* 553 U.S. 35 (2008) that took place on January 7, 2008.

26. Ibid.

CHAPTER 12. "ACTUAL INNOCENCE"

1. Marcia Coyle, "A Question of Innocence," in *A Year In The Life of The Supreme Court,* ed. Rodney A. Smolla et al. (Duke University Press, 1995), p. 148.

2. The facts of the case are taken from the decision of the Texas Court of Criminal Appeals, which affirmed Herrera's conviction and sentence. *Herrera v. State,* 682 S.W.2d 313 (Tex. Crim. App., 1984).

3. See "Habeas Corpus Curbs Sought by Reagan Aide," *New York Times,* January 31, 1982. The Reagan administration's determination to sharply limit the so-called Great Writ was finally realized in 1996 after bombings at the World Trade Center in New York City in 1993 and the Federal Building in Oklahoma City in 1995. The Antiterrorism and Effective Death Penalty Act of 1996 (AEDPA), among other things, precludes prison inmates from bringing successive habeas claims absent a credible showing of actual innocence.

4. Hector Villareal, interview with authors for *ABC World News Tonight,* Sunday, October 4, 1992.

5. Ex parte Herrera, No. 81-CR-672-C (Tex. 197th Jud. Dist., Jan. 14, 1991), p. 35. The Texas Court of Criminal Appeals affirmed (Ex parte Herrera, 819 S.W.2d

528 [1991]), and the U.S. Supreme Court denied review. *Herrera v. Texas,* 502 U.S. 1085 (1992).

6. See *Jackson v. Virginia,* 443 U.S. 307 (1979).

7. United States District Court for the Southern District of Texas, D.C. Docket No. CA-M-92-30, Judge Ricardo H. Hinojosa.

8. *Herrera, Petitioner-Appellant v. Collins, Respondent-Appellee,* 954 F.2d 1029 (5th Cir. 1992).

9. Delia Carrisalez, *ABC World News News Sunday,* October 4, 1992.

10. Talbot "Sandy" D'Alemberte, telephone interview with authors, August 21, 2012.

11. A transcript of the argument in this case, *Herrera v. Collins,* and an audio recording can be accessed at "*Herrera v. Collins,* Director, Texas Department of Criminal Justice, Institutional Division," Oyez Project at IIT Chicago-Kent College of Law, http://www.oyez.org/cases/1990-1999/1992/1992_91_7328 (accessed November 28, 2012).

12. *Herrera v. Collins,* 506 U.S. 390 (1993).

13. Ibid. at 446.

14. Ibid. at 417.

15. Ibid. at 428.

16. See the federal Antiterrorism and Effective Death Penalty Act (AEDPA) (1996), which specifically states: the writ of habeas corpus shall not be granted unless the lower court adjudication "resulted in a decision that was contrary to, or involved an unreasonable application of, clearly established Federal law as determined by the Supreme Court of the United States or resulted in a decision that was based on an unreasonable determination of the facts in light of the evidence presented in the State court proceeding."

17. *O'Dell v. Netherland,* 521 U.S. 151 (1997).

18. The statements of this case are adapted from the decision by the Supreme Court of Virginia affirming O'Dell's conviction and sentence. *O'Dell v. Commonwealth,* 364 S.E.2d 491 (1988).

19. Editorial, "Afraid of a Shadow of a Doubt," *Washington Post,* May 7, 2000, p. B8.

20. *Simmons v. South Carolina,* 512 U.S. 154 (1994).

21. See *Teague v. Lane,* 489 U.S. 288 (1989), a landmark ruling on the retroactivity of the new rules of criminal procedure.

22. Helen Prejean, *The Death of Innocents: An Eyewitness Account of Wrongful Executions* (New York: Vintage Books, 2006).

23. Helen Prejean, *Dead Man Walking* (New York: Random House, 1993).

24. *O'Dell v. Netherland,* 519 U.S. 1050 (1996); No. 98-6867; A-424.

25. Lisa Miller, "Justice Scalia Speaks for Himself on Death Penalty Not Catholic Church," *Washington Post*, October 27, 2011.

26. *O'Dell*, 521 U.S. at 151.

27. Prejean, *Death of Innocents*, p. 152.

28. "Know the Cases: Stephan Cowans," Innocence Project, http://www .innocenceproject.org/Content/Stephan_Cowans.php (accessed November 28, 2012).

29. "Justice Dept., FBI to Review Use of Forensic Evidence in Thousands of Cases," *Washington Post*, July 10, 2012.

30. "Man Executed on Disproved Forensics," *Chicago Tribune*, December 9, 2004.

31. For more information about the Innocence Project, go to http://www .innocenceproject.org.

32. See the file on this case maintained by the Innocence Project: "Know the Cases: Frank Lee Smith," http://www.innocenceproject.org/Content/Frank_Lee _Smith.php (accessed November 28, 2012).

33. The DeLuna case is examined in meticulous detail in James S. Liebman et al., *Los Tocayos Carlos, Columbia Human Rights Law Review* 43 (Spring 2012). We are indebted to Professor Liebman for his assistance with this chapter.

34. Constitutional Conversation with Justices Breyer, O'Connor, and Scalia, moderated by *Meet the Press* host Tim Russert, presented by the National Constitution Center and Broadcast on C-SPAN, April 21, 2005. See the Program Archives of the National Constitution Center, http://ratify.constitutioncenter.org/visiting/PublicPrograms/ ProgramArchives/ConstitutionalConversationwithSupremeCourtJustices.shtml (accessed November 28, 2012).

35. *Herrera*, 506 U.S. 390 at 435.

36. Ibid. at 427.

CHAPTER 13. INEFFECTIVE ASSISTANCE OF COUNSEL

1. *ABC World News Tonight*, ABC News, November 21, 1994.

2. *McFarland v. State*, 928 S.W.2d 482; Tex. Crim. App. LEXIS 19 (1996). The statement of the case is taken from this decision by the Texas Court of Criminal Appeals.

3. Henry Weinstein, "A Sleeping Lawyer and a Ticket to Death Row," *Los Angeles Times*, July 15, 2000, p. A1.

4. Ibid.

5. John Benn, interview with authors for *ABC Good Morning America Sunday*, ABC, May 4, 1997.

6. Ibid.

7. See "Asleep on the Job? Slaying Trial Boring, Lawyer Says," *Houston Chronicle*, August 15, 1992.

8. "Single Witness Central to Appeal; Death Row Inmate Asserts Innocence," *Houston Chronicle*, June 15, 2003.

9. Judge Doug Shaver, interview with authors for *ABC Good Morning America Sunday*, ABC, May 4, 1997.

10. *McFarland v. State*, 928 S.W. 2d 482; Court of Criminal Appeals of Texas (Tex. Crim. App. 1996).

11. Ibid. at 527.

12. *McFarland v. Texas*, 510 U.S. 1002; 114 S. Ct. 575; 126 L. Ed. 2d 474; U.S. LEXIS 7492 (1993).

13. *United States v. Mills*, 535 U.S. 1120; 122 S. Ct. 2347; 153 L. Ed. 2d 174; U.S. LEXIS 4179 (2002).

14. George McFarland, interview with authors for *ABC Good Morning America Sunday*, ABC, May 4, 1997.

15. For an example, see "The Eighth Amendment and Ineffective Assistance of Counsel in Capital Trials," *Harvard Law Review* 107, no. 8 (1994): 1923.

16. Marcia Coyle et al., "Fatal Defense: Trial and Error in the Nation's Death Belt," *National Law Journal* 12 (June 1990): 30.

17. See Andrew Rutherford, *The International Sourcebook on Capital Punishment*, ed. William A. Schabas (London: Center for Capital Punishment Studies, 1997), p. 5.

18. Judge Clarence Peeler, interview with authors for *ABC World News Tonight*, ABC News, November 21, 1994.

19. In re Venable, S.C. No 730, Supreme Court of Georgia, 1989 Georgia LEXIS 406, July 27, 1989.

20. The facts of this case are taken from the initial opinion of the Georgia Supreme Court upholding Ross's conviction and death sentence in *Ross v. State*, 326 S.E. 2d 194 (1985).

21. Ibid. at 197.

22. *Smith v. State*, 236 Ga. 12, 222 S.E.2d 308 (1975); see also William Cotterell, "Apprentice Hit Man Is Second Person Executed in Two Days," United Press International, December 15, 1983, AM cycle.

23. *Smith*, 236 Ga. at 14.

24. *Smith v. Kemp*, 715 F.2d 1459, cert. denied, 464. U.S. 1003 (1983).

25. "Georgia Executes Smith for Murder," United Press International, December 15, 1983.

26. *Machetti v. Linahan*, 679 F.2d 236 (June 25, 1982).

27. Stephen Bright, "Counsel for the Poor: The Death Sentence Not for the Worst Crime but for the Worst Lawyer," *Yale Law Journal* 103, no. 7 (May 1994).

392   NOTES

28. Ibid., p. 4.

29. Richard J. Wilson, "Empty Handed Justices," *Judges Journal* 22 (1983): 20, 22.

30. Prepared by Jon Gould and Lisa Greenman, "Update on Cost, Quality, and Availability of Defense Representation in Federal Death Penalty Cases," Office of Defender Services of the Administrative Office of the U.S. Courts, June 2008.

31. Richard Dieter, interview with authors, November 26, 2012.

32. Gary Hengstler, "Attorneys for the Damned," *American Bar Association Journal* (January 1987): 56–60.

33. Howard McGlasson, interview with authors, November 9, 1994, with portions broadcast on *ABC World News Tonight*, ABC News, November 21, 1994.

34. *Nelson v. Zant*, 261 Ga. 358, 405 S.E.2.d 250 (1991).

35. Gary Nelson, interview with authors, November 1, 1994, with portions broadcast on *ABC World News Tonight*, ABC News, November 21, 1994 and on *Good Morning America Sunday*, ABC, May 4, 1997.

36. Stephanie Saul, "When Death Is the Penalty: Attorneys for Poor Defendants Often Lack Experience and Skill," *N.Y. Newsday*, November 25, 1991, p. 8.

37. *Strickland v. Washington*, 466 U.S. 668 (1984).

38. Ibid. at 689.

39. David Washington was executed on July 14, 1984, two months after the Supreme Court's decision.

40. *Washington*, 466 U.S. at 711.

41. See "Eighth Amendment and Ineffective Assistance of Counsel."

42. Stephen Bright, "Counsel for the Poor," p. 6.

43. See Coyle et al., "Fatal Defense," pp. 30, 44.

44. Richard Dieter, interview with authors at the Death Penalty Information Center, January 9, 2012.

45. Ala. Code Sec 15-12-21 (d); See also Justice Ruth Bader Ginsburg's opinion for the Court in *Maples v. Thomas*, Comm'r Alabama Department of Corrections, 132 S. Ct. 912 (2012) 556 U.S. (2012), in which she takes Alabama to task for its failure to provide adequate representation in capital cases.

46. "Eighth Amendment and Ineffective Assistance of Counsel," p. 1930.

47. Lise Olsen, "Death Row Lawyers Get Paid while Messing Up," *Houston Chronicle*, April 20, 2009.

48. Details of this case were reported on *ABC World News Tonight*, ABC News, August 30, 1982.

49. *McFarland v. Scott*, 512 U.S. 849 (1994).

50. *Wiggins v. Smith*, 539 U.S. 510 (2003).

51. In the interest of full disclosure, coauthor Tim O'Brien is a life member of the American Law Institute.

52. "Message from ALI Director Lance Liebman," American Law Institute, October 23, 2009, http://www.ali.org/_news/10232009.htm (accessed November 29, 2012).

53. E-mail to the authors, December 17, 2012.

CHAPTER 14. CLOSING ARGUMENTS

1. For a transcript of the presidential debate in St. Louis, MO, see "October 17, 2000 Debate Transcript," Commission on Presidential Debates, http://www.debates .org/index.php?page=october-17-2000-debate-transcript (accessed November 29, 2012).

2. See "Table 5: Crime in the United States, by State," U.S. Department of Justice, Criminal Justice Information Services Division, 2009, http://www2.fbi.gov/ ucr/cius2009/data/table_05.html (accessed November 29, 2012); "Deterrence: States without the Death Penalty Have Had Consistently Lower Murder Rates," Death Penalty Information Center, 2012, http://www.deathpenaltyinfo.org/ deterrence-states-without-death-penalty-have-had-consistently-lower-murder-rates (accessed November 29, 2012).

3. "Studies: 2009 FBI Crime Report—Murder Rate Highest in the South, Lowest in the Northeast," Death Penalty Information Center, http://www.death penaltyinfo.org/studies-2009-fbi-crime-report-murder-rate-highest-south-lowest -northeast (accessed November 29, 2012).

4. Isaac Ehrlich, "The Deterrent Effect of Capital Punishment: A Question of Life and Death," *American Economic Review* 65 (June 1975): 397.

5. Written by English jurist William Blackstone in his *Commentaries on the Laws of England* published in the 1760s. The principle is much older than Blackstone's formulation. An early example appears in the Bible (Genesis 18:23–32) as: "And Abraham drew near and said, 'Wilt thou also destroy the righteous with the wicked? . . . That be far from thee to do after this manner, to slay the righteous with the wicked: and that the righteous should be as the wicked, that be far from thee: Shall not the Judge of all the earth do right?' And the Lord said, 'If I find in Sodom fifty righteous within the city, then I will spare all the place for their sakes.'"

6. "Presidential Debate at the University of California in Los Angeles, October 13, 1988," American Presidency Project, http://www.presidency.ucsb.edu/ws/ index.php?pid=29412 (accessed November 29, 2012).

7. Jeffrey M. Jones, "Support for the Death Penalty 30 Years after the Supreme Court Ruling," Gallup, June 30, 2006, http://www.gallup.com/poll/23548/ Support-Death-Penalty-Years-After-Supreme-Court-Ruling.aspx (accessed November 29, 2012).

8. John Paul Stevens, "On the Death Sentence," review of *Peculiar Institution: America's Death Penalty in an Age of Abolition*, by David Garland, *New York Review of Books* (December 2010). In the same essay, Justice Stevens also takes issue with *Witherspoon v. Illinois*, 391 U.S. 510 (1968), in which the Court held that prosecutors may exclude jurors whose scruples would prevent them from returning a death sentence. Stevens suggested a system in which jurors are "selected with less regard to their death penalty views than occurs today—in that respect, a truer cross-section of the community."

9. See our discussion of the Robert Alton Harris case in Chapter 3.

10. For an insightful analysis of this proposition, the authors highly recommend the following: Charles E. Silberman, *Criminal Violence, Criminal Justice* (New York: Vintage Press, 1980).

11. Stephen B. Bright, "Counsel for the Poor: The Death Sentence Not for the Worst Crimes but for the Worst Lawyer," *Yale Law Journal* 103, no. 7 (May 1994).

12. The decision, arguably, might not apply where the new evidence proves conclusively that the inmate could not possibly have committed the crime, such as in the case of DNA evidence.

13. "Death Term Is Commuted by Governor," *Lodi News-Sentinal* (Lodi, CA), June 26, 1967.

14. "Connecticut Voters Split on Death or Life without Parole, Quinnipiac University Poll Finds; But Voters Say Abolishing Death Penalty Is Bad Idea," Polling Institute release, Quinnipiac University, April 2012, http://www.quinnipiac.edu/institutes-and-centers/polling-institute/connecticut/release-detail?ReleaseID=1739 (accessed November 29, 2012).

15. E. J. Dionne, "Connecticut's Death Penalty Message," April 30, 2012, http://www.realclearpolitics.com/articles/2012/04/30/connecticuts_death_penalty_message_113989.html (accessed November 29, 2012).

16. "Connecticut Voters Split."

17. *Simmons v. South Carolina*, 512 U.S. 154 (1994).

18. Jabari Asim, "A Chilling Look at the Death Penalty," *Washington Post*, July 26, 2004.

19. *Trop v. Dulles*, 356 U.S. 86 (1958).

20. Scott Turow, *Ultimate Punishment—A Lawyer's Reflections on Dealing with the Death Penalty* (New York: Farrar, Straus & Giroux, 2004).

21. An amendment to the Constitution would also do the trick. The likelihood of that would seem slim.

22. John C. Jeffries Jr., *Justice Lewis F. Powell, Jr.: A Biography* (New York: Charles Scribner's Sons, 1994), pp. 422–30.

23. Charles Lane, *Stay of Execution: Saving the Death Penalty from Itself* (New York: Rowan & Littlefield, 2010).

24. "No Need for the Execution Express," *New York Times*, October 3, 1989.

25. *Baze v. Rees*, 553 U.S. 35, 86 (2008), quoting from *Furman v. Georgia*, 408 U.S. at 455.

26. John Paul Stevens, "Our 'Broken System' of Criminal Justice," review of *Our Broken System of Criminal Justice*, by William J. Stuntz, *New York Review of Books* (November 2011).

27. *Callins v. Collins*, 510 U.S. 1141 (1994); Blackmun's words, which struck a responsive chord in many quarters, were actually penned by one of Blackmun's clerks, Michelle Alexander. See Linda Greenhouse's Pulitzer Prize–winning biography *Becoming Justice Blackmun: Harry Blackmun's Supreme Court Journey* (New York: Times Books, 2005).

28. Greenhouse, *Becoming Justice Blackmun.*

29. *Callins*, 510 U.S.

30. Callins was executed on May 21, 1997, but not before sending Justice Blackmun a handwritten note thanking him for writing the dissenting opinion in his case.

LIST OF FIGURE CREDITS

Figure I.1. Justice Harlan's note to Chief Justice Earl Warren. *From the papers of William O. Douglas, part 2, box 1470, no. 13, Library of Congress.*

Figure 1.1. The public hanging of John Morgan. *Courtesy of West Virginia Archives and History.*

Figure 1.2. Kemmler execution as reported in the *New York Herald* on August 7, 1890.

Figure 1.3. *New York Times* article from August 7, 1890.

Figure 1.4. Warden Frank Blackburn. *Courtesy of ABC News.*

Figure 1.5. Execution by lethal injection. *Artist sketch courtesy of United Press International ©Bettman/CORBIS.*

Figure 1.6. Warden Burl Cain. *Courtesy of ABC News.*

Figure 2.1. Troy Gregg. *Courtesy of Georgia Department of Corrections.*

Figure 2.2. William Furman. *Courtesy of Georgia Department of Corrections.*

Figure 3.1. Professor Anthony Amsterdam. *Courtesy of New York University School of Law.*

Figure 3.2. Murder victims John Mayeski and Michael Baker. *Courtesy of ABC News.*

Figure 3.3. Robert and Daniel Harris. *Courtesy of ABC News.*

Figure 3.4. One of the boys' bodies. *Courtesy of ABC News.*

Figure 3.5. Mug shot of Robert Alton Harris. *Courtesy of California Department of Corrections.*

Figure 3.6. Robert Harris arrested. *Courtesy of California Department of Corrections.*

Figure 3.7. Detective Steven Baker. *Courtesy of ABC News.*

Figure 3.8. California Deputy Attorney General Michael Wellington. *Courtesy of ABC News.*

Figure 3.9. Michael Wellington surveying the crime scene. *Courtesy of ABC News.*

Figure 3.10. Last-minute reprieve. *Courtesy of ABC News.*

Figure 3.11. Daniel Harris mug shot. *Courtesy of California Department of Corrections and Rehabilitation.*

Figure 3.12. Sandra Lockett. *Courtesy of Ohio Department of Corrections.*

Figure 3.13. Albert O. Young. *Courtesy of Ohio Department of Corrections.*

Figure 4.1. Officer Frank Schlatt. *Courtesy Atlanta Police Department (Public Record Department).*

Figure 4.2. Officer Schlatt's family at graveside. *From the* Atlanta Journal-Constitution, *May 16, 1978.* © 1978 Atlanta Journal and Constitution. *All rights reserved. Used by permission and protected by the Copyright Laws of the United States. The printing, copying, redistribution, or retransmission of this Content without express written permission is prohibited.*

Figure 4.3. Warren McCleskey. (Photograph by Marlene Karas.)

Figure 4.4. Jury verdict in *State of Georgia v. Warren McCleskey.*

Figure 5.1. Earl Warren. *Photograph by Harris and Ewing, courtesy of the Collection of the Supreme Court of the United States.*

Figure 5.2. Eric Nesbitt family photo. *Photograph used as evidence admitted in court exhibit;* Commonwealth v. Daryl Atkins, *Case No. RI-8229.*

Figure 5.3. Eric Nesbitt, shortly before being shot to death. *Courtesy* Newport News Daily Press.

Figure 5.4. *Courtesy* Newport News Daily Press.

Figure 5.5. Nesbitt's body at the crime scene. *Photograph used as evidence in court exhibit;* Commonwealth v. Daryl Atkins, *Cir. Ct., York Cty., Va. No. RI-8229.*

Figure 5.6. Autopsy sketch. *Photograph used as evidence in court exhibit;* Commonwealth v. Daryl Atkins, *Cir. Ct., York Cty., Va. No. RI-8229.*

Figure 5.7. Justice Antonin Scalia. *Photograph by Mollie Isaacs, courtesy of the Collection of the Supreme Court of the United States.*

Figure 5.8. Daryl Atkins. *Courtesy of Virginia Department of Corrections.*

Figure 5.9. William A. Jones. *Courtesy of Virginia Department of Corrections.*

Figure 5.10. Ellis turned the country around. *Photograph by Mark Holm, courtesy of the University of New Mexico School of Law.*

INDEX

AAMR (American Association on Mental Retardation), 118

Addison, Eileen, 107, 114, 131, 377

Aguirre, George, 305

Aikens, Ernest, 40–41

Albritton, Mary Lee, 222–23, 385

ALI. *See* American Law Institute

Alito, Samuel, 278
> in *Baze and Bowling v. Rees*, 278
> in *Kennedy v. Louisiana*, 211, 217

American Law Institute, 332, 392–93

Amnesty International, 300, 378

Amsterdam, Anthony, 38, 40, 61, 63–64, 75

Angola State Penitentiary, 26, 214

Appelbaum, John, 142

Arcene, James, 140

Arguello, Alvin, 194–95

Armstrong, Jeanette, 222–24, 385

Armstrong, Sampson, 222–23, 225–26, 400

Atkins, Daryl, 103, 109–12, 114, 125–29, 145, 160, 398

Atkins v. Virginia, Virginia Supreme Court decisions, 115–17, 119, 122, 126, 128

Auburn State Prison, 23

Baez, Joan, 79

Baird, Charlie, 315

Baker, Kevan, 303–304

Baker, Michael, 67–68, 81, 85, 397

Baker, Steven, 72, 74–75, 81, 339, 397

Baker, Tammy, 71

Baldus, David, 95–96

Baldus study, 97–99

Banner, Stuart, 15, 48, 275, 369–71, 387

Baze, Ralph, 278

Baze v. Rees, 209, 383, 388, 395

Benitez, Judy, 213

Benjamin, Charlie, 133, 136–39, 141

Benn, John, 313–15, 328, 390

Billington, John, 20

Black, Hugo, 11, 14, 101, 272

Blackburn, Frank, 26–27, 397

Blackmun, Harry A., 64–66, 80, 97, 99, 247, 262, 289, 296, 347–48, 350, 395, 402
> on failure of death penalty, 349
> in *Herrera v. Collins*, 296, 310
> in *Lockett v. Ohio*, 64–66
> on "machinery of death," 347
> in *McCleskey v. Kemp*, 99

Booth, John, 240, 267, 400

Booth v. Maryland, 237, 249–50, 253–54, 261, 263, 265, 267, 359, 385–86

Borger, Jack, 98

Bork, Robert H., 47–48, 154–56, 249, 337, 379

Dennis, James, 184
Dershowitz, Alan, 38–39, 232
Deutsch, Stanley, 28, 277–78, 370
Dew, Nathan, 56–58, 60
Dickson, Del, 11, 369, 371, 387
Dieter, Richard, 326, 392
Dixie Furniture store, 89
DNA testing, 195, 299, 302–303,
    342–43, 394
Douglas, William O., 12, 39, 41, 43,
    48, 369, 397
Dred Scott, 266–67, 386
Duffy, Clinton T., 388
Dukakis, Michael, 339
Durkes, Herbert L. Jr., 167, 380

Edison, Thomas, 23, 370
Edwards, Judy, 238, 242, 385
Eighth Amendment, 19, 39–41, 64,
    104, 106, 124–25, 161, 217, 224,
    266, 278–79, 391
    and claim of innocence, 294, 310
    and cruel and unusual punish-
        ment, 19, 33, 38–39, 47, 64,
        116, 141, 145–46, 200, 205,
        208–209, 218
    and excessive and dispropor-
        tionate punishment, 224
    and ineffective assistance of
        counsel, 391–92
Ellis, Jim, 117–20, 130–31, 376, 398
Enmund, Dewey, 221, 224
Enmund, Earl, 222–25, 232, 400
Enmund v. Florida, 85, 221, 232, 374,
    377, 385
Evans, John, 273–75, 387, 401
Evans, Offie, 94, 96, 273–74

evolving standards of decency,
    7, 105–107, 109, 111, 113, 115,
    117–21, 123, 125–27, 129, 131,
    145–46, 156, 161, 344, 376

fair trial, Sixth Amendment right
    to, 125–26, 176, 206, 288, 291,
    311, 324, 328–29, 377
Fierro v. Gomez, 374
Fifth Amendment
    and double jeopardy, 380
    and self-incrimination, 62–63,
        288, 320
First Amendment, 154, 218
Florida State Prison in Starke, 224
Florida State University, 291
Fones, William H. D., 237
Ford, Alvin Bernard, 174–75, 184, 194
Ford v. Wainwright, 381
Forrester, Owen, 96
Fortas, Abe, 13, 15
Foster, Allen, 275
Fourth Amendment, unreasonable
    search and seizure, 288
Francis, Willie, 184, 238, 244,
    270–73, 387, 401
Frank, Daniel, 20
Frankfurter, Felix, 104, 272–73, 387
French Declaration of the Rights of
    Man, 157
Funderburg, Ellen, 321
Furman, William Henry, 35–37, 40,
    52–53, 184, 397
Furman v. Georgia, 41–43, 46–49,
    55–57, 61, 65–66, 73–74, 76, 100,
    199, 209, 224, 342, 349, 353,
    371–72, 383, 395